THE SUNNI-SHI'A DIVIDE

ALSO BY ROBERT BRENTON BETTS

Christians in the Arab East: A Political Study (1978)

The Druze (1988)

The Southern Portals of Byzantium:
A Concise Political, Historical and Demographic Survey of the
Greek Orthodox Patriarchates of Antioch and Jerusalem (2009)

RELATED TITLES FROM POTOMAC BOOKS

Radical Islam in America: Salafism's Journey from Arabia to the West
—Chris Heffelfinger

Virtual Caliphate: Exposing the Islamist State on the Internet
—Yaakov Lappin

Islam without a Veil: Kazakhstan's Path of Moderation
—Claude Salhani

Searching for a King: Muslim Nonviolence and the Future of Islam
—Jeffry R. Halverson

THE
SUNNI-SHI'A
DIVIDE

*Islam's Internal Divisions
and Their Global Consequences*

Robert Brenton Betts

Potomac Books
Washington, D.C.

Potomac Books is an imprint of the University of Nebraska Press

Library of Congress Cataloging-in-Publication Data
Betts, Robert Brenton.
  The Sunni-Shi'a divide : Islam's internal divisions and their global consequences /
Robert Brenton Betts. — 1st ed.
    p. cm
  Includes bibliographical references and index.
  ISBN 978-1-61234-522-2 (hardcover : alk. paper)
  ISBN 978-1-61234-523-9 (electronic)
  1. Sunnites—Relations—Shi'ah. 2. Shi'ah—Relations—Sunnites. 3. Islam and
world politics. I. Title.
  BP194.16.B48 2013
  297.8'042—dc23

                                                                2013007562

Printed in the United States of America on acid-free paper that meets the American National
Standards Institute Z39-48 Standard.

Potomac Books
22841 Quicksilver Drive
Dulles, Virginia 20166

First Edition

10 9 8 7 6 5 4 3 2 1

In memory of my brother,
Richard Allen Betts (1933–2004)

Contents

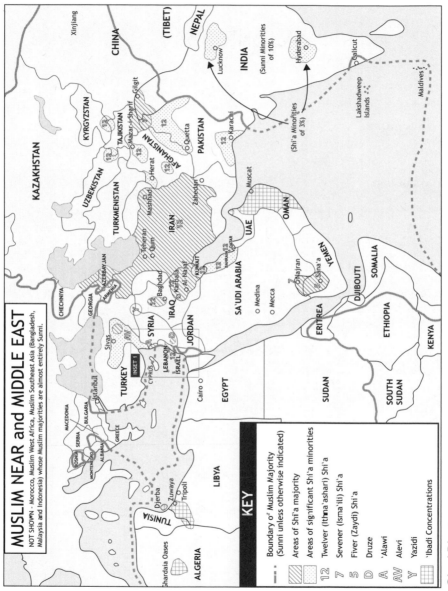

MUSLIM NEAR and MIDDLE EAST

NOT SHOWN - Morocco, Muslim West Africa, Muslim Southeast Asia (Bangladesh, Malaysia and Indonesia) whose Muslim majorities are almost entirely Sunni.

KEY

- – – – Boundary of Muslim Majority
  (Sunni unless otherwise indicated)

  Areas of Shi'a majority

  Areas of significant Shi'a minorities

- **12** Twelver (Ithna'ashari) Shi'a

- **7** Sevener (Isma'ili) Shi'a

- **5** Fiver (Zaydi) Shi'a

- **D** Druze

- **A** 'Alawi

- **AV** Alevi

- **Y** Yazidi

  'Ibadi Concentrations

Chad Blevins

ALGERIA
Ghardaia Oases
TUNISIA
Djerba
Zuwaya
Tripoli
LIBYA
EGYPT
Cairo
SERBIA
BOSNIA
MONTENEGRO
MACEDONIA
ALBANIA
BULGARIA
GREECE
Istanbul
TURKEY
Sivas
CYPRUS
LEBANON
ISRAEL
JORDAN
SYRIA
'IRAQ
Baghdad
Karbala
Al-Najaf
KUWAIT
SA'UDI ARABIA
Medina
Mecca
CHECHNYA
GEORGIA
ARMENIA
AZERBAIJAN
IRAN
Teheran
Qum
Mashhad
Zahedan
KAZAKHSTAN
UZBEKISTAN
TURKMENISTAN
KYRGYZSTAN
TAJIKISTAN
AFGHANISTAN
Herat
Mazar-i-Sharif
Gilgit
Quetta
PAKISTAN
Karachi
Xinjiang
CHINA
(TIBET)
NEPAL
INDIA
(Sunni Minorities of 10%)
Lucknow
Hyderabad
Calicut
(Shi'a Minorities of 3%)
Lakshadweep Islands
Maldives
BAHRAIN
QATAR
UAE
Muscat
OMAN
YEMEN
Najran
Sana'a
SA'UDI ARABIA
ERITREA
DJIBOUTI
SOMALIA
ETHIOPIA
SUDAN
SOUTH SUDAN
KENYA
INSET 1

Acknowledgments

I would like to thank my three editors: Hilary Claggett, Aryana Hendrawan, and Kathryn Owens. In addition, Dr. Seta B. Dadoyan deserves our collective thanks for offering her valuable suggestions and corrections to typographical errors in the text that would have otherwise gone unnoticed. I would also like to make special mention of Chad Blevins, my cartographer, for his beautiful execution of the two maps from my own rough, sketchy drafts. Contrary to the old caveat, he succeeded in making silk purses out of sows' ears, for which I am very grateful.

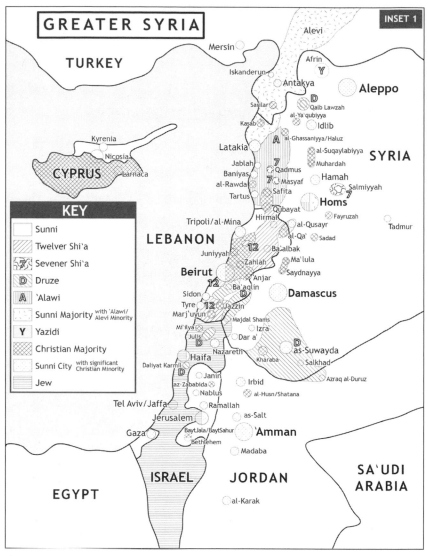

Chad Blevins

Introduction

Until the September 11, 2001, attacks on New York's Twin Towers, Islam for most Americans was a vague concept, a religion embracing hundreds of millions of non-Europeans with strange and exotic practices that had little or no impact on their daily lives apart from the price of gasoline. The painful shattering of this comfortable isolation from a major world force drew the United States into bitter and costly military conflicts in 'Iraq and Afghanistan. Few Americans knew anything about Islam, let alone the distinction between Sunni and Shi'a, Sufi and Wahhabi, the origins of the Holy Qur'an and Shari'a law, and the respect with which all Muslims, even secular ones, hold for the Prophet Muhammad, his family, and Islamic traditions. Divisions within Islam, as I noted nearly a quarter century ago in the British Catholic weekly *The Tablet*, were originally political in nature since, in classical Islam, there was no separation between "church" and state, but acquired distinctive approaches to Muslim theology that deepened the split over time.[1]

As American soldiers continue to die while reluctant allies bail out or distance themselves, it becomes even more essential that the average citizen be made aware of the fractured structure of Islam with its internal weaknesses, which, if properly understood, will have a long-lasting impact on our country's future. Why did the Arab Spring succeed in toppling long-standing dictatorial regimes in Tunisia and Egypt in a matter of days and weeks? Why did it fail in Bahrain? Why did it continue for eight months in Libya before the ruling tyrant of forty-two years, Mu'ammar Qadhafi, deposed and in hiding, was finally hounded down and savaged to death on October 20, 2011? Why have other leaders managed to survive? Why are Iran and Pakistan opposed to each other in Afghanistan, yet cooperating at some levels in efforts to restore a form of Taliban rule there? At the same time, it is essential that we understand the internal forces in

1

America that brought it into confrontation with the Muslim world, despite presidential disclaimers to the contrary.

The Sunni-Shi'a Divide provides a succinct historical summary of the sectarian divisions within Islam and takes a hard look at their political and demographic implications. Beginning with the splits in the fabric of the Muslim religious community that began to appear within the first generation after the death of the Prophet Muhammad, the book traces the intricate, sometimes confusing, and often bloody history of the most important of these divisions, the Shi'a departure from and refusal to accept Sunni "orthodoxy," along with the fascinating smaller remnants of movements outside the two principal Islamic allegiances that often play an important role in local politics of individual countries.

Although at least four-fifths of all Muslims remain faithful to their Sunni heritage, they are by no means a single monolith, separated as they are by internal religious disagreements, with Sufis at one extreme and the Wahhabis of Sa'udi Arabia (and their *Salafi* or Sunni ultra-traditionalist sympathizers throughout the world) on the other, as well as tribal, secular, and nationalist divisions. The total number of Muslims is probably approaching 1.5 billion and growing. Of these, an estimated 15 percent subscribe to the "Twelver" Shi'a creed, a majority in Iran, 'Iraq, Azerbaijan, Bahrain, and the Eastern Province of Sa'udi Arabia where most of the country's vast oil reserves are found. A particularly important, and heavily armed, minority is found in Lebanon and tens of millions of others live in central Asia, Pakistan, and India. Another 2 to 3 percent are followers of smaller Shi'a offshoots such as "Fiver," "Sevener," 'Alawi, Alevi, Druze, Bohra, and the more recent Baha'i sects, the modern Sunni spin-off group called Ahmadis that appeared and grew in British Imperial India, and the earliest sect of all, the present-day Ibadis who dominate the southeastern Arabian Sultanate of 'Uman (Oman), which along with Iran controls the flow of international oil supplies through the Strait of Hormuz.

In order to better understand these divisions, the following narrative also considers the varying schools of the diverse Islamic legal systems, which in the West are mistakenly lumped together under the much-maligned and oft-misunderstood term of Shari'a law. It also attempts to clarify the principal religious differences separating both Sunni and Shi'a Islam from traditional Christianity and Judaism whose beliefs traditionalist Muslims claim to have "purified." Yet in both the case of Sufism and Shi'ism, Christianity has most probably had its own input, and possibly Hinduism as well, leading extremist Sunnis to criticize them as "worse than unbelievers."

The relations between Sunni and Shi'a Muslims may have been and continue to be fractious, but one thing that has brought them together at one level was the creation of the state of Israel on what they believe to be Arab and Muslim soil in 1948. Long a Sunni concern since all Palestinian Muslims, apart from the Druze of Galilee, are Sunnis, it has become a Shi'a one as well, especially for the Hizbollah movement in Lebanon and the Islamic Republic of Iran. Israel's very existence is viewed by nearly all followers of Islam—Sunni or Shi'a—to be the last effort of Western colonialism to control the Islamic world, and militant opposition to the "Judaization" of the third-holiest Muslim site, Jerusalem, has proved to be the one issue on which all Muslims can agree, an impassioned belief that most of the Western world has as yet failed to comprehend fully.

Another important factor in understanding modern Sunni Islam is the loss of central leadership that occurred with the dissolution of the institution of the caliph by Kemal Atatürk in 1924. This political vacuum in a religion that since its inception has depended on a strong religious and political authority has allowed extremists like the 9/11 terrorists and the groups behind them like al-Qa'ida and the Taliban to attempt to fill. What is at stake is the security and future of not just Israel but Western civilization, particularly if such extremism were to succeed in overthrowing the traditional regimes in the oil rich Arabian Peninsula. If they were to be replaced by the forces of Taliban-style movements, much of the world's oil supply could be cut off and the years of American efforts in 'Iraq and Afghanistan would result in nothing but a ruined economy.

The threat that Shi'a Iran might join the nuclear weapons club of which Sunni Pakistan and Jewish Israel are already members has added a very dangerous factor to the existing equation. Despite saber-rattling from both Israel and the United States, there remains little either country can do in the long run to prevent Iran from achieving its goal. Whether its success could place sufficient pressure on Israel to come to terms with the Palestinians and achieve the two-state solution that most countries of the world would prefer remains to be seen. But the consequences for world stability if this solution is not worked out, and soon, are likely to be dire. As the historic rivalries within the Islamic world continue to play out on the international stage, the challenges they pose to the region and the world can only be understood in the context of the societies in which they developed.

1

The Rise of Islam
and Its Early Divisions

Islam is the only major modern religion to have emerged in relatively recent history. Judaism's roots are ancient but subject to serious scholarly conjecture, and virtually nothing is known of Jesus other than that which is revealed in the Gospels, carefully edited by Eastern Roman authorities once Christianity was accepted as the official religion of the empire in the late fourth century. Nevertheless, there is much that is not known about the faith revealed to Muhammad—as Muslims believe—by Allah through the archangel Gabriel (Jibril) in the collection of 114 chapters (*suras*) that make up the Qur'an, or, more particularly, the circumstances in which the revelation occurred. Arabia at the time was known to the West as the periphery of empire, both Roman and Persian. For the Romans, there were three divisions, Arabia Petraea ("stony" Arabia, primarily Sinai and today's Hashemite Kingdom of Jordan), Arabia Felix ("happy" Arabia, because unlike most of the rest of the peninsula, it receives enough rainfall to support agriculture, embracing large portions of Yemen as well as Oman with its Green Mountain, the Jabal al-Akhdar), and the vast, barren, and sandy expanse of Arabia Deserta ("sandy" or "wasteland" Arabia), ruled today by the Kingdom of Sa'udi Arabia and the princely states of Kuwait, Qatar, and the United Arab Emirates. Even in ancient times, however, the desert was inhabited by nomadic Beduin tribes, and it also boasted several urban centers built around oases, principally the trading centers of Mecca and Yathrib (later al-Madina) in the Red Sea coastal region of al-Hijaz, strategically positioned along the spice and frankincense trade route linking Syria with Arabia Felix.

Christianity was introduced into the Arabian Peninsula in the very earliest years of the faith. Arabic was one of the languages spoken by the disciples at Pentecost after the Holy Spirit, promised by Christ and descending in "tongues of fire," gave them the gift of conversing in languages they had not previously known. In an often-overlooked event of deep significance for nascent Christianity, St. Paul departed to "Arabia" (which of the three provinces is unclear) for as many as three years immediately after recovering from the spiritual and physical trauma of his Christophany on the road to Damascus.[1] Missionaries from the established church, albeit mostly from heterodox branches, entered the peninsula from three directions—Palestine/Syria and Mesopotamia from the northwest and northeast, respectively, and Ethiopia from the southwest, while the Orthodox Byzantines became involved in Yemen very early in the era of Justinian I (525). The Beduin were largely pagan, although some tribes are known to have adopted Christianity, and both Judaism and Christianity were widespread in the few urban areas. Yemen had a significant Christian presence, especially in Najran, as well as major long-established Jewish settlements. Yathrib was inhabited by Jewish tribes whose ancestors had fled Roman persecution following the destruction of the Second Temple by the armies of Emperor Titus in 70 AD, or had possibly settled there even before, and who over time actively and successfully proselytized among their pagan neighbors.

Eastern Church sources also claim a Christian presence in Yathrib by that time as well. Half a century before the birth of Muhammad, the Christians of Najran had been the victims of a massacre instigated by the Jewish tyrant Yusuf Dhu Nuwas ("Joseph of the curly hair"), the last Himyarite king (ca. 515–525), who came to power by murdering his predecessor, allegedly during a paid sexual encounter. According to local tradition, in 524 he had some 20,000 of the Najrani Christians burned to death *en masse* in an eerie (if reverse) foreshadowing of the Holocaust, though some sources suggest other methods of murder. In the Orthodox Church, one of those massacred is remembered as a saint, al-Harith, along with his fellow martyrs ("The Great Martyr Arethas, and all those with him in Arabia") every year on October 24, particularly by the Arabic-speaking Orthodox of the patriarchates of Antioch and Jerusalem. It was in response to this massacre that Justinian, then in charge of the affairs of his uncle, the emperor Justin I, sent a mission aimed at overthrowing its perpetrator by forces from nearby Christian Ethiopia under its emperor Caleb, and also in hopes of wresting control of the vital sea-link to the spice and silk markets of India from the Persians. Arab tradition, preserved in Greek Church writings, has it that Dhu Nuwas, faced with certain defeat, committed suicide by riding his horse into the Red Sea.

Mecca was the center of Arab paganism, which focused on the sanctuary of its gods, a cube-shaped monument called the Ka'ba that housed a sacred black stone, a site of pilgrimage later embraced by Islam once the pagan idols had been destroyed. Yet even Mecca had a Christian community. Waraqa Ibn Nawfal, the cousin of Muhammad's first wife, Khadija, is reputed to have been the city's bishop, and there are contemporary Arabic sources that allude to the Prophet's possible Jewish ancestry. There is no doubt that he had more than passing familiarity with the Old Testament since many of its prophets, two in particular, Abraham and Moses, as well as Joseph, David, and Solomon, crop up frequently in the Qur'an, as does the person of Jesus, the son of Mary, who is highly revered in Islam as the final authority regarding the fate of all souls on the Day of Judgment. Some of the more familiar biblical stories are also found in the Qur'an, notably the testing of Abraham, who in Muslim tradition was prepared to sacrifice his first son, Ishmael (Isma'il), by the bondswoman Hagar rather than his second, Isaac (Ishaq), by his wife Sarah in old age. The virgin birth of Jesus occurred in the shade of a date palm, rather than in a cave or a stable according to the Eastern Orthodox and Western Catholic traditions, respectively. God created the world and all that is in it in six days, but not strictly according to the slightly differing schedules related in the first two chapters of Genesis. Like extreme Evangelical Christians, traditionalist Muslims view the story of creation as an undeniable fact. Darwin's theory of evolution is for them, therefore, seriously problematic.

Muhammad is traditionally thought to have been born in 570, "the Year of the Elephant," which marked the failed siege of Mecca by Christian Ethiopian armies moving north from Yemen with what must have included at least one of these magnificent beasts previously unknown to the inhabitants of the Arabian Peninsula. Perhaps it was felt necessary years later to link the Prophet's birth with such a dramatic event when in fact the precise date was not known. What is known is that he was orphaned at an early age (his father died before his birth and his mother when he was only six) and that he was raised by an uncle and other members of his extended family, the clan of Hashim who belonged to the leading Quraysh tribe of Mecca. As a youth he is reputed to have travelled to Syria as part of a family trading caravan that spent an evening encamped outside the city of Bosra, some seventy miles south of Damascus, where a monk, Sergius Bahira, of the Christian Nestorian or, as often described, Arrian sect, met the young man and immediately recognized him as a future prophet.

Some years later, Muhammad married a wealthy Meccan widow, Khadija, traditionally thought to be in her late thirties or even forty, some twelve years his senior. Despite her age, she bore him four daughters and two sons, according to Sunni tradition, only two of the daughters reaching adulthood, Fatima and Zaynab. The Shi'a claim that she bore only Fatima and that the others were from Khadija's sister. One of Muhammad's later wives, an Egyptian Christian, Maryam al-Qubtiyya (Mary the Copt), is also said by Sunnis to have given birth to a son who died in infancy. Both Sunnis and Shi'a, however, acknowledge that the only grandchildren of the Prophet were Fatima's two sons, Hasan and Husayn.

Meanwhile, Muhammad continued to work as a merchant until the age of forty when he suddenly began receiving divine messages from the angel Gabriel as he meditated in the desert wastes outside the city. These revelations continued for more than twenty years until his death in 632. Muhammad, who was admittedly illiterate, memorized these verses, as did many of his followers who continued to recite them in his presence. Early Christian critics of Islam, notably St. John of Damascus, were convinced that Muhammad was either deranged, epileptic, a soothsayer, or—even worse—a heretic, and that the circumstances of his revelations were highly suspect. For St. John, who served the early Umayyad rulers as a senior administrator before retiring to the monastery of Mar Saba near Bethlehem, Muhammad had "concocted his own heresy, from the Old and New Testaments which he had chanced upon, and from conversations with an Arian monk," and that from these "laughable revelations he taught his followers to worship God."[2] For Dante, both Muhammad and his son-in-law 'Ali, the fourth Sunni caliph and first Shi'a imam, deserved to languish at the bottom of hell enduring hideous tortures befitting "sowers of scandal and division."[3]

Whether divinely inspired or the delusions of a deranged but calculating mind, as some contemporary Christian critics believed, these revelations were to become the sacred text of Islam, the Holy Qur'an, Arabic for "that which is written or recited," and which Muslims hold to be the literal word of God. The thrust of the new faith was that there is but one God, Allah, and that Muhammad is the final prophet (*nabi*), or *rasul*—the "messenger" chosen by God to restore the true monotheism of Abraham which Muslims believe had been distorted by both Judaism and Christianity. The word "Islam," which the Prophet used to describe his faith, translates as "submission" (to the will of God), and he demanded absolute adherence to his revelations. All history before the divine revelations was decried by Muslims as the age of ignorance (*jahiliyya*). Muhammad's rejection of pagan Arab belief with its many gods did not go over well with the ruling powers in Mecca, whose prosperity relied on income derived from the worship of the gods whose idols reposed in the Ka'ba. Three years after the first Qur'anic verses were revealed in 610, Muhammad began preaching his new religion in Mecca, and his handful of early followers started praying in public. Faced with persecution, a small number of the faithful fled to Ethiopia for sanctuary on several occasions, but all had returned by 629. In the year 622 Muhammad, his wife, and his Meccan followers were forced to flee north to Yathrib (al-Madina) where they were initially welcomed by the city's large Jewish population, giving rise to some questions as to the Prophet's possible Jewish ancestry. This desperate migration in search of refuge—*al-hijra* in Arabic and *hegira* in Latin—marks year one of the Muslim calendar.

During his eight years in Yathrib/al-Madina, Muhammad gradually increased his influence, initially by ingratiating himself with the Jewish community there and by trying to win them over to his new faith, which the Arabs of Mecca had thus far rejected. To this end, his followers made their daily prayer rituals facing Jerusalem, not Mecca. The year before the hijra, Muhammad had performed his spectacular feat of bi-location by journeying to heaven via the place in Jerusalem where the Second Temple had once stood, described as the *masjid al-aqsa* ("the farthest house of worship"), on the back of a graceful white steed called al-Buraq, often portrayed with a human face (especially in Persian and Indian miniatures), accompanied by the angel Gabriel, while simultaneously remaining at the Ka'ba in Mecca. According to the Hadith, or verified oral tradition that is the source of the account, Muhammad, having tethered al-Buraq at the Western Wall while he prayed, then ascended to the highest heaven where he negotiated with God the number of daily prayers required of Muslims at five, substantially down from the original fifty demanded. He also met and prayed with Adam, Noah, Abraham, Joseph, Moses, John the Baptist, and, finally, Jesus. The seven circles of heaven, home to these prophets, are described as being made of precious metals and stones, much as the Christian heaven is portrayed at the end of the Book of Revelation—a city of pure gold with jasper walls, pearly gates, and foundations of sapphire, emeralds, and other precious stones. By virtue of this miraculous event, known to Muslims as *al-isra' wa'l-mi'raj* (the Night Journey or Ascent) and celebrated every year on the twenty-seventh day of the Islamic month of Rajab, Jerusalem over time became the third holiest place in Islam (after Mecca and Medina) and the site of the magnificent Dome of the Rock Sanctuary (Masjid Qubbat al-Sakhra), completed in 691 over the site of Muhammad's reputed heavenly ascent and on the reputed site of Abraham's aborted sacrifice of his son Isaac. The nearby al-Aqsa Mosque was completed a few years later, and the compound containing both mosques is known to Muslims as the "Noble Sanctuary"(al-Haram al-Sharif). To Jews it is the Temple Mount, the remaining foundations of which, called the "Western Wall," are the focus of their prayers for the restoration of an earlier, long-vanished holy site.

Unimpressed by Muhammad's remarkable journey to God's dwelling place via their holy city and other arguments in support of his divine mission, the Jews of Medina refused to acknowledge him as their messiah and disparaged the Prophet as a fraud. Angered at this rejection, Muhammad and his flock took final control of the city by violent means. Some Jewish tribes were forced into exile, but one Jewish clan, the Qurayzah, was dealt with particularly harshly. All the adult males were killed and their women and children sold into slavery or taken into Muslim households—one-fifth of the captives reserved for the Prophet himself—where up to four wives (not to mention concubines, means of support permitting) were sanctioned by divine revelation, and divorce became a relatively easy procedure.[4] Shortly thereafter, the largest remaining Jewish town in the region, Khaybar, was conquered and all its inhabitants subjugated.

In the meantime, a number of the Arab clans of Medina accepted Muhammad's teaching, perhaps as many as ten thousand new followers. The Prophet and his now-substantial power base succeeded in fighting off several attempts by the pagan elite of Mecca to overthrow him, and in 630 he returned to his natal city in triumph. Two years later, however, he was dead. As the earliest biographer of the Prophet, Muhammad Ibn Ishaq (704–768), tells us in his *Sirat al-Rasul Allah* (*The Life of the Prophet of Allah*), Muhammad's death was the ultimate outcome of an initially failed attempt by one of the justifiably bitter Jewish widows of Medina to poison him.[5] Commenting on these events, eminent Scottish scholar of Islam W. Montgomery Watt noted that "the Jews had opposed Muhammad to the utmost of their ability, and they had been utterly crushed," but also speculated "on what would have happened had they come to terms with him instead of opposing him," and concluded that "they could have secured very favourable terms from him, including religious autonomy, and . . .

might have become partners in the Arab empire and Islam a sect of Jewry. How different the face of the world would be now, had that happened! . . . A great opportunity was lost."[6]

As soon as news of the Prophet's death became known, many of the loose alliances that had been hastily established with Beduin tribes began to unravel almost immediately, but the fervor of faith and the strength of leadership exhibited by Muhammad's closest companions, in Arabic the *ansar*, held the followers of the new religion together. Muhammad left no living male heir, only his surviving daughter, Fatima, who was married to her cousin 'Ali, by whom she bore her two sons, Hasan and Husayn. A bitter split over who was to succeed the Prophet surfaced immediately, leading directly to the Sunni-Shi'a divide that has plagued Islam ever since. The ansar favored the election of a successor (*khalifa* or caliph) by tribal elders from among their own number, while a large number of the faithful supported a hereditary line of leadership under the Prophet's first cousin and son-in-law. 'Ali was an undeniably formidable warrior but a leader who, despite his legendary prowess on the battlefield cleaving opponents cleanly in two with his famous double-pronged sword (Dhu al-Faqar or zulfikar) at a crucial moment—the Battle of Siffin in 657—lacked the "killer instinct," the will to win at all costs.

In the crucial choice of a first successor the companions prevailed, and Abu Bakr, the father of Muhammad's favorite wife, the child-bride 'A'isha, was chosen. He died just two years after his election, but during that volatile period the rule of Islam over Arabia was consolidated in what are known as the Riddah (secession/apostasy) Wars. He was succeeded by the second of the so-called orthodox or rightly guided (*al-rashidun*) caliphs, 'Umar Ibn al-Khattab, under whose inspired leadership the new religion began its expansion into the rich and fertile lands of the Eastern Roman (Byzantine) and Persian empires which bordered the barren and desolate wastes of Arabia Deserta. A devoutly religious man who personally eschewed the trappings of wealth which had suddenly overwhelmed his victorious armies, 'Umar also promoted tolerance of other religions, as exemplified by his covenant protecting the Christian holy sites in Jerusalem following its capture in 637. By the time of his death in 644 (he was murdered by a disgruntled Persian convert), Islamic armies had overrun Palestine, Syria, and Mesopotamia, defeating Byzantine and Persian armies in 636 at the Battles of Yarmuk and al-Qadisiyya, respectively, and were poised to conquer Egypt, Persia, and beyond.

How did this transformation of the power structure of the ancient world, unimaginable at the time, occur? As the religiously motivated but primitive forces of Islam were soon to discover to their delight and surprise, the two great empires that bordered Arabia were not the invincible powers they were thought to be. For nearly two decades (610–629), they had been at war with each other, and by the time the Byzantines had driven the Persians back to Mesopotamia and recovered Jerusalem and the holy relic of the True Cross in the process, they were both financially and militarily exhausted. The emperor Heraclius was already well into a terminal illness and unable to rally his forces against what should have been an insignificant threat from a few thousand Beduin tribesmen whose ancestors had occasionally troubled the southern desert frontiers by the odd raid, only to be bought off time and again by gifts and titles.

This time it was different. The wealthy provinces of Syria, Palestine, and Egypt were in open rebellion against the Orthodox Christian faith of the emperor, his patriarchs, and their Greek-speaking subjects. Since the middle of the fifth century, the majority of the inhabitants of the southern provinces bordering Arabia who spoke Aramaic (Syriac) and Coptic (a mixture of ancient Egyptian and Greek) had broken from the mainstream Orthodox Church to follow rival Christian creeds, Nestorianism and Monophysitism, which were condemned by the Ecumenical Councils of Ephesus (431) and Chalcedon (451), respectively, and survive to this day. The Christians of the patriarchates of Antioch (Syria), Jerusalem (Palestine), and Alexandria (Egypt), as well as the Armenians inside the Byzantine Empire deeply resented the persecution of their heterodox beliefs and political positioning by the emperor and his Greek clergy, and saw in Islam a tolerant ally against a common enemy. Many openly sided with the invaders, or at best stood passively by as the imperial forces were defeated. The Monophysites of Syria, called Jacobites after one of their earliest spiritual leaders, Jacob (Ya'qub) Barada'i, were particularly supportive of their new rulers in the years following the Islamic conquest, just as they had been of the Persian invaders a generation earlier. In return, they were treated deferentially by their new Muslim rulers and may have even influenced the manner in which Muslims pray. In another striking similarity, the turbans of Shi'a divines are very similar to those worn by bishops of the Syriac and Coptic Orthodox and Maronite Catholic churches. In Persian Mesopotamia, the Semitic majority, which had abandoned the official Zoroastrian faith of their Aryan masters in favor of non-Orthodox Christianity, also welcomed their Arabian cousins as liberators.

The victorious armies did not initially impose their own religion on their newly subjugated peoples, and for many years did not mix with them, but kept to themselves in purpose-built settlements outside the major cities of the conquered territories more suited to their nomadic way of life. The conquered peoples were permitted to keep their religion provided they were "People of the Book" (*ahl al-kitab*), that is, followers of a written scripture like Christians and Jews, and provided their adult males paid a poll tax (*jizya*) in lieu of military service, which was reserved for Muslims. In Islam these subject peoples were referred to as dhimmi, or protected citizens. They and recent Islamic converts were also subject to the *kharaj*, or property tax, from which Arab Muslims were exempt.

Followers of Islam were expected to adhere to the so-called Five Pillars (*arkan*)—witness to the oneness of God and to Muhammad as his final prophet; prayer five times a day at prescribed times and in a prescribed manner, preceded by prescribed ablutions; charity (*zakat*) to the poor and to the community, usually set at around 2.5 percent of one's income; fasting from dawn to dusk during the entire month of Ramadan (in which Muhammad received his first revelations) and on several other specific occasions; and pilgrimage (*hajj*) to Mecca and Medina during the Islamic month of Dhu al-Hijjah at least once in a believer's lifetime, circumstances permitting. Individual pilgrimages conducted at other times during the year, known as the '*umra*, were deemed laudable but did not count as the proper hajj performed at the proper time in the company of thousands of fellow believers. For some Muslims, especially the Shi'a discussed later, a sixth obligation was that of Holy War (*jihad*) to protect and spread the religion revealed by the Prophet from the Dar al-Islam (areas controlled by the new faith) to the rest of the world, known to Muslims as the Region of War (Dar al-Harb), or territories yet to be conquered. This is actually the secondary meaning of "jihad," since it originally meant (and still means) "struggle over an adversary," which can be something abstract such as adversity or evil. This meaning is still conveyed in the word's use as a proper or family name, as often borne by Christians (especially Orthodox), male and female, as well as by Muslims. The Shi'a also add to the first pillar, the *shahada* or "witness to the oneness of God," the phrase "and 'Ali is his [Muhammad's] *wali* or caretaker" and prescribe other requirements, such as to love the family of the Prophet and to hate and curse their enemies, and subscribe to the infallibility (*ismah*) of 'Ali and the imams who would succeed him.

Under 'Umar's successor, 'Uthman Ibn 'Affan (644–656), the armies of Islam expanded rapidly—west into Egypt, east into the Persian heartland,

and north into the Greek-speaking regions of Antioch and Cilicia, and Armenia beyond. It was also during his reign that the Qur'an took its present written form, having until then survived somewhat precariously as a largely oral tradition. Its integrity came under threat as those of the generation of the Prophet who had committed it to memory began to die out. Many were lost in warfare, including an estimated ten thousand men in the lengthy Battle of the Camel, which took place near Basra in southern Mesopotamia in 656 between the supporters of 'Ali and those of 'A'isha, the wife of the Prophet, known to Muslims as Umm al-Mu'minin (mother of Muslim believers).

On the death of 'Uthman—like his predecessor, the victim of assassination—the followers of 'Ali, who had never given up on their determination to achieve the goal of rule by the Prophet's descendants, finally succeeded in electing him the fourth, and final, "orthodox" caliph. It proved to be a short-lived victory. After his election, he was challenged by his opponents, the old-guard elite of Mecca who were among the last to accept Islam, led by the governor of Syria, Mu'awiya, who was a relative of the murdered caliph 'Uthman. He demanded that 'Ali deliver up the assassin. 'Ali refused. A battle between the two sides took place in 657 at Siffin in the desert between Syria and 'Iraq. Just as the tide appeared to be turning in his favor, 'Ali yielded to an appeal for a negotiated peace. A significant number of the caliph's supporters saw this as a sign of weakness and abandoned him and the Islamic *umma*, or community, calling for an entirely new order.

Islam's Earliest Dissenters—The Kharijites

Those who threw off their allegiance to the last of the Rashidun caliphs are known as Seceders (*al-Khariji* or *al-Khawarij*/Kharijites)—literally "those who broke away" from the heretofore undivided community of the Prophet's followers. The doctrine which they developed in support of their departure was based on a radical democratic view of the caliphate which held that any Muslim, including a non-Arabian convert or, even more dramatically, a woman, could aspire to the leadership of the faithful. The first of what were to be many Islamic sects, it still survives today in a more moderate, nonviolent form, chiefly in Oman (1.2 million followers, or 75 percent of the population) where its followers came to be known as Ibadis (*al-Ibadiyyah*) after an early reformer. The remaining 25 percent of Oman's population are Sunnis centered in the southwestern province of al-Salalah. Ibadis are also found in Zanzibar (under Omani suzerainty from 1698 to 1890) and in a few isolated Berber-speaking pockets in North Africa (the Mzab oases around Ghardaïa in Saharan Algeria, Djerba island off the southern coast of Tunisia, and the Jabal Nafusa region of northwestern Libya), the remnants of the Ibadi Rustamid dynasty that dominated the central Maghreb from 776 to 909. The total Ibadi population outside Oman totals barely 250,000.

It was one of these Khariji dissidents who succeeded in assassinating the caliph/imam 'Ali in 661 as an act of revenge for the defeat of this separatist faction at the Battle of Nahrawan in 658. In the chaotic aftermath of 'Ali's violent death, the Meccan elite in the person of Mu'awiya were able to seize power. He ruled from Damascus over a vastly expanding Muslim Empire from 661 until his peaceful death in 680, during which time the Umayyad dynasty was firmly established. His successors held on to power until 750. Not noted for their strict adherence to the tenets of Islam (some of Mu'awiya's successors were notoriously addicted to wine, forbidden to the faithful in the Qur'an), the Umayyads were from the start deeply mistrusted by many Muslims. Based in Damascus, the civilized comforts of which Mu'awiya preferred to the austere, religious environment of Medina, the Umayyads were faced with open rebellion by the followers of 'Ali who, on his death, transferred their allegiances initially to his elder son, Hasan. When Hasan died in Medina in 670, either "from excesses of the harem," according the Umayyads, or by poisoning, as claimed by 'Ali's followers, his younger brother, Husayn, inherited the mantle of his father along with the loyalty of 'Ali's devoted supporters.

Rise of the Shi'a Movement

When Mu'awiya died in 680, Husayn challenged the caliph's son and successor, Yazid I, and marched from Arabia with a handful of family members, including his half-brother 'Abbas Ibn 'Ali, and followers into southern Mesopotamia (al-'Iraq) at the invitation of the people of the city of Kufa. He was intercepted by forces loyal to Yazid at a barren desert site near the town of Karbala'. In the confrontation and battle that ensued during the first ten days of the Islamic month of Muharram, the Prophet's grandson was brutally cut down, along with his seventy-two companions, on the tenth day (October 10, 680, though some sources put it on the 13th) and his severed head taken to Yazid as proof of Umayyad triumph. The surviving women and children were taken captive and forced to cross the Syrian Desert in the early October heat, as the result of which a number perished.

The followers of 'Ali never forgave the Umayyads for shedding the blood of Husayn and many of the other members of the Prophet's family who had accompanied him. The slaughter of the Prophet's younger grandson marks the defining moment of the Sunni-Shi'a divide. His body was buried in Karbala', and the grave is today the site of a grand mosque marking, along with the companion mosque containing the tomb of his father 'Ali in nearby al-Najaf, the two holiest of Shi'a shrines.

From the very earliest years following the murder of Husayn, devotees have reenacted his martyrdom annually at a religious festival known as 'Ashura'—the ten days that commemorate his suffering and, on the last of these, his death—during which self-flagellation has traditionally played a major role. Shi'a banners displayed on public occasions are black, signifying a perpetual state of mourning for their martyred hero, as opposed to those of the Sunnis which, like the Sa'udi Arabian flag, are green—Muhammad's favorite color, as one might expect from someone who lived all his life in a mostly barren, treeless, desert environment.

After the Karbala' killings, the Shi'a refused to recognize Umayyad rule, instead looking for guidance to the descendants of 'Ali and his two sons, most of whom had to live in hiding and suffered martyrdom. Their opponents and oppressors came to be known as Sunnis, or followers of the sunna (path) of the Prophet Muhammad. As the years passed, the differences between the two branches of Islam began to widen and their mutual enmity deepen to such an extent that for some Sunnis, especially the extremist Wahhabi sect of Sa'udi Arabia, founded in the eighteenth century by a puritanical scholar named Muhammad Ibn 'abd al-Wahhab, the Shi'a are not even considered to be truly Muslim.

Division Breeds Division—Shi'a Rise to World Power

One of the more famous Hadith, a collection of orally transmitted sayings attributed to the Prophet through reputable sources that supplement the Qur'an as the basis of Sunni religious law (Shari'a), predicts that after his death the unity of Islam would be riven by division.[7] As we have seen, the Kharijites were the first to break away, but with the assassination of the fourth "orthodox" caliph, 'Ali, by one of their followers, a second and far more important split divided Islam led by his supporters. Known as Shi'a (a shortened form of Shi'at 'Ali or followers of 'Ali), they referred to themselves as People of the Mantle (*ahl al-'aba'* or *al-kisa'*), recalling the tradition that the Prophet blessed 'Ali, Fatima, and their two sons by holding his mantle or cloak over them while praying to God that they might be purified. For the Shi'a, these five holy figures—Muhammad and the four members of his family to whom he gave special blessing—have their five treacherous Sunni counterparts who are reviled and cursed: the first three "orthodox" caliphs (Abu Bakr, 'Umar, and 'Uthman), the first Umayyad caliph, Mu'awiya, and his son and successor Yazid I, who ordered the Karbala' massacre. 'Ali is held in particular reverence, even in some cases eclipsing the Prophet himself, having a divine aura that Muhammad never claimed. Matti Moosa in his study *Extremist Shiites: The Ghulat Sects* (1987) concluded that "for all intents and purposes, the relationship between 'Ali and God is similar to that [in Christianity] of Jesus to God."[8]

The Shi'a rejected the concept of a caliphate based on power struggle and dynasty—the pattern followed by their neighboring Christian Byzantine Empire—and looked to the Prophet's lineal heirs as their religious and political leaders, whom they called imams. In Sunni Islam, an imam is simply the person who leads communal prayer rituals and usually preaches the weekly sermon (*khutba*) in the mosque on Friday. There is no clergy as such and no liturgy like the celebration of the Eucharist in both Orthodox and Catholic Christianity that would require any. All Muslims in the Sunni tradition are theoretically equal regardless of their worldly status. The Shi'a, however, believed their imam to have divine powers by virtue of their blood link to 'Ali and the Prophet. Sunnis also deeply revere the family of the Prophet (*ahl al-bayt*, literally "people of the house" or family of Muhammad), but from the beginning of the split they viewed the Shi'a as a direct threat to the emerging caliphate, and their imams were continuously harassed and their followers persecuted by both the Umayyads and their Abbasid successors. They were in constant fear for their lives and for good reason all imams, according to "Twelver" Shi'a tradition, were murdered except for the twelfth, who went into hiding and will return at the end of time. The imams exercised their leadership through an underground network of authority, which was not strong enough to prevent further division. Throughout the Umayyad period, the Shi'a were confined to southern 'Iraq and the eastern shores of the Arabian Peninsula, but gradually they began to expand to other areas of the growing Islamic Empire, particularly in central Asia (Turkestan), parts of what is today Afghanistan, and southern Pakistan (Sind).

Fivers, Seveners, and Twelvers

Loyalty to the earliest imams was sufficient to maintain a unity of a belief among the earliest Shi'a faithful, but the pressure of constant persecution from the Sunni Umayyads and early 'Abbasids, compounded by internecine bickering over not only succession but also theological issues (in particular those pertaining to the divine nature of 'Ali and access to the extent of divine inspiration attributed to later imams), gradually led to division and fragmentation.

Fivers, Also Known as Zaydis

The first split in the Shi'a movement grew out of the disputed succession of the fifth imam, Muhammad al-Baqir, following the death of his father and predecessor the fourth imam, 'Ali Ibn Husayn, in 712. Those who favored his brother Zayd, known today as Zaydis or "Fivers" (*al-mukhammisa*), established an imamate in Yemen which survived until 1962 when a Sunni-led revolution backed by Egypt under Nasser overthrew the Zaydi establishment. Nearly 50 percent of the population of Yemen, concentrated in the northwest of the country, still adheres to Zaydi Shi'ism, and it is the force behind the long-simmering revolt against the secular republican government which has the city of Sa'dah (where the medieval Zaydi imamate was established) near the Sa'udi border as its base. Large numbers of Zaydis also live in the Sa'udi Arabian province of 'Asir across the border from northern Yemen and provide refuge and support for the rebels. Unlike the later "Sevener" and "Twelver" Shi'a discussed later, the Zaydis did not require a hereditary inheritance of the imamate, asserting that any direct descendant of the Prophet could succeed to the title. They also rejected the later Twelver doctrine that the imam was divinely inspired and infallible in matters of faith and morals, as well as their belief in *ghayba*, or the "hidden" imam who will appear at the end of time to usher in an era of justice. For Zaydis, justice in this world can only be achieved by means of a constant struggle, which the imam was duty bound to lead.

Several other Zaydi Shi'a movements achieved success in the early Islamic Empire, notably in Morocco (al-Maghrib) under a dynasty known as the Idrisids (named after their first sultan, Idris), which ruled from 788 to 974 and whose ancestry is still claimed by the present royal family. The king of Morocco bears the ancient title of the Sunni caliphs, *amir al-mu'minin* (Prince of the Believers) but does not assert this claim beyond the borders of his country. In addition, the later Abbasid Empire was effectively controlled for over a century (934–1055) by the Iranian Buwayhid dynasty, whose leadership subscribed to Zaydi Shi'ism but did not have any long-term impact on the beliefs of the populace.

Seveners, Also Known as Isma'ilis

The second and most important division in the Shi'a movement occurred in the late eighth century over the issue of succession to the sixth imam, Ja'far al-Sadiq, following his death in 765. His eldest son, Isma'il, was designated to succeed him, but he died before his father. Those who supported Isma'il as the rightful seventh imam and his son Muhammad as the eighth came to be known as Isma'ilis, or Seveners. Their leadership has passed through male heirs up to the present day, the forty-ninth of whom in the Nizari line of succession is the current imam, Prince Karim IV Aga Khan, born in 1936. They number some 15–20 million and are mostly found in Pakistan (particularly in the Gilgit-Baltistan region, also known as Balawaristan, in the far northeast of the country, including the idyllic Hunza Valley), western India (Gujarat, Maharashtra/Mumbai, and Rajasthan), Afghanistan (especially the strategic Wakhan corridor linking it with China), neighboring Uzbekistan and Tajikistan, plus small but historic concentrations in Syria (numbering some 200,000), where the movement began. In addition, substantial communities of the Isma'ili subsect known as Bohras are found in western India and in the city and region of Najran in southern Sa'udi Arabia and across the border into Yemen (see under "Fatimids, Druze, and Bohras"). Large numbers of Indian Isma'ilis emigrated to British East Africa during the Raj, and later to England or back to India after the independence of Kenya, Uganda, and Tanganyika, due to persecution by the new African governments who resented the community's wealth. In recent years, small numbers have returned to their former East African homes.

Having broken with majority Shi'a community, the Isma'ilis began to spread their doctrine with its combination of outward (literal) and esoteric (inner) readings of the Qur'an and a spiritual interpretation of Islam that denied the necessity of ritual forms of worship. They were particularly successful in North Africa and ultimately Egypt, where they established the Fatimid Empire.

Twelvers, or the Mainstream Shi'a of Today

The vast majority of the world's Shi'a, however, believe that because Isma'il had predeceased his father, the sixth imam Ja'far, the imamate passed to

Ja'far's surviving third son, Musa al-Kathim (Kazem), and his successors, the last of whom—the twelfth imam by their reckoning, Muhammad al-Mahdi—disappeared at the age of five in 874 following the death of his father, the eleventh imam. According to them, he went into a cave at Samarra in central 'Iraq, now beneath a cellar in the Golden Mosque built over it, and entered into a state of occultation where for the next sixty-eight years he remained in touch with his followers through four deputies in succession. This period is known as the Minor Occultation (*ghaybat al-sughra*). In 941, when the fourth of these intermediaries felt death approaching, he announced that there would be no more deputies and that a period of Major Occultation (*ghaybat al-kubra*) would begin. The twelfth imam would have no further contact—indirect or direct—with the faithful until he emerged from hiding at the end of time as the *mahdi*, or precursor-redeemer—a figure expected by all Muslims, who will initiate the process of bringing in the *yawm al-din*, or Day of Judgment. In the meantime, he was the "Hidden Imam" from whom Shi'a religious leaders were given divine direction through the Word of God. His followers came to be known as Twelvers (Ithna'ashari) and held the loyalty of the majority of Shi'a faithful in their traditional homeland of southern 'Iraq and, far more significantly, in Iran when it converted to Shi'ism many hundreds of years later under the Safavid dynasty in the mid-sixteenth century.

In the absence of a divinely guided imam, a religious hierarchy developed over time within Twelver Shi'ism, beginning with Islamic scholars or *mujtahids*, a word derived from the same Arabic root as "jihad" with the general meaning of "struggle," in this case the struggle to achieve divine wisdom. The mujtahids' struggle to achieve religious knowledge is known as *ijtihad*, from the same root. The most respected and revered are known by the general term *marja'*—an authority to whom one turns or appeals—and more specifically as the *marja' at al-taqlid*, or those worthy of emulation. Their followers, the *marja'iyya*, are usually congregated around a Shi'a seminary, or *hawza*. The most famous of these are found in al-Najaf and Karbala' in 'Iraq and at Qom and Mashhad in Iran. The highest of these religious scholars with the largest followings are recognized as "ayatollahs," a term based on a Qur'anic reference to "a sign of/from God" that will guide believers in a manner similar to that by which the Holy Spirit was sent by Christ to lead his followers to a closer understanding of their faith. A particularly respected few members of this rank hold the title of grand ayatollahs (*ayat-allah al-uthma*), chief among them at the present is 'Ali al-Sistani of al-Najaf. Such spiritual leaders, exercising ijtihad, give guidance to the Shi'a faithful in all aspects of their personal life and the practice of their religion. In the absence of an imam, the believer is required to follow a qualified mujtahid's directives.

In most cases, followers of a marja'al-taqlid are expected, on his death, to shift their allegiance to another spiritual leader. An exception was Lebanon's leading Shi'a scholar, the Grand Ayatollah Sayyid Muhammad Husayn Fadlallah, who died on July 4, 2010, aged seventy-five. He believed that deceased religious leaders were also deserving of emulation, and large numbers of his followers, not only in Lebanon but in 'Iraq, the Gulf, and the Indian subcontinent, continue to revere him through the enduring social and religious institutions administered in his name by his eldest son, Sayyid 'Ali Fadlallah, from a southern Beirut suburb. A liberal on many social issues, he strongly supported the equality of women and their right to defend themselves from both physical and social discrimination and abuse, in particular "honor" killings of women suspected of besmirching a family's reputation as the result of sexual relations outside of the bonds of marriage. Born to Lebanese parents in the holy city of al-Najaf, he was often referred to as the spiritual adviser to Hizbollah, but Fadlallah in fact was frequently at odds with the Lebanese militant group, particularly their belief in *wilayat al-faqih*, or the theocratic rule espoused by Grand Ayatollah Khomeini of Iran. Where he did support Hizbollah was in its fierce resistance to Israel's occupation of southern Lebanon and the very idea of a Jewish state in Palestine. In 1985 he was the target of a failed assassination attempt, claimed by Hizbollah to be by the American government and its allies, that killed or wounded hundreds of innocent women and children returning from their Friday noon prayers.

Approximately 15 to 20 percent of the Islamic faithful today are Shi'a, the majority of them Twelvers. They form the bulk of the population in Iran (where some 16 million of 65 million Iranian Shi'a, or nearly 25 percent, are Turkish-speaking Azeris living in the northwest of the country on the border with Azerbayjan), 'Iraq, Azerbayjan, Bahrain, and the eastern province of Sa'udi Arabia. They are a large minority (30 percent or more) in Lebanon and have major concentrations in Pakistan (Kashmir, Punjab, Sind, and Baluchistan), India (e.g., Hyderabad and Lucknow, the location of two Shi'ia holy sites: the Asfi Imambara, built in 1784—a national focus of celebration during 'Ashura'—and the Shah Najaf Imambara), and the former Soviet Republics of central Asia and Afghanistan. The largest

Shi'a group in the last country is made up of the Mongol-descended Hazara tribes, who make up about 10 percent of the population. Most are Twelvers, though there are Isma'ili Hazaras (and even a few Sunnis) as well. Several hundred thousand Hazaras are also found in southwest Pakistan (Baluchistan region), especially the city of Quetta, where like Shi'a elsewhere in the country they have been frequent targets of murderous attacks by Sunni extremists. As many as 3 million Hazaras have fled Afghanistan for Iran, but despite being fellow Twelver Shi'a they have not been granted citizenship, probably because of their distinctive Central Asiatic physical features and language, something the Iranian 'Aryan Shi'a majority deny.

Many Afghan and other central Asian Shi'a hold that the first imam 'Ali is buried not in the holy city of al-Najaf but in the northern Afghan city of Mazar-i-Sharif ("The Noble Shrine") at the Blue Mosque/Shrine of Hazrat 'Ali. Some scholars believe, however, that the tomb is actually the final resting place of Zarathustra, the founder of Zoroastrianism.

Isma'ili Qarmatians vs. Sunni Abbasids

An early division in the history of Isma'ilism occurred in Bahrain and the eastern Arabian Peninsula, where Shi'a Islam had taken early root. Known as Qarmatians (al-Qaramita) after their founder, Hamdan al-Qarmat, this breakaway group established their own state in the region in 899. They subscribed to a belief that held that Isma'il, the eldest son of the sixth imam and imam-designate Ja'far al-Sadiq, had not died before his father but had entered into a state of occultation, a radical interpretation of Sevener theology that died out with them in the eleventh century. These radical Isma'ilis espoused communistic and utopian ideals and, something unheard of in other branches of Islam, a strict vegetarian diet.

A century and a half before the Qarmatian rise to power, the Umayyad dynasty of Damascus had been overthrown in 750 by a combination of forces, principally 'Iraqi and Persian, known as the Abbasids after their first caliph, 'Abdallah Abu'l-'Abbas, whose son and successor, al-Mansur, moved the capital of his empire east from Damascus to a new city on the Tigris river called Dar al-Salam, "the abode of peace," but popularly called by the name of the small Christian village it replaced, Baghdad. Initially supported by many Shi'a because of their hatred for the Umayyads, the Abbasids soon declared their true Sunni colors, and the struggle between the two principal forces within Islam continued unabated. The Umayyads, however, managed to reestablish themselves in one of the farthest corners of Dar al-Islam: Spain (or in Arabic, al-Andalus), where a lone survivor of the massacre of the royal family in Damascus proclaimed himself as the caliph 'Abd al-Rahman I in Cordoba in 756. He and his heirs presided over a dominion of exceptional wealth, culture, and scientific achievement that lasted for nearly three centuries. The Abbasid caliphs remained in Baghdad, albeit with little real power or authority after the tenth century, until the last of their line was killed by the Mongol invaders led by Hulagu Khan, the son of Genghis, in 1258 and the city destroyed. When the Isma'ili Fatimids came to power in Cairo in 969, there were three rival caliphates vying for the loyalty of the Muslim umma, two Sunni and one Shi'a.

It was this divided Islamic milieu that allowed the Crusaders from Western Europe to achieve their amazing success in establishing four Latin Christian statelets—the Kingdom of Jerusalem, the two Counties of Edessa and Tripoli, and the Principality of Antioch (known collectively in medieval French as the "Outremer" or "overseas lands")—a presence in the heart of the Muslim world that was to endure for nearly two hundred years (1099–1291).

The Qarmatians were responsible for launching one of the earliest threats to the early Abbasid Empire just as its age of glory attained under the caliph Harun al-Rashid was coming to an end in the late eighth and early ninth centuries. Southern 'Iraq had already undergone a terrible upheaval from 869 to 883 with what became known as the Zanjid Revolt, led by a man claiming to be the descendant of 'Ali and supported by tens of thousands of East African slaves called *zanj* living in and around the city of Basra. No sooner had this rebellion been finally and ruthlessly crushed by the Abbasid authorities than the Qarmatians appeared on the scene in the zanjis' wake. Although they never succeeded in reaching Baghdad, the forces of this extremist Isma'ili Shi'a movement did manage to plunge all of 'Iraq south of the imperial capital once again into turmoil. In 930 they briefly captured Mecca, slaughtering thousands of pilgrims, throwing their bodies into the sacred well of Zamzam (the mildly brackish but potable waters of which Muslims believe saved the lives of Ishmael and his mother, Hagar), and absconding with the holiest of holies, the Black Stone from inside the Ka'ba shrine. This relic was eventually ransomed at great cost by the Abbasids in 952, but there still remains doubt if the stone they returned was the real one. Following military defeat in 976, the weakened Qarmatians slowly declined, finally vanishing from power in 1074, but Twelver Shi'ism remained strong in the region with no interruption until today; its followers form the majority of the population of both Bahrain and Eastern Sa'udi Arabia (al-Hasa province) as well as an important minority in Kuwait. Nearly 10 percent of Sa'udi Arabians (some 2 million out of a total of 23 million) are Shi'a, most of them centered in and around the oil-rich city of al-Dammam. Between one-quarter to one-third of Kuwaiti citizens (who number barely one-third of the country's total population of 3.5 million) are Twelver Shi'a. Most of the Kuwaiti Shi'a are Arabs of 'Iraqi, Bahraini, and Eastern Sa'udi origin, though a significant minority are descended from Farsi-speaking immigrants from Iran, including the commercially prominent Bebehani family. The remaining two-thirds of the population are foreign immigrant workers (largely other Arabs, Indians, and Pakistanis) who are not entitled to Kuwaiti citizenship.

Fatimids, Druze, and Bohras

At the same time the Qarmatians were defeated, other Isma'ilis had begun one of the major movements (*da'wa*, or "call") of medieval Islam based initially at the town of Salmiyya in central Syria, still a center of that country's small Sevener community. This movement was to take them to the pinnacle of power in Egypt with their own caliphate, that of the Fatimids (969–1171), whose rulers claimed descent through Fatima, daughter of the Prophet. Over time they developed their unique theological approach to Islamic scripture that stressed an esoteric, inner meaning (*bataniyya*) that could be understood only by the few.

An extreme movement within Fatimid Isma'ilis led to the founding of the Druze sect, first in Cairo and later in Lebanon and Syria, between 1017 and 1043. This sect survives among a million followers who hold secret beliefs with which only an enlightened few among them—both men and a high proportion of women—are entrusted. Strictly monogamous,[9] they do not outwardly observe any of the Sunni Five Pillars and believe in *tanassukh*, or the transmigration of souls after death. After the *Druze da'wa* was closed in 1043, no new members were admitted to the faith and the number of its followers was believed to have been fixed for all time. Although they refer to themselves as *muwahhidun*, or strict unitarians, they are called by the name of one of their early leaders, Neshtighin al-Darazi, who was later murdered and discredited. They are also known and refer to themselves as the Bani al-Ma'ruf because of their widely acknowledged generosity and proverbial hospitality. Unlike all other Shi'a offshoots, the Druze hold no special reverence for 'Ali or his family. They believe that the Fatimid imam caliph al-Hakim bi-Amr Allah was the final of a series of incarnations of the Supreme Deity (*al-'aql al-kulli*). Their secret scriptures (*al-Hikma al-Sharifa*, or *Noble Knowledge*) are contained in 111 documents and epistles received from al-Hakim after he mysteriously disappeared in 1021 (either reappearing later in the Far East as the Druze believe, or having been murdered at the order of his sister as his opponents claimed) and also from the two leading propagators of the Druze faith, Hamza Ibn 'Ali al-Zuzani and *Muqtana* Baha' al-Din al-Samuqi.

The principal geographical stronghold of the Druze has always been in the mountains of what is today southeastern Lebanon, where they developed a reputation early on as formidable warriors. Travelers from the West, in addition to admiring the military prowess of these mysterious people, were almost unanimously lavish in their praise of Druze hospitality as well as the comeliness of their women, who did not veil themselves in Muslim fashion, adopting rather an almost transparent scarf called the *mandil*. During Ottoman dominion, they achieved considerable political power under the Ma'nid dynasty, founded by Fakhr al-Din II in 1617, whose rule extended north into Cilicia, east to Palmyra, and south into Galilee. An admirer of the West, he invited Catholic missionaries to establish schools, which led to the introduction of printing presses and other innovations of the modern world. Although for political reasons he outwardly professed Sunni Islam, he was able to remain inwardly Druze, thanks to the widespread concept of *taqiyya* (dissimulation) or lying about one's faith common to all Shi'a in situations where it was necessary to do so in order to avoid persecution. Fakhr al-Din is also thought by many Christians to have secretly become a member of the Maronite church. It was in response to these allegations of apostasy that he was arrested on the orders of Sultan Murad IV in 1633, taken to Istanbul, and executed along with two of his sons two years later.

Because of Fakhr al-Din's enlightened rule and receptivity to Western ideas, he is regarded by Druze and Christians to be the father of modern Lebanon. After his death, an internal power struggle led to a civil war that forced a large number of Druze belonging to the Qaysi or Yazbaki factions to flee Mount Lebanon after 1711 for the uninhabited wastes of southern Syria, where they established a second major population center around the present-day city of al-Suwayda', known unofficially as the Mountain of the Druze (Jabal al-Duruz). A substantial number of the defeated Yazbakis, however, remained in their ancestral homes in Mount Lebanon and, under the leadership of the Arslan family based in 'Alayh, form the principal opposition to the dominant Druze political force in Lebanon led by the Junbalat clan.

Over the succeeding centuries, many Western observers became fasci-
nated by the secrets of the Druze religion, and there is a strong similarity
between this secrecy and the practices of Freemasonry, which may have
arisen out of early contact with the Crusaders. Indeed female Masonry,
known as the Order of the Eastern Star, has as its symbol the five-pointed
Druze star whose five colors of green, red, yellow, blue, and white embody
the cosmic ranks (*al-hudud*) represented by a specific dignitary, green being
that of Hamza as the personification of the Universal Mind or Intelligence
(al-'aql al-kulli).[10] Formal Druze worship is confined to weekly meetings
on Thursday evenings, during which all members of the community gather
together to discuss local issues before those not initiated into the secrets
of the faith (the *juhhal*, or the ignorant) are dismissed, and those who are
(the *'uqqal*, or enlightened) remain to read and study their holy scriptures.
There are also shrines (*maqamat*) built around the tombs of holy men and
women, usually on mountaintops, which are sites of retreat and pilgrimage. Religious leadership is exercised by the *ajawid*, or highest-ranking
members of the *'uqqal* who comprise the *masha'ikh al-din* (leaders of religion), as opposed to the *masha'ikh al-zaman*, or secular community leaders.
The highest religious authority is the *shaykh al-'aql*, who is chosen by the
religious leadership (with the tacit agreement of the political leaders) in
Lebanon, Syria, and Israel. Lebanon and Israel each have a single shaykh al-
'aql, whereas in Syria there are three, though that of al-Suwayda is generally
regarded as the first among equals.

Probably because of their secret religious beliefs and refusal to marry
outside their own community, strange practices ranging from incestuous
orgies to the worship of a Golden Calf were attributed to the Druze by
outsiders, but modern scholarship has dismissed such stories as examples
of disinformation spread by their enemies. The worst insult that can be
hurled at a Druze by an enemy is "*ya 'ajl*" (you calf), a reference to this
alleged object of adoration. Because the Druze believe in a form of reincarnation and refuse to observe most outwardly Sunni or Shi'a practices, many
within the wider Islamic community do not believe them to be really Muslim. Many if not most Druze themselves would privately agree, although in
Lebanon they have been regarded as Muslim since independence in 1944
for mainly political considerations. They do retain some Islamic customs,
notably the observation of 'Id al-Adha, or the Feast of Sacrifice that follows
the annual Pilgrimage to Mecca, and the recitation of the opening verse of
the Qur'an (al-Fatiha) at religious gatherings and at funerals. Their total
numbers of over a million include approximately 500,000 to 600,000 in

Syria, at least 350,000 in Lebanon, over 100,000 in Israel (Galilee), and another 100,000 in diaspora, chiefly the United States and Brazil.

Another important result of the Isma'ili religious ferment of eleventh-century Cairo that gave birth to the Druze came about with the death of the Fatimid imam caliph al-Mustansir in 1094. He was succeeded by his elder son, Nizar, but when he and his family were murdered shortly thereafter his followers fled to Iran, where they established the Nizari branch of Isma'ili Shi'ism that today is followed by 90 percent of all Isma'ilis. In the late thirteenth century, they fled further afield to the Indian subcontinent in the wake of defeat at the hand of the Mongol invaders of Genghis Khan. A breakaway group, however, gave their allegiance to Nizar's younger brother, Musta'li, and his successors. They remained in Egypt, but when Fatimid rule came to an end in 1171 they fled to Yemen and ultimately also to India, where they are known popularly as Bohras. Thus ended two centuries of Isma'ili presence in Egypt, whose population during the Fatimid era had remained in majority Sunni, especially outside Cairo, with a large but gradually declining community of Coptic Christians that has since remained stable for the last several centuries at about 10 percent of the total population. Official government censuses in the twentieth century put their numbers at only 6 percent, but this figure is widely regarded as a deliberate, politically motivated undercount.

The largest group of Bohras, the Dawudi branch, survives primarily in western India and numbers over one million. Two-thirds live in the province of Gujarat, and most of the remainder is found in the neighboring states of Maharashtra (Mumbai) and Madhya Pradesh, alongside a smaller group who claim to be Sunnis. The smaller Sulaymani branch is centered in northern Yemen and southern Sa'udi Arabia, especially the city of Najran, mixed with larger numbers of Zaydi Shi'a, and number about three hundred thousand followers. Bohras are frequently seen in Cairo as pilgrims in the old Fatimid area of the city at the mosque of the Druze founder, al-Hakim bi-Amr Allah, whom they, like the Druze, revere.

The majority Nizari Isma'ilis are best known in the West, unfairly, by the pejorative term Assassins (hashashshun) given to them by the Crusaders, some of whose leaders, like those of their Sunni Abbasid rivals, were victims of political murder by agents of the Nizari leadership, allegedly drugged on hashish before being sent out on their deadly missions. They remained a political and military force to be reckoned with until their power was curtailed in the mid-thirteenth century when their headquarters was overrun by the Mongols in Iran (Alamut) and by the Mamlukes, although their Syrian strongholds remain Isma'ili Shi'a population centers to this day. Most Nizaris in Iran fled to what are today Afghanistan, Pakistan, and India, and over the centuries they have evolved into one of the most liberal branches of Islam. The Nizari Isma'ili followers of the Aga Khan today bear no resemblance to the hashashun made infamous by the Crusader tales of "the Old Man of the Mountain." They, as well as the minority Isma'ili Bohras, are known for their skill and success as merchants and for their charitable works, especially through the Aga Khan Foundation, a private organization that focuses on hunger, poverty, illiteracy, and sickness in regions of Africa, Asia, and the Middle East.

'Alawi and Alevi—Same Name, Very Different People and Beliefs

The Sevener Shi'a were not alone in their sectarian fragmentation. The majority Twelvers also spawned their own divisions that survive today primarily in Syria and Turkey—the 'Alawi (Alawites) and Alevi, respectively. These two sects, along with several smaller groups in northern Mesopotamia, such as the Shabak and Bajwan as well as the Iranian Ali Ilahis, make up the extremist *ghulat* (from the Arabic root *ghlu*, "to exaggerate") Shi'a sects. These sects hold a common belief in the divine authority of 'Ali and his twelve successors.

'Alawi

The 'Alawi (Alawite) sect forms the majority of the population outside the capital city and smaller towns of the coastal province of Latakia (al-Ladhiqiyya) in northwestern Syria, known during the French Mandate of Syria as the Pays or État des Alaouites, and makes up about 12–13 percent of the country's population overall. They also spill over into the neighboring provinces of Hama and Homs and across Syria's international borders into northern Lebanon (the city of Tripoli and the province of 'Akkar—each of which sends one 'Alawi deputy to the 128-member Lebanese parliament) and the southernmost province of Turkey (Hatay/Alexandretta). Their total population is approximately 2.5 million, 90 percent of whom live in Syria. Among the most curious and syncretic quasi-Islamic sects, embodying many pagan and Christian elements in their secret practices, they are often paired with the Druze because of their shared belief in the transmigration of souls and their denial of the outward trappings of Islam (mosques, public prayer, and pilgrimage to Mecca) but have little else in common on closer examination.

'Alawi Islamic roots can be traced back to the ninth century and the shadowy figure of Abu Shuʻayb Muhammad Ibn Nusayr (d. 874, reputedly a disciple of the eleventh Twelver imam, Hasan al-ʻAskari), and they are also known as Nusayris after their alleged founder. But the term "Nusayri" can also be translated as a diminutive of an Arabic word for Christian (Nasira/Nasara, or Nazarene), which makes them, for Sunnis, into "little" followers of Christ.

And indeed there are many 'Alawi practices which smack of a heretical form of Christianity. They believe in a "trinity" of sorts ('Ali, Muhammad, and Salman al-Farisi, an early companion of the Prophet and, just to make things more complicated, a person who also figures in the Druze religious belief).Yet they claim to be, like the Druze, absolute unitarians, though God is fully manifested for them in the historical personage of 'Ali, which for Sunnis is total anathema. They practice a form of the Mass (*quddas*) in secret in which wine (but no bread) is consecrated by a religious leader (*naqib*)—in which the person of 'Ali, like Christ in the Orthodox and Catholic consecrated bread and wine, is believed to be present—and shared among the adult men in attendance. Women and children are not allowed. Since 'Alawis have no formal places of worship, these Masses are celebrated in homes or in hidden places.[11] 'Alawis are also frequently given Christian names such as Helen, Matthew, Gabriel, Catherine, and Elias.

Unlike other Muslims, 'Alawis bury their dead in sarcophagi above ground. Yet they observe the 'Id al-Fitr, the three-day feast that comes at the end of the month of Ramadan (but without observing the fast that precedes it), and the 'Id al-Adha, the feast that follows the annual pilgrimage to Mecca (without, like the Druze, performing the pilgrimage itself). They observe the ancient Persian New Year (Nowruz), the Christian feasts of the Epiphany, the feast days of St. John Chrysostom and St. Mary Magdalene, revere the Muslim figure of al Khidr (usually associated with St. George or Elias/Elijah), and practice *taqiyya*. Also in common with Christians, the 'Alawi women do not normally wear any head-covering in public, and when they do, mostly in villages, it is token and minimal. While subscribing to the concept of the transmigration of souls, they apply it only to men since women are deemed unworthy of religious knowledge and therefore not privy to the secrets of faith, unlike the Druze whose women have played an important role in their history and are well represented in their religiously initiated elite.

Historically, the 'Alawi formed the lowest socioeconomic class of Syria but rose to power recently through the military, most prominently in the person of the late president Hafiz al-Assad, who was succeeded in 2000 by his son Bashshar. Both Asads officially subscribed to Sunni Islam since the Syrian Constitution requires it of their presidents, but this was a political, not religiously motivated, decision. But whereas Hafiz's wife is 'Alawi, Bashshar's is from a prominent Sunni family from Homs. Although the 'Alawi are not recognized by Sunnis as Muslims, the Lebanese Twelver Shi'a declared them to be fellow faithful by means of a fatwa by the late cleric Musa al-Sadr, later supported by Iranian religious figures. Like many Shi'a young men of Lebanon, the 'Alawi often wear around their necks a gold talisman of the famed sword of 'Ali, Dhu al-Faqar. Ironically, the ultra-Sunni who ordered the 9/11 attacks, the late Usama bin Ladin, was born to a Syrian woman who came from the 'Alawi sect, universally reviled by Wahhabis and their extremist allies.

Alevi

The Alevi, or 'Alawi of central Anatolia, also known in Turkish as Qizil-bashi, have even stronger Twelver religious roots but share little else with their similarly named fellow sectarian Shi'a of Syria, least of all their crypto-Christian tendencies and their belief in reincarnation. Much larger in number—forming anywhere from 15 to 20 percent of Turkey's population of over 70 million (double that by their own reckoning)—they are concentrated in central Asia Minor (especially the provinces of Sivas and Tunceli) but are found throughout the country and in all the major cities. They claim a pure Turkoman ancestry via the first invaders of Anatolia from central Asia, the Seljuks (eleventh century). A number of their religious practices may indeed harken back to their pre-Islamic, central Asian roots. Despite their strong ancient Turkish associations, an estimated 20 percent of Alevis are ethnic Kurds, the large majority of whom in Turkey and elsewhere in the Middle East are Sunnis.

Strictly monogamous, the Alevi are politically very secular and supportive of Kemal Atatürk's modernizing changes to the traditionally Islamic Ottoman society. Their women do not wear the *hijab*, or Muslim head covering, one of the few things they do share with the 'Alawi of Syria whose women, as noted previously, also appear uncovered in public. Unlike their Syrian cousins, however, the Alevi women are regarded as religious equals and participate with men in worship services. Alevis were frequently targeted and persecuted, even subjected to mass killings and forced conversion under the Ottomans and consider Atatürk a kind of secular messiah or mahdi sent to rescue them. Even under Atatürk, though, the Alevi were subject to persecution, notably in the Tunceli region, where from 1936 to 1939 they were victims of what are known today as the Dersim Massacres, during which the Turkish Army slaughtered an estimated fourteen thousand Zaza Kurdish Alevi over their resistance to relocation, taxation, and conscription, while another 12,000 were forcibly resettled elsewhere. Today the province has the fewest number of inhabitants in the country (under a hundred thousand) and the lowest population density.

Harassment has continued into modern times, a notable example being the Massacre of Sivas on July 2, 1993, when Sunni fundamentalists attacked Alevis emerging from a religious celebration in that central Turkish city, setting fire to the hotel in which it was being held resulting in the deaths of thirty-seven people. Alevis claim the death toll was much higher and allege that they are constantly being harassed by the Sunni majority and are not fairly represented in government or the military despite their deep allegiance to the founder of modern Turkey and his secular views. They claim Atatürk as a fellow Alevi even though he was outwardly very dismissive of religion and may have had Jewish ancestry. A popular, widely circulated theory holds that his father was a Doenme, a secret Messianic Jew who outwardly professed Islam. His native city of Salonica, the Thessaloniki of ancient and modern Greece, was in majority Jewish (a plurality by the time of its incorporation into Greece in 1912) from the sixteenth century onward—mostly refugees from Spain whose Catholic kings began expelling them along with Muslims after the re-conquest of Granada in 1492—until they were rounded up, deported, and ultimately killed following the German occupation of Greece in 1941.

Alevi society is divided into two groups—a small spiritual elite who claim descent from 'Ali and Husayn and the majority lay membership—which do not intermarry. Religious knowledge is passed orally through the religious families. Turkish, not Arabic (as is the case with the 'Alawi of Syria), is the language of their rituals, the most important of which is a regular commemoration of the sufferings of the twelve Shi'a imams, especially 'Ali and Husayn. They celebrate a ceremony similar to the 'Alawi Mass or quddas, which, like theirs, is always conducted in secret and includes the consumption of a ritual alcoholic drink. In common with the Druze and other esoteric Shi'a ghulat sects, the Alevi focus on the inner (*batini*) meaning of their faith, reject the external practices of Sunni Islam and its Five Pillars, and in times of persecution have practiced dissimulation. They do not fast during

Ramadan but do so during the ten days of 'Ashura'. Traditional Alevi villages do not have mosques or the daily calls to prayer—unless forced on them by the government, which they allege is a deliberate form of persecution. They believe that they are true Turks who have preserved the traditions of their pre-Islamic Turkoman ancestors from central Asia and are critical of the Turkish Sunnis for having been "Arabicized" by means of the Hadith (or Tradition) of early Salafi transmitters. They are tolerant of all other religious and social groups, including Christians, Jews, and even homosexuals.

Shi'a Collapse in Egypt and Their Rise to Power in Iran

At its height in the first century of the second millennium, the Fatimid Shi'a caliphate ruled from al-Maghrib (Morocco) in the west to Syria in the east and controlled the Holy Cities of Mecca and Medina. Their power ended abruptly in 1171, however, following the conquest of Cairo two years earlier by the great Kurdish Sunni military campaigner Salah al-Din al-Ayyubi (Saladin) as part of his bid to surround the Crusading States of the Outremer and drive the European Christian interlopers into the sea. Although he succeeded in recapturing Jerusalem for Islam following the Battle of Hattin in 1187, the Crusaders hung on precariously for another century, and it was left to Saladin's Mamluke successors, notably the ruthless sultan Baybars, to complete the re-conquest of Palestine ending with the capture of Acre ('Akka) in 1291 by the sultan al-Ashraf Khalil.

But in the meantime, the Shi'a dominance of Egypt and North Africa had collapsed like a house of cards. Since the late twelfth century, Egypt has been resolutely Sunni, although a number of non-Sunni practices remain firmly entrenched in the popular religious culture of the country, attributable both to the earlier Christian and Sevener Shi'a and later Sufi traditions. The festive spring holiday of Shamm al-Nasim, universally observed with great enthusiasm by both Muslim and Christian Egyptians, is a moveable feast that always coincides with Coptic Easter Monday. The popular mosque of al-Husayn in the center of the old Cairo houses a shrine said to contain the head of the third Shi'a imam, brought there by the Fatimid Vizier in 1153 and revered today by Egypt's entirely Sunni Muslim community. The Shi'a deny the Egyptian claim and believe that Husayn's head is buried with his body in the grand mosque dedicated to him in Karbala', their holy city in 'Iraq.

In similar fashion, the great Umayyad mosque at Damascus in Sunni-majority Syria, which incorporates an earlier Christian cathedral of St. John the Baptist, boasts a shrine that claims to house the remains of the hirsute Forerunner of Christ (including his head, famously severed by order of King Herod's son at the request of his niece, Salome), revered by both Christians and Muslims alike. Also in Damascus, which has no indigenous Twelver Shi'a population, is the famous mosque built over the tomb of the daughter of 'Ali, Sitt (the Lady) Zaynab—sister of the second and third imams, Hasan and Husayn—the object of pilgrimage by tens of thousands of Iranian and other Shi'a pilgrims, especially Indian and Pakistani and predominantly women every year. Sunni Cairo also has a claim to 'Ali's daughter with its famous mosque bearing her name, a testament, along with the mosque of Husayn, to Egypt's Isma'ili/Fatimid heritage.

The Safavid Dynasty

With the collapse of the Fatimid caliphate, the Shi'a lost their only base of political domination in the Islamic world and reverted to living at the mercy of their unrelentingly hostile Sunni overlords for more than three centuries. At the beginning of the sixteenth century, however, this situation changed dramatically with the rise of the Safavid (Qizilbashi) dynasty in Iran. Up until this time, Iran had been a Sunni stronghold, although Shi'a communities had existed there since the eighth century in such places as Qom, now the country's holiest Shi'a center, and later in the mountain redoubts of the Nizari Isma'ili "Assassins." During the tenth and eleventh centuries, as was noted previously, Iran had been ruled by the Buwayhid dynasty (934–1055), whose leadership subscribed to the moderate Zaydi branch of Shi'ism, although the population remained largely Sunni. But when the Safavid leader Ismail conquered Tabriz in northwestern Iran in 1501 and declared himself to be the shah (political and spiritual ruler) of all Shi'a and the *shahinshah* (emperor) of Iran, Sunni dominance came to an end.

Originally from Azerbayjan, the Safavids came from Turkic-speaking Persian Sunni stock, but the grandson of their founder converted to Shi'ism at some point in the early fifteenth century. Shi'a influence in the Turkish regions of central Asia was strong in the Middle Ages, and Tamerlane (Timur i-Lang) the famed Turkified Mongol conqueror from Samarkand (ruled ca. 1370–1405) was thought to have strong Shi'a leanings. His chief spiritual mentor, Sayyid Baraka, who is buried next to him, was a Shi'a leader from Balkh in what is today Afghanistan, and he is known to have held 'Ali and the twelve imams in the highest esteem. Tamerlane's chief political adviser, however, was a Sunni of the Hanafi School of Law, and the ruler's own beliefs are far from certain. His defeat and capture of the Ottoman sultan Bayezid I at the Battle of Ankara in 1402 plunged the empire into more than a decade of internal strife over the succession of the sultan who had died in captivity the following year.[12] The Byzantine Empire, by then in terminal decline, was unable to take advantage of the ensuing political hiatus, and Tamerlane's death three years later ended any possible Shi'a threat to Ottoman rule.

One of the first acts of Shah Isma'il I was to order the conversion of all Sunnis in his realm; during the rule of the Safavid dynasty Iran became firmly Shi'a and a base for the expansion of the sectarian faith. At its height during the reign of Shah 'Abbas I (ruled 1587–1629), Safavid power stretched from the Euphrates in the west as far eastward as the Indus in what is today Pakistan, north to the Oxus in Khorasan (the northwestern Iran, Turkmenistan, and Uzbekistan of today), and south as far as Bahrain. The Safavids also expanded their traditional base in Azerbayjan to include the Christian states of Armenia and Georgia in the western Caucasus. In 1598 Shah 'Abbas moved his capital to Isfahan, where imposing monuments today bear witness to his wealth and power. Following the collapse of the Safavids in 1736, succeeding dynasties maintained Iran's strongly Shi'a religious orientation, although pockets of Sunni populations survived, especially in Kurdish areas on the Ottoman border in the west and in Baluchistan, the region that today includes southeastern Iran, the southwestern area of Pakistan, and parts of southern Afghanistan.

Sufi and Wahhabi—the Opposite Poles of Sunni Islam

The majority of Sunni Muslims, probably 80–85 percent, adhere to a moderate interpretation of the sunna of the Prophet and Shari'a law that is tolerant of other faiths and stresses a message of peace but still proclaims the faith of Islam as the final and unalterable revelation of God to mankind. On their religious extremes, however, there are two divergent and mutually incompatible movements within Sunni Islam that have exerted considerable influence, more so now than ever before, on how Muslims should practice their religion. The earlier of the two, Sufism, introduced many nontraditional ideas of worship and religious practice, embracing non-Muslims in a larger spiritual family. Its polar opposite, the Wahhabi movement of the early eighteenth century, propounds Islam in its most militant and puritanical form, rejects all other divisions of Islam (especially

Shi'ism) as being the same or worse than Christianity and Judaism—in other words *kufr*, or blasphemy—and calls for a return to the rigid religious practices of the Muslim community of Medina in the time of the Prophet. On the one hand, we have tolerance, religious pageantry, and mysticism, and on the other rigid adherence to and interpretation of Shari'a law, intolerance and condemnation of any beliefs other than its own, and willingness to resort to any and all means of advancing them at the expense of other interpretations of Islam and all other religious faiths. These two opposing forces within the Sunni world are constantly at odds, and often in deadly confrontation, with the Sufis being on the receiving end of Wahhabi violence. Sufis, in contrast, are not, and never have been in any way, violent in their propagation of Islam.

Sufis

Sufism, the mystical Muslim approach to God, appeared very early in the history of Islam. It probably originated through contact with other religions, especially Christianity, whose strong tradition of asceticism was firmly established in its monastic movement by the time of the Prophet Muhammad. Islam from the beginning rejected the idea of celibacy and living apart from the world and the umma. Sufism, with its concept of devotional male orders with establishments (*tekkes*) similar to monasteries and the religious hermit or dervish (*darwish*) dedicated to living a life that would bring them into a closer relationship with God, has always been viewed with distrust by many Sunnis. The term *sufi* is thought to have derived either from the Arabic *suf* ("wool"), referring to the simple garments with which devotees clothed themselves, or the word *saf* (from the Arabic *saf*, clear, denoting "purity"), which characterized the type of life they aspire to live, or perhaps both. All Sufi orders claim to trace their origins to the Prophet and/or his cousin/son-in-law 'Ali, except for the Naqashbandi order, which believes it was inspired by the first caliph, Abu Bakr. Although Sufis are overwhelmingly Sunni, they share much in common with Shi'ism in their outward expressions of spirituality, especially their love for 'Ali and his family, and Shi'a orders of Sufis do exist, notably the Nematollahi of Iran.

To become a Sufi, one must attach oneself to a teacher and learn from him by example until the student has actually experienced ("tasted," *dhawq*) religious ecstasy (*nashwa*). Sufis believe that through fasting and constant repetition of the word "Allah" and the recitation of his 99 Divine Names and Attributes they can be drawn away from the everyday world and transported to the actual presence of God for a brief but overpowering spiritual encounter. Some do this through music, especially drums and flutes; circular dancing, or "whirling" as early Western observers called it; and increasingly loud and frenetic chanting of the Divine Names. Traditional Islam has always been suspicious of such behavior and Sufis were often persecuted, even killed. The Prophet himself is known to have frowned upon musical instruments and secular songs, and according to Ibn Ishaq, on his triumphant return to Mecca in 630 demanded the killing of two slave girls who were reputed to have sung mocking songs about him while he was in Medina.[13] Only one was actually executed, however, the second having begged for clemency, which the Prophet granted.

The most famous of the early Sufis, Mansur al-Hallaj, was crucified in Baghdad in 922 after eleven years in prison, having declared, "I am the way" in much the same way as Christ. Nevertheless, Sufi teachings continued to hold great appeal. The leading Muslim theologian who brought a virtual end to Islamic philosophical speculation, al-Ghazali (1058–1111), was a strong proponent of Sufism and found it to be the most satisfactory, if most demanding, path toward knowledge of God. The later philosopher Ibn Tufayl (1105–1185) tried to show how reason could bring his mythically orphaned hero of his philosophical novel *Hayy Ibn Yadzan* into a similar, Sufi-like encounter with the Divine, while his fellow Andalusian Ibn Rushd (1126–1198, Averroës in Latin), the *qadi* (judge) of Cordoba, the last and greatest of the Islamic philosophers who translated Aristotle into Arabic, attempted to demonstrate that religion and philosophy were "milk sisters" (those who have suckled from the same breast). When his works were later translated into Latin, they provided Thomas Aquinas and the Catholic Church with the means for establishing rational argument as the basis of their theology. But in the Muslim world, Ibn Rushd's writings were widely criticized, even burned, and in Islamic theology reason remained forever subservient to faith.

The greatest of all Sufi figures, one who has come into recent vogue in the West, is Jalal al-Din al-Rumi (1207–1273). Born in Balkh in what is today Afghanistan, he and his family fled the onslaught of the Mongol hordes of Genghis Khan and found refuge in Anatolia, recently conquered from the Byzantine (Eastern Roman) Empire in what was known as the Sultanate of Rum, hence his appellation, al-Rumi or "the Roman," Rome for Arabs being the "New Rome" of Constantinople. He eventually settled in the city of Konya, where he lived for most of his adult life. He founded a Sufi order known as Mawlawi (Mevlevi in Turkish) and was buried in a shrine at Konya that remains the site of pilgrimage and devotion to this day. He left a voluminous literary legacy but is primarily remembered for his mystical poetry, which appeals to adherents of all religions. Although he remained a devout Sunni Muslim all his life, he preached a message of tolerance, finding truth in all faiths with an emphasis on love for all mankind.

Sufism is found throughout the Islamic world and is particularly strong in Egypt, Pakistan, India, and Bangladesh. In Pakistan, it has recently been challenged by the growing strength of Wahhabism imported by al-Qaʻida and the Taliban. A substantial majority of Sunnis in both India and Pakistan (especially Punjab) follow Sufi traditions. They are known locally as "Barelvi Hanafis," opposed to the more conservative "Deobandis" who deem the Barelvis to be shrine-worshipping, grave-revering heretics. It is the Deobandis who have been increasingly infiltrated and influenced by Wahhabi missionaries. The holiest Sufi shrine in the subcontinent is Dargah Sharif at Ajmer, the ancient capital of the Indian province of Rajasthan. Its two marble mosques built in the late sixteenth/early seventeenth centuries by the Moghul emperors Akbar and his eldest surviving son, Jihangir, honor the Afghan-born saint Khawaja Muʻin al-Din Chishti (1141–1230), a contemporary of St. Francis of Assisi to whom he is often likened because of his strong advocacy of charity, aid to the poor, and a life abjuring all worldly pleasure and luxury. The Chishti order of Sufis is very active in the subcontinent, and every year in October millions of pilgrims converge on Ajmer to commemorate the saint's death anniversary (*urs*). On April 8, 2012, the president of Pakistan, Asif ʻAli Zardari, made a special pilgrimage to Ajmer as part of a brief state visit to India, the first in four years after the bomb attack in Mumbai, becoming the fifth Pakistani head of state to pay homage at the shrine, a gesture that did not go unnoticed by the Wahhabis and Deobandis.

The following year, however, on March 8, 2013, the day before a scheduled visit to the *dargah* (shrine) by the prime minister of Pakistan, Raja Pervez Ashraf, its spiritual head, a descendant of the Sufi saint Muʻin al-Din Chisti, announced that he would not receive his prominent guest as a protest against "the continued atrocities against minorities in Pakistan" and the attack that had killed two Indian soldiers near the Line of Control (ceasefire line) in Kashmir two months earlier, one of whom had been beheaded. This "inhuman act" not only violated international military norms, he said, but also "violated the basic tenets of Islam."[14] The prime minister's visit went ahead despite the snub, but while he was offering prayers for peace in the world and peace and prosperity in Pakistan, the city of Lahore was reeling from jihadist attacks on a Christian area of the city that left more than one hundred homes burning following the arrest of a local Christian man on charges of insulting the Prophet Muhammad under the country's infamous blasphemy laws.

In the lawless border regions of northwest Pakistan, centuries-old Sufi shrines have been destroyed, and their colorful ceremonies featuring music, dancing, and the participation of women have been discouraged through bombings and other acts of violence. Most recently, these attacks have spread to the cities: first in Lahore in July 2010, leaving forty-two people dead, and three months later in Karachi on October 7, killing seven people and wounding another sixty-five. Less than three weeks after that, a motorcycle bomb killed five more people near another shrine in a small town in Punjab province. An interesting aspect of the controversy over the construction of an Islamic cultural center with a mosque and prayer rooms near the site of the World Trade Center bombing in 2001 is that the leadership of those Muslims who built this center was originally in the hands of a Sufi imam who is as opposed to the methods of the 9/11 terrorists as anyone and the target of death threats from extremist Islamists. The center opened on September 22, 2011, with much celebration including an orchestra playing Arabic music, something conservative Sunnis must have disapproved of, but which is very much in the Sufi tradition.

On another front, armed Sufi forces in Somalia recently joined the weak central government and the forces of neighboring African countries, especially Ethiopia and Uganda, in an attempt to dislodge the armed militia of al-Shabab ("the boys/guys/youths" in Arabic), a group with alleged ties to al-Qa'ida that wants to impose a strict, conservative version of Shari'a law on the war-torn country from their strongholds in the capital, Mogadishu, and the port of Kismayu. In August 2011 the Shabab forces suddenly abandoned their bases in the face of a terrible famine caused by drought, allowing Western aid groups to send aid to tens of thousands of victims of this tragedy.

Wahhabis

The Wahhabi approach to Islam could not be further from that of the Sufi. Taking its name from the eighteenth-century religious figure Muhammad Ibn 'Abd al-Wahhab, who preached against moral decadence and worldliness, the Wahhabi movement took root in the central Arabian region of al-Najd around 1740 under the sponsorship of its ruling shaykh, Muhammad Ibn Sa'ud. Wahhabis are also referred to as Salafis, from the Arabic *salaf* (ancestors), or those who look to the earliest followers of Islam for their inspiration. They rejected any authority in Islam except for the Qur'an and the Hadith and saw all religious shrines, even the tomb of the Prophet himself, as potentially idolatrous. The Shi'a were (and are) particularly abhorrent to them, and in 1801 and again in 1802 Wahhabi forces raided the cities of Karbala' and al-Najaf, killing many Shi'a faithful and severely damaging the great mosque and shrine of Husayn. The following year, they raided the holy cities of Mecca and Medina, destroying what they viewed as idolatrous monuments. But for the most part they remained confined to their isolated desert base until the collapse of the Ottoman Empire in 1918. They rejected the attempt by the victorious Western powers to establish their ally in World War I, Sharif Husayn of Mecca, as king of the Hijaz in 1917 with control over former Ottoman territories, including the Holy Cities. Husayn was swept from power by the Sa'ud family of al-Najd in 1924 and died the following year. The Kingdom of Sa'udi Arabia was proclaimed in 1932 under the dynasty of 'Abd al-'Aziz Ibn Sa'ud (1876–1953) with the Wahhabi sect of Sunni Islam as its religious base. A religious police force was organized to impose and enforce strict Wahhabi rules of behavior.

All other forms of Islamic and non-Islamic belief and worship were rejected and prohibited, an exception being made for the dominant Shi'a population of the Eastern Province (al-Hasa), which was very grudgingly tolerated, probably because it occupied the area where vast oil reserves had been recently discovered and today straddles the pipeline that takes millions of barrels a day to the port of Ra's Tannura for shipment abroad. Nevertheless, Sa'udi Arabia's Shi'a citizens were officially viewed as infidels, not as fellow Muslims of a different sect, and subject to harassment and discrimination. Even today, there are no Shi'a mayors or police chiefs in the Eastern Province, and not one of the three hundred Shi'a girls' schools there has a Shi'a principal. The government has restricted the names that the Shi'a can use for their children in order to discourage them from calling attention to their identity. In his efforts to modernize Sa'udi society, King 'Abdallah's predecessor, King Fahd, created a stir by deciding to appoint two Shi'a members, the first ever, to his handpicked 120-member *majlis al-shura*, or Royal Council, before his death on August 1, 2005. 'Abdallah increased the number to four soon after becoming king when the membership was raised to 150. The Eastern province, however, where the Sa'udi Shi'a population has its strongest concentration, remains underrepresented on the council—8 percent of the membership as opposed to their 16 percent share of the total population.

Still, Sa'udi school textbooks excoriate Shi'ism as a heresy, even worse than Christianity and Judaism.[15] A second, smaller Shi'a concentration is located in the mountainous southwestern province of 'Asir bordering on Yemen, whose long-established Zaydis dominate the northwestern part of that country. A smaller number of Sulaymani Bohra Isma'ilis are found in and around the city of Najran, a part of Yemen until 1933 when it was annexed to Sa'udi Arabia. They view the pre-Islamic Christian community of that city, forced to emigrate to Mesopotamia by Caliph 'Umar, as their spiritual ancestors because both were persecuted for their faith—the Christians by a Jewish tyrant in 524 AD and the sectarian Muslims by the hard-line Sunni Wahhabi Sa'udis, despite promises by King 'Abd al-'Aziz to respect their traditions when he conquered the city nearly eighty years ago.

Followers of the Sa'udi-based sect dislike being referred to as either Wahhabis or Salafis, preferring to call themselves unitarians (muwahhidun) even though this is the term that the Druze, from whom the Wahhabis could not be further removed theologically and socially, have attributed to themselves for nearly a millennium, not to mention that the 'Alawis of Syria also use the term with considerably less justification than the Druze.

Wahhabism is also the dominant religion of the neighboring Gulf state of Qatar, although imposed there in a less strict form that allows Christians to worship publicly and build churches, unlike in Sa'udi Arabia where this is absolutely forbidden. The tenets of the Wahhabi movement have also spread to other parts of the Islamic world, especially India, Pakistan, and the Muslim diaspora in Europe, and have provided a religious basis for some of the more extreme anti-Western Islamic groups of the present day, notably the Taliban and al-Qa'ida. In the wake of the 9/11 attacks, the Sa'udi government has made very serious attempts to curb the influence of al-Qa'ida, forcing its leadership to flee the country to the remote, and more religiously hospitable, Sunni regions of southern and eastern Yemen. Sa'udi king 'Abdallah made genuine attempts to bring extreme Wahhabi social views more in line with moderate Islamic practice, particularly in regard to the treatment of women and religious tolerance for non-Wahhabi Muslims, appointing thirty women members to the Royal Council, the king's nonelective consultant parliament in January 2013, decreeing that their numbers should never fall below 20 percent but specifically stipulating that they should be veiled. At the same time, he appointed a Shi'a woman to join her three male colleagues.

He has also attempted to rein in the authority of individual Wahhabi religious leaders whose increasingly numerous fatwas, often proclaimed over the Internet, have been a growing source of irritation to the government. He is, however, approaching ninety and ill. Whether his successor will continue his programs of reform remains in serious doubt, especially after the death of his long-serving deputy, Crown Prince Sultan Ibn ʿabd al-ʿAziz in October 2011. Sultan ibn ʿabd al-ʿAziz's replacement was the seventy-eight-year-old Naʾif Ibn ʿAbd al-ʿAziz, known to be an ultra-conservative, but he also suffered from ill health and died the following June after heart surgery in Geneva. His younger brother Salman became the third crown prince in less than nine months and at seventy-seven is not thought to have any life-threatening illnesses. He is also regarded as more moderate on social issues. Despite ʿAbdallah's reforms, however, Wahhabi extremism has remained strong at many levels, as exemplified by the 1998 bulldozing of the grave of Aminah bint Wahb, the mother of Muhammad, to the dismay of moderate Muslims throughout the world. Gasoline was poured over the site to discourage any attempt to turn it into a religious shrine, anathema to Wahhabi thought and practice. In another example of Wahhabi intolerance of any but their own interpretation of Islam, the extremist Salafi group Ansar Dine, which took over northern Mali in January 2012, made headlines by destroying centuries-old shrines built over the graves of Sufi saints in Timbuktu, claiming they were "idolatrous," much as the Taliban did in Afghanistan when they blew up the ancient giant statues of Buddha at Bamyan in March 2001. The Islamic jihadists in Northern Mali, days prior to the recovery of Timbuktu by French and Malian army forces in late January 2013, also attempted to torch the ancient city's libraries containing priceless Sufi texts and manuscripts, but most of the treasures escaped permanent damage.

Communities on the Periphery of Sunni and Shiʿa Islam: Ahmadis, Bahaʾis, and Yazidis

In addition to peripheral sects like the Druze and Bohras with Sevener roots, and the Syrian ʿAlawis and Turkish Alevis that have a historic connection with Twelver Shiʿism, there are another three communities with ties to Islam that deserve mention: the Ahmadis of Pakistan and India who emerged from the majority Sunni tradition just over a century ago, the Bahaʾis of Iran who grew out of Twelver Shiʿism there more than a half-century earlier, and the Yazidis of ʿIraq and Syria whose origins are much older and more confusing.

Ahmadis

Descendants of Sunnis in British India, the Ahmadis are followers of Mirza Ghulam Ahmad (d. 1908), who proclaimed himself to be the long-expected mahdi in 1889. The Ahmadiyya Muslim Community was officially organized in 1900, but following the death of Ahmad's first successor in 1914 the group split. The original movement, which is by far the larger of the two, continued to recognize their founder as the redeemer even though his name was not Muhammad, as required by both Sunni and Shi'a tradition. Ahmad got around this by explaining that his name is simply the superlative form of the Prophet's name, which refers to Muhammad's holy mission, earthly achievements, and personal qualities. The splinter group, known as the Lahore Ahmadiyya Muslim Movement, rejected Ahmad's claim to prophet status and viewed their movement as a reforming force in Islam. The original Ahmadis believe all Muslims who reject their founder are unbelievers. Both Sunnis and Shi'as reject Ghulam Ahmad's claim and view his followers as heretics.

Following the partition of India in 1947, nearly half of the world's estimated 10 million Ahmadis found themselves in the newly created state of Pakistan, where they were initially accepted as Muslims. The first foreign minister of Pakistan, Muhammad Zafr Allah Khan (1947–1954), was an Ahmadi, but over time the government's position hardened. In 1974, after anti-Ahmadi riots nationwide in which many were killed, Ahmadis were prohibited by law (in an amendment to the constitution that declared them to be heretics) from calling themselves Muslims. They are regularly the target of Sunni animosity; on May 28, 2010, two of their mosques in Lahore were bombed resulting in a considerable loss of life. In India, where the second-largest number of Ahmadis are found, they are still legally accorded Islamic status. In Bangladesh, formerly East Pakistan, they are barely tolerated and often subject to persecution and attack. Ahmadis are found outside the Indian subcontinent in many countries but in small numbers, the largest of these concentrations being in England, where they were among the first Indian immigrants to arrive. Their small community in Indonesia was the target of a February 2011 attack by Sunni villagers in central Java who beat three Ahmadis to death while torching two churches.

Since the split in 1914, each group of Ahmadis has had a succession of five religious leaders known in the original community as caliphs (*khulafā'*) and for the Lahore group as emirs (*umarā'*, or princes). Both groups practice a traditional form of Islam based on the Qur'an and the Hadith and even make the traditional annual pilgrimage to Mecca but refrain from declaring their Ahmadi beliefs on arrival because of the strict Wahhabi Sunni allegiance of the Sa'udi religious authority that rejects them. Their theology preaches a nonviolent form of jihad as a perpetual striving for justice and peace, similar to the Zaydi Shi'a of Yemen.

In addition to the main group's claim that their founder was the mahdi, there is another interesting belief that sets them apart from other Muslims, namely that Jesus was indeed crucified and appeared to die but recovered in his tomb and travelled to Kashmir, where he died of old age and is buried. They view his return at the Last Day as allegorical, whereas both Sunnis and Shi'as hold that he will return in the flesh to preside over the Last Judgment at the end of the world.

Baha'is

Members of the Baha'i faith, as their faithful refer to it, are followers of Sayyid 'Ali Muhammad of Shiraz, who in 1844 declared himself to be the *Bab* (door), or the hoped-for mahdi of Twelver Shi'a tradition. The Persian government arrested him, and he died in prison six years later. His small group of followers rallied around Mirza Husayn 'Ali, an early disciple who took the name of Baha'Allah (Splendor of God) and after whom believers in the Bab came to be called. In 1853 he was exiled to Baghdad, then a part of the Ottoman Empire, and later moved to Istanbul, where in 1863 he assumed his messianic mantle. In 1866 he proclaimed himself to be a messenger of God in letters to both Queen Victoria and Pope Pius IX; he was arrested by Turkish authorities in 1868 and imprisoned at 'Akka (Acre) in Palestine, where he died in 1892. His shrine there is the world's holiest site for Baha'is, a place of pilgrimage and the *qibla*, or direction they face when praying. Nearby on Mount Carmel, overlooking the city of Haifa, Israel, at a place designated by Baha'Allah a year before he died, is the tomb and shrine of the Bab, whose remains were smuggled out of Iran to the Holy Land and interred there when the shrine was completed in 1909. It is the second-holiest site for Baha'is and also the site of their world headquarters, which since 1963 has housed the governing administrative body of the Baha'i Faith. Baha'Allah's eldest son Abbas, known as 'Abd al-Baha' (d. 1921), inherited the leadership of the movement from his father and was succeeded as Guardian of the Faith by Shoghi Effendi (d. 1957). During this period, the movement spread to centers outside the Middle East and today counts 5–7 million followers, chiefly in India (over 2 million), Iran (an estimated

350,000), and the United States (150,000), with smaller communities in most countries of the world, especially in the West.

The principal message of the Bab and BahaʾAllah is that all humanity is one, men and women are equal, science and religion are in harmony, and world peace is the ultimate objective. The history of religion is written in the lives of great prophets—Abraham, Buddha, Jesus, Muhammad among them—and ultimately the Bab. Bahaʾis have no liturgy, often meeting in private homes and rented premises, and leave obligatory prayer up to the conscience of individual believers. They follow very little of traditional Muslim practice, though they do fast from dawn to dusk for nineteen days in March, and like all branches of Islam they frown on pre-marital sex and homosexuality. Both Shiʻas and Sunnis consider Bahaʾis to be apostates from Islam, and they have been persecuted in Iran since their inception there, particularly since the Islamic Revolution of 1979, which has encouraged violent repression, including murder.

In direct contrast, the ancient faith of Zoroastrianism, along with Christianity and Judaism, is tolerated as that of one of the three Peoples of the Book who were allowed to follow their faith under traditional Islamic rule so long as they paid the *jizya*, or "poll tax." There are about 50,000 Zoroastrians in Iran, especially in Yazd where they have a temple; a larger community of 75,000–100,000, originally from Iran, lives in India, chiefly Mumbai, where they are known as Parsees (from the Persian word for their own language, Farsi). That Bahaʾis survive in significant numbers in Iran is a tribute to their faith and tenacity. They are considered by both Sunnis and Shiʻa as apostates, who under Shariʻa law are deserving of the death penalty. In Egypt and a number of other Muslim countries, they are not legally recognized.

Yazidis

The Yazidis, sometimes referred to as an "extremist Shiʻa sect," are in fact followers of a syncretic religion that embodies elements of Zoroastrianism, Mithraism, Manichaeism, Nestorian Christianity, Sufism, and Shiʻa Islam. They revere Shaykh ʻAdi Ibn Musafir (d. 1162), a twelfth-century Muslim religious figure (either a Sufi or an Ismaʻili Shiʻa), whom they hold to be their founder. His tomb and shrine are at Lalish, some forty miles north of Mosul in northern ʻIraq, which is the site of an annual pilgrimage in October. It lasts for a week and is marked by ritual bathing, the slaughtering of an ox, and much music, dancing, and general celebration. The Yazidis are Kurdish-speaking (apart from two neighboring Arabic-speaking villages east of Mosul, Ba'shiqa and Bahazani, where they live side-by-side with Syriac Orthodox Christians), and all of their religious traditions, only recently written down, have been transmitted for centuries in the Kurmanji dialect of Kurdish.

The Yazidis' religious beliefs are very distinctive and peculiar to them. They believe that God created the world and then left it in charge of seven archangels. The chief of them is the Peacock Angel, known as Malak Ta'us, who is always portrayed in the form of that iconic bird. The Yazidis believe Malak Ta'us to be the embodiment of Iblis, the Qur'anic name for Lucifer, the rebellious angel cast out of heaven by God for refusing to bow down to the newly created Adam, thus incurring divine wrath for disobedience. Yazidis deny that he is a fallen angel and revere him and his six companions in order to placate the evil that rules this world. Out of fear and respect for him, they will not utter his Arabic name, Shaytan, and refuse even to say any other word beginning with the sound "sh," including, rather ironically, *shirir* (evil-doer). They believe that they are the descendants of Adam, but not of Eve. As to how such a curiosity should have come to pass, Yazidi belief has it that after the traditional stages of the Creation process, Eve (Hawa in Arabic) announced to Adam that he was to have no part in the business of producing children. He challenged her to a test, placing some of his saliva into a sealed jar and asking Eve to do the same. After nine months, Adam opened his jar and found inside a beautifully formed boy and girl, "whereas Eve's jar contained nothing but corruption."[16] They also have curious dietary restrictions beyond the normal proscription of pork, including fish (which cannot be killed in halal fashion) and green-colored vegetables like okra, lettuce, and haricot beans. Sunnis regard Yazidis as devil-worshippers and have persecuted them for most of their existence, especially during the Ottoman period and into recent times.

Yazidis believe that their name comes from the Kurdish word *yazdan*, meaning God, but another tradition holds that it derives from the second Umayyad caliph, Yazid I, who is embodied in another of their seven archangels. That they revere the memory of the man who ordered the killing of their third imam, Husayn Ibn 'Ali, makes the Shi'a distrust them even more than the Sunnis. Yazidis pray five times a day facing the sun, except at noon when they turn toward the tomb of Shaykh 'Adi. Like the Druze and 'Alawis, they believe in the transmigration of souls and observe the general Shi'a practice of *taqiyya*, or lying about one's true faith, in order to avoid persecution, bodily harm, and death. Also like the Druze and the Alevi, they are divided between an elite group that has access to the secrets of their religion and those who do not. Like the Druze, they believe that you are born to the faith and no one may join it by marriage or conversion. Therefore women are not allowed to marry outside the faith (Druze women increasingly can and do) and are required to be virgins at marriage. There have been recent cases of "honor killings" in which Yazidi girls were murdered for violating these taboos. In April 2007 a seventeen-year-old Yazidi in Ba'shiqa, the mixed Yazidi-Syriac Christian village west of Mosul mentioned earlier, was stoned to death for wanting to marry a Sunni man. Five years later in Germany, an eighteen-year-old Yazidi girl from Turkey was murdered by her four brothers for living openly with her German boyfriend. Again, whereas Druze women were also killed at one time to preserve the "family honor," there has not been such a case, to the author's knowledge, in Lebanon at least since the 1950s. Yazidis observe the fast at the end of Ramadan and also celebrate a feast honoring Jesus that usually coincides with Easter. They have a particularly close relationship with Syriac Orthodox and Nestorian Christians in northern 'Iraq with whom they tend to live in close proximity.

Yazidi leadership is divided among a spiritual head, the Baba Shaykh who lives near Lalish and has infallible authority in the interpretation of their scripture, and a secular leader known as the *amir* (prince) who represents the community in its dealings with civil authority. Estimates of their total numbers vary widely, from 450,000 to 800,000, but the smaller figure is probably closer to being accurate as their population has declined due to war and persecution. Roughly three-quarters of the population is in northern 'Iraq, divided among the Shaykhan district north of Mosul where the tomb of Shaykh 'Adi is located and the low mountain range of Jabal Sinjar to the west of Mosul on the border with Syria. The latter country is also home to some ten thousand to fifteen thousand Yazidis in the province of al-Jazira, just across the border from Jabal Sinjar and in the hilly region north and west of Aleppo. Another estimated fifty thousand are found in Armenia and neighboring states of the Caucasus (mainly Georgia), with an additional thirty thousand to forty thousand or so in Russia proper. Until recently, there was a significant number in southeastern Turkey around the city of Mardin, but most of them—numbering ten thousand or more—along with many of their Christian neighbors and refugees from 'Iraq, have immigrated to Western Europe either to escape persecution or seek employment (or both). There are estimates of some forty thousand Yazidis in Germany, with smaller numbers in Sweden (four thousand), Ukraine (two thousand), and about five thousand elsewhere, chiefly Holland, the United Kingdom, and North America.

Sunni, Shi'a, and Other Schools of Islamic Law

All branches of Islam have their own school (*madhhab*) or schools of Religious Law (Shari'a) and Jurisprudence (*fiqh*) peculiar to them. The Twelver Shi'a follow the Ja'fari School (established by the sixth imam, Ja'far al-Sadiq). Unlike sectarian Muslims, the Sunnis have four schools of varying degrees of strict interpretation of Islamic dictates. The earliest, largest, and most moderate of these is the Hanafi School, named after Abu Hanifa al-Nu'man of Kufa (699–767), which is followed today in those countries that once made up the Ottoman and Moghul Empires—the Balkans, Turkey, Syria, Lebanon, Palestine, Egypt, 'Iraq, Pakistan, India, and Bangladesh—representing just over half of the world's Sunni population. They base their rulings on the Qur'an, the Hadith, consensus (*ijma'*) of the educated elders (*'ulama'*) and theological scholars (*fuqaha'*), and, finally, reasoning (*qiyas*).

The second-largest, and also moderate, legal code is that founded by Abu 'Abdallah Muhammad Ibn Idris al-Shafi'i of Gaza (767–820). It stresses the importance of reasoning and allegory and is the predominant school of Sunnis in East Africa, Southeast Asia (Indonesia, Malaysia, and the Muslim areas of the southern Philippines), and the Kurdish populations of northern 'Iraq and eastern Turkey. An estimated one-quarter of the world's Sunnis follow the Shafi'i school.

The more conservative Maliki school is based on the teachings of Malik Ibn Anas and relies on the same four components as Hanafi and Shafi'i jurisprudence with the added element of the practices of the *salafa* (earliest Muslims) of Medina. It is followed by the Sunnis of North and West Africa, Kuwait, the United Arab Emirates, and Bahrain, who make up about 15 percent of the world's Sunnis.

The most conservative Sunni legal code is that laid down by Ahmad Ibn Hanbal (d. 855), which relies entirely on the Qur'an, the Hadith, the model of earliest Islamic practice, and the consent of the faithful. Only 5 percent of Sunnis adhere to Hanbali teachings, principally in Sa'udi Arabia and Qatar, though a number of individual Muslims throughout the world find its rigid principles preferable to the more moderate teachings of the other three schools. It also prescribes its own particular rules of ritual prayer.

The deep misconceptions about traditional Islamic legal practice in the West have led to recent efforts, so far isolated but increasingly draconian and bordering on hysterical, to prevent Shari'a law from gaining a foothold there, especially in the United States among the Christian Right and spearheaded by the American Jewish anti-Shari'a alarmist David Yerushalmi and his followers. First of all, Shari'a law is far from universally agreed upon by Muslims, as seen from the previous discussion of the various Islamic schools, and can only be applied in a country where Muslims of a similar religious orientation are a dominant majority. In fact in only one country, Sa'udi Arabia, is a form of it the single legal code. In the rest of the Muslim world, it is applied in combination, to varying degrees, with civil codes brought in from the West during the colonial period. For most Muslims, it is a part of their tradition that they apply selectively, particularly in personal matters of marriage, divorce, and inheritance.

There is one common practice followed almost universally by the vast majority of both Sunnis and Shi'as: male circumcision. Yet it is not specifically prescribed in the Qur'an nor the Hadith (though several allude to it), but based entirely on custom and tradition, and it is thought to have pre-Islamic, probably Pharaonic, origins. Since early Muslims had close contact with Jews, especially in Yathrib/Medina, and were briefly allied to them, the practice could have stemmed from this association. One popular belief is that the Prophet was born without a foreskin (a common indicator in ancient times of divinely ordained leadership) and therefore worthy of emulation. Another tradition has it that he personally ordered the circumcision of his grandsons, Hasan and Husayn, seven days after birth. Unlike Judaism, which requires circumcision on the eighth day (which is why January 1 for Catholic Christians is the "Feast of the Circumcision" of Jesus), there is no agreement in Islam when the procedure should be undertaken, and in many Muslim societies it occurs at age seven or eight (e.g., Turkey), or even older with great ceremony and celebration as a rite of passage to adulthood. A small minority argues that since the Qur'an stresses the "perfection of creation" on a number of occasions, the human body should not be disfigured or tampered with in any way. Only the Druze do not ritually observe it, though in recent years the popular dictates of modern hygiene have made it more common among them.[17]

Female genital mutilation, sometimes erroneously referred to as "female circumcision," is not required by any Islamic school of law, is officially frowned upon, and was recently proscribed by legal declaration or fatwa by the religious authorities of al-Azhar, the leading Sunni institution of higher learning in Cairo. The Lebanese Shi'a grand ayatollah, Muhammad

Fadlallah, also issued a fatwa condemning the practice even though it is rarely encountered among Shi'as, if at all. It is nevertheless widespread in large areas of Sunni Islamic society, especially Egypt, the Sudan, Ethiopia, Somalia, and Central and parts of Western Africa in varying degrees of severity that increase as one moves south from the Nile Delta. It is also practiced by Christians in rural Egypt, further confirming ancient Pharaonic roots, despite being condemned by Coptic Church authorities. Only among the small Coptic Protestant community, strongly influenced by Western missionaries, has this horrific and despicable practice been thoroughly abolished.[18]

Summary: The Principal Differences Dividing Sunni and Shi'a Islam from Each Other, and from Christianity and Judaism

Islam is considered along with Judaism and Christianity to be one of the three Abrahamic religions—those which acknowledge the scriptural patriarch to be the father of the monotheistic faith they all share. In theory, all three worship the same one God—originally referred to as *El* in Hebrew and other related Semitic languages from which *ilah* (god) and *Allah* (the God) in Arabic are related. The dying Christ called to his Father in despair from the cross using the Aramaic form "*El-i, El-i, lama sabachtani*" ("My God, My God, why has Thou forsaken me?"). El, later called Yahweh (Jehovah) by the Jews, is found in many commonly used biblical names and places such as Emmanu-el (God is with us), Beth-el (House of God), the prophets El-ijah ("El is my God"), Samu-el ("God has heard"), and Nathani-el ("Gift of God"), as well as Eli-shiva (Elisabeth—"God's Promise or Oath"), and the three archangels, emissaries of El (Micha-el, Gabri-el, and Rafa-el). In addition to angels, Islam also has lesser supernatural spirits (*jinn*) which can be both good and evil in nature, a word which comes into the English language as "genie" from the *One Thousand and One Nights* story of Aladdin and his magic lamp.

The two principal differences separating Islam and Christianity are the rejection by the former of the latter's belief in the divinity of the man Jesus and the concept of the Trinity—that God is one but manifested in three different natures: father, son, and holy spirit. For Muslims, this is a denial of the absolute unity of the Godhead and Christians are polytheists who believe in three gods, even though for most Christians they are three aspects of the same single essence. All traditional Christian scholars from St. Augustine onward, however, have had to admit that the Trinity is a "mystery" which cannot be logically explained. Yet it has been suggested by a number of theologians and scholars, most recently Dr. Joseph L. Cumming of Yale University, that the definition of the three basic attributes (*sifat*) of Allah by the great tenth-century Sunni theologian al-'Ashari (d. 935)—power, knowledge, and life—correspond remarkably to the three basic hypostases (attributes) of God enshrined in the Trinity: God the Father as power, God the Son (Jesus) as knowledge or *logos* (word), and God the Holy Spirit as life and love. As interesting as this parallel may be, the fact remains that the Qur'an commands believers, "Do not say 'Three.' Cease! Believe in God alone."[19]

The nature of Jesus is more complicated. Islam views him as a great teacher and prophet, second only to Muhammad, who did not die on the cross but was taken directly to God on his death without the agony and suffering claimed by Christians as a means of removing the stain of original sin from mankind, known in Christian theology as "the atonement." The Qur'an alludes that someone else was crucified in his place—a case of mistaken identity—the same belief as that held by early Christian heretics (Marcionites and Docetists) who had the same difficulty as Muslims in believing that an omnipotent God would allow himself in the person of his son Jesus to be humiliated and tortured in such a hideous manner in order to save mankind.[20] Although the Marcionites had been anathematized in the third century and disappeared shortly thereafter, Docetism as a force contesting the basic theological beliefs of Christian orthodoxy still existed at the time of Muhammad and could quite plausibly have influenced him.

For Christians, Jesus is "the Word" (*logos* in Greek) as proclaimed at the beginning of St. John's Gospel. For Islam, "the Word" is the Qur'an, the literal utterances of God delivered word for word to Muhammad by the angel Gabriel, though for some Sunnis (especially Sufis) and many Shi'a "the Word" also includes the messenger himself, Muhammad, as the perfect human being. A minority of Shi'a, especially the extremist sects (even in the case of the 'Alawis and Alevis, for example), regard 'Ali as the acme of human perfection, a being with divine properties eclipsing both the Prophet and his revealed book. Though refusing to go that far, the more mainstream Ithna'ashari (Twelver) Shi'a believe he is God's deputy and a possessor of divine knowledge which has been transmitted to his descendants, the imams.

For mainstream Sunni Islam, the Qur'anic Word was not created but was in existence from the beginning. What the angel Gabriel revealed to

Muhammad was a verbatim copy of the archetype of the Qur'an in heaven. An attempt in the ninth century to view the Qur'an as having been created by God in time for the purpose of enlightening mankind was soon discredited as heresy and its followers, known as *al-mu'tazila* (Mu'tazilites), were condemned, though Ibadis and most Shi'a accepted the concept. For opponents of the Mu'tazilites, God's word (a "*kalam*") as part of his being could not come at a later time. For the Mu'tazilites to say that God's word is as old as he is to imply the existence of two Gods. Whereas Christians believe their holy scriptures to have been written by men inspired by God, all Muslims, when they read the Qur'an, hear the voice of God himself speaking. Muhammad is not the author of the Qur'an, merely the recipient of it, a singular honor in itself. One of the most convincing arguments for their religion's veracity is what they call "the miracle" (*i'jaz*) of the Qur'an, a reference to the beauty of the Arabic in which it is written. Until relatively recent times, it was forbidden to translate the holy book, and there is no doubt that it does lose a great deal of its impact in other languages.

Muslims would agree with the first two statements of St. John that "in the beginning was the Word, and the Word was with God," except they would be referring to their Holy Book, not Jesus, and would take absolute exception to the next statement of the Gospel: "the Word was God" and later that "the Word was made flesh." The concept of Jesus as the Christ and his Divine Nature is anathema to Islam. Nevertheless, in Islam Jesus and his mother are deeply revered. Mary is the only woman to be mentioned by name in the Qur'an, where there is more about her than there is in the New Testament. According to the forty-second verse of the third chapter, she is preferred by Allah "above all the women in creation," and she is mentioned in no fewer than thirty-three other Qur'anic verses. The nineteenth chapter bears her name, *surat Maryam*, and appears to be adapted from St. Luke's Gospel and a non-canonical gospel of James, "the brother of Jesus," which was still in use by Christians at the time of the emergence of Islam, especially with those outside the Byzantine tradition with whom Muhammad would have come into contact. "The recitation of *Sura* 19, an act of piety practiced especially by Muslim women, is believed to impart blessings on both the speaker and the listener."[21] Mary's virginity is never called into question by Muslims as it is by many Protestant and even some Catholic Christians and theologians. Moreover, the overall Islamic veneration of Mary for her purity and holiness presages the relatively recent (1854) Catholic dogma of her Immaculate Conception, celebrated on December 8, something that Eastern Orthodoxy has tacitly recognized since St. John of Damascus, writing in the early years of the Umayyad caliphate, defended her absolute purity based on the virginal birth of Christ.[22] Jesus will preside at the Last Day according to Islamic belief, deciding which souls are destined for Heaven and which for Hell, and one tradition has it that he will descend to one of the minarets of the Umayyad Mosque in Damascus which bears his name to announce the end of the world.

Both Sunni and Shi'a traditions accept that he will be preceded by the previously discussed forerunner al-Mahdi. They agree that this person will bear the name of the Prophet; that he will be a direct descendant through the line of both of his grandsons, Hasan and Husayn; that his appearance will be preceded by natural phenomena similar to the signs and portents the final book of the Christian New Testament says will presage the second coming of Christ; and that he will usher in an era of peace and justice (the length of which varies according to interpretation) before the Last Judgment. Where Twelver Shi'as differ from Sunnis is that this belief is at the very core of their religion and that the expected mahdi is a specific person named Muhammad—namely their twelfth imam who went into a final state of occultation in 941 and whose reappearance is expected at any moment. It is no coincidence that President Mahmud Ahmadinejad of Iran has made frequent reference to this devoutly hoped-for eschatological event in his frequently impassioned speeches. There is, however, nothing in the Qur'an that refers to the appearance of a messianic figure such as the mahdi, whereas the pivotal role of Jesus at the end of time is rooted in Muslim scripture. Nevertheless, the concept of the mahdi is found in several Hadith attributed to both Muhammad and 'Ali (though their veracity has been questioned), and both the Twelver fifth and sixth imams (Muhammad al-Baqir and Ja'far al-Sadiq) prophesized his coming. In addition to the natural phenomena that will precede this apocryphal event, Muslims share the belief that it will be initiated by the advent of the Antichrist (al-masih al-dajjal).

The late well-known Lebanese authority on the history of religion, Kamal Salibi, a Protestant of Greek Orthodox ancestry, has questioned whether the Jesus of the Christian Bible is the same as the one mentioned in the Qur'an and has presented a serious, if not absolutely convincing, argument that the man the Prophet Muhammad had in mind was in fact an earlier prophet of that name, a common one in Hebrew related to Joshua.[23]

One significant fact that backs up this possibility is that the Muslim name for Jesus, 'Isa, is different than the one used by Christians, Yasu'. Although both Muslims and Arab Christians use the former as both given and family names, the latter is never used for either. Both Arabic-speaking Christians and all Muslims refer to God as Allah, something that the Muslims of Malaysia recently ignored when contesting the right of Christians in their country to refer to him as such.

In many respects Islam is closer to Judaism in that both are religions based on a strict interpretation of religious law. While Christianity has its legalistic aspects, especially in the theology of St. Thomas Aquinas, its law can be reduced, as Jesus himself declared, to loving God and your neighbor as yourself. Moreover, both traditionally religious Muslims and Jews share an unequivocal belief in the administration of criminal justice based on the doctrine of "an eye for an eye." God may be "merciful and compassionate" (*al-rahman, al-rahim*) as described in the opening chapter of the Qur'an, but his Law is not necessarily so. As we have seen, in his early days in al-Madina, Muhammad tried to convince the Jews who dominated the city that he was their anticipated Messiah. When they refused, he took control of it by force, killing many of the adult Jewish males and attaching their women and children to his followers' families. Many of the strict punishments, still administered in Sa'udi Arabia where a fundamentalist interpretation of Shari'a law holds sway, are common with those of Jewish tradition. These include the stoning of women accused of adultery and of men for blasphemy and heresy, as in the case of the first Christian martyr, Stephen, whose brutal execution was led by none other than Saul of Tarsus. Saul was a rigid Pharisee who was to become the St. Paul of epistle fame following his conversion on the road to Damascus, where he had intended to punish other Jewish followers of the crucified miracle worker. Muslims also share the Jewish refusal to portray the human form in any way, considering statues, icons, and other works of art that do so to be idolatrous.

Largely because of these shared beliefs and traditions, Islamic political authority wherever it spread treated both Jews and Christians as protected citizens so long as they peacefully followed their religions and paid special taxes. In fact, Jews were in practice viewed with even more tolerance because of the suspected loyalty of Orthodox Christians in Muslim domains to the still-powerful Byzantine emperor in Constantinople. It should be remembered that Christians are widely believed to have remained a majority in Greater Syria (Lebanon, Syria, Jordan, and Palestine/Israel of today) until the Crusades, nearly five centuries after the death of Muhammad. In the Arabian Peninsula itself, all Christians were forced to convert or leave very early in the Islamic era, whereas the Jews of Yemen were allowed to remain until most were resettled in Israel after its establishment in 1948–1949. Only a few hundred remain today, and their numbers are dwindling because of continued emigration, but no Islamic authority has ever ordered them to leave. In Sa'udi Arabia, the many foreign Christian workers there on a temporary basis are not permitted to worship publicly, and no churches may be built anywhere in the kingdom. This is not the case elsewhere in the Arabian Peninsula; even in Wahhabi-dominated Qatar there are houses of Christian worship. Both Kuwait and Bahrain even have non-Muslim citizens—a few hundred Christian families in Kuwait, the descendants of early Palestinian refugees who were granted full nationality rights in the early 1950s, and a handful of Jews in Bahrain (around forty, down from fifteen hundred before 1948), one of whom, a woman named Houda Noono, was appointed that country's ambassador to the United States in May 2008. Christian Kuwaitis have also been given diplomatic posts, which must surely aggravate conservative Sa'udis and extremist Salafis elsewhere.

Most of the differences that separate Sunnis and Twelver (and most other) Shi'as as well as some of the similarities they share have already been mentioned. Paramount among the differences is the refusal of the Shi'a to recognize the Sunni caliphate but rather to look to the authority of a direct descendant of Muhammad through 'Ali and the Prophet's daughter Fatima and their two sons, known as imams. Additionally, whereas the Sunnis acknowledge that Muhammad had other children who predeceased him, for the Shi'a Fatima was his only child. For Sunnis, an imam is just a prayer leader with no spiritual or political authority, but for all Shi'a sects he is a direct, divinely inspired descendant of the Prophet Muhammad. Twelver Shi'a have their own school of Islamic Law (Ja'fari). When standing to perform their requisite prayers, Sunnis hold their arms crossed in front, one hand resting on the other, while Shi'as keep their arms at their sides, with hands pressed flat against the outside of their thighs. During the month of Ramadan, Sunnis add a sixth communal prayer at night, called *al-tarawih*, which the Shi'a pointedly do not observe. Many religiously observant Sunni and Shi'a men grow beards, but the latter usually trim theirs while Sunnis often do not. No Shi'a family would name their son after either the second or third caliphs, 'Umar and 'Uthman (Osman), whereas the names are commonly given to Sunni boys. Some Sunni extremists have even been known to bestow the names of the Umayyad caliphs Mu'awiya and his son Yazid, hated and cursed by the Shi'a, on their offspring. The names of 'Ali, Hasan, and Husayn are commonly borne by Shi'a men, but they are not necessarily an indication of sectarian allegiance since Sunnis also employ them, especially in countries like Egypt and Palestine where no Shi'a minority exists and the issue of identity does not arise. In countries like Lebanon where Sunni and Shi'a live side by side, and often in daily confrontation, there are few Sunnis named 'Ali unless they are Palestinian refugees.

Martyrdom is viewed in a favorable light by both Sunnis and Shi'as, though until the recent advent of suicide bombing by extremist Sunnis it was more common for Shi'a to fit the pattern of voluntary self-sacrifice. The word "martyr" in both Christianity and Islam comes from the word "witness" (*martyros* in Greek, *shahid* in Arabic), but for Muslims, both Sunni and Shi'a, martyrdom is achieved through death in the advancement of Islam, usually on the battlefield, rather than by peacefully accepting torture and even death for refusing to deny Christ as it is for Christians.

In matters of marriage, divorce, and inheritance, there are a few significant differences between Sunni and Shi'a, especially the latter's practice of trial or temporary marriage (*mut'a*), which allows a woman, more often than not divorced or widowed, to move in with a man for a specified period of time in exchange for a token gift. Not all Shi'a approve of it, and the Sunnis heap scorn on the practice. Another difference involves inheritance. In Sunni Islam if a man has only daughters, they must share his estate with close male relatives. Under Shi'a law, daughters can inherit everything. This has led to instances of wealthy Sunnis, including a former prime minister of Lebanon, Salim al-Hoss, converting to Shi'ism in order to ensure the inheritance of his only child, a daughter. Adoption is not legal in any Muslim tradition, but it is expected that relatives will take in and look after orphans, widows, and other members of the immediate family in need. Although homosexuality is a major taboo for all Islamic groups, few people would deny that it is a common but mostly unspoken feature of Muslim societies, especially in the more conservative ones where the sexes are strictly segregated and sexual contact between them restricted to marriage.

In Sunni Islam, there is no clergy per se except for administrative posts such as imam or *mufti* (leader of a specific town or city), whereas the mujtahids of the Shi'a definitely exercise spiritual as well as political authority in the absence of their divinely guided imam. Mujtahids can and do issue legal judgments (fatwas) based on Islamic legal statutes and tradition, most famously that by Iran's late Ayatollah Khomeini calling for the death of British Indian author Salman Rushdie for what he and many traditional Muslims believe to be blasphemy in his book *The Satanic Verses*, which had brought attention to a rather embarrassing incident in Muhammad's early revelationary period where it appeared that he was prepared to compromise on the issue of absolute monotheism in Islam but relented in a later chapter, blaming Satan for the misguided verses.

A major difference between Sunni and Shi'a theology is the question of Divine Revelation. For Sunnis, Muhammad is "the seal" of the prophets, the final and absolute word from God. There can and will be no further revelation before the end of time. Shi'as, who, unlike Sunnis, generally accept that the Qur'an was created (as do Ibadis), do not rule out the possibility of further revelation via the last imam, Muhammad al-Mahdi, in a state of occultation for over a millennium. The annual celebration of 'Ashura' by the Shi'a is also a major sticking point. Strict Sunnis do not tolerate any kind of religious frenzy of the kind brought on by the self-flagellation practiced by some Shi'a during this ten-day period to commemorate the suffering and death of Husayn, in the same way they abhor the music and dancing that accompanies Sufi ceremonies. Moreover, the adulation the Shi'a accord Husayn and his grieving mother Fatima in connection with the third imam's suffering and death strikes some Sunnis and outside observers as having an uncomfortable resemblance to the particular reverence Christians give to Jesus and Mary during Holy Week and at the Stations of the Cross throughout the year when Christ's physical torture and Mary's sorrows are brought home to Catholics and in parallel fashion to Orthodox Christians through the spiritual power of their beloved icons. Moreover, the Shi'a reenactment of Husayn's sufferings on the final day of 'Ashura' has been likened by some to the tradition of Christian Passion Plays during Holy Week. All Muslims hold that unbelievers are condemned to Hell for eternity, but for most (except Ibadis), flawed believers are thought to remain there only until their sins have been purified, after which they enter Paradise, in much the same way that the Catholic doctrine of Purgatory allows for all but unrepentant sinners to purify themselves before reaching the gates of Heaven.

2

The Sunni-Shi'a Divide
in Modern Times

Over the centuries, the rivalry of the two branches of Islam has been hardened by mutual distrust and intolerance. It can safely be said that in places where they live side by side, such as Lebanon, 'Iraq, and parts of Iran, Sa'udi Arabia, and Pakistan, their dislike, even hatred, of each other is stronger than that felt toward other religions. This is especially the case in Lebanon, where Sunni and Shi'a members of parliament (MPs) are not at all comfortable in their politically dictated alliance (half of the national assembly is Sunni, Shi'a, and Druze, the other half Christians of various sects) and both reach out to the other side—Sunnis to the Greek Orthodox, Shi'as to Maronite Catholics—to form governments. In Pakistan, the Shi'a represent about 20 percent of the total population of 190 million, most of them Twelvers but a significant minority made up of Nizari Isma'ilis (Seveners) in the northeast. Sunnis make up the overwhelming majority (75 percent), but there are strong internal divisions pitting a growing Wahhabi/Salafi element against the traditional Sufi base. The remaining 5 percent (9–10 million) are made up of roughly equal numbers of Ahmadis, Hindus, and Christians, and much smaller communities of Baha'is, Zoroastrians, Sikhs, and Buddhists.

Open conflict between Sunnis and Shi'as in Pakistan and Afghanistan is frequent and bloody. Sunni attacks on Shi'a mosques, processions, and individuals have been common since independence, and the growing influence of Wahhabism and a local Taliban movement have increased these incidents in recent years. On March 25, 2011, a convoy of Shi'a travelling in a tribal region in northwest Pakistan was ambushed and thirteen were killed. On December 6, 2011, during the holy period of 'Ashura', fifty-five Shi'a pilgrims were killed in two suicide bombings in Afghanistan. The first bomb exploded in Kabul as chanting Shi'a men in the *ta'ziya* procession were whipping their bare backs as a sign of mourning, and the second went off outside the mosque of Hazrat 'Ali in Mazar-i-Sharif. On February 28, 2012, eighteen men and boys were killed execution style in Pakistan after their bus, en route from Rawalpindi to the Isma'ili Shi'a city of Gilgit, was stopped by men in military uniforms (whom the Pakistani authorities denied were regular soldiers). Those with identifiably Shi'a names on their ID cards were separated from the rest and shot. On September 1, 2012, in a Shi'a area of the city of Quetta in Baluchistan province, seven Hazara tribesmen were shot dead by unknown but presumably Sunni assailants. The Shi'a Hazaras, refugees from Afghanistan, have become popular targets of Sunni extremists. Over a hundred Hazaras were killed there in 2012, many in broad daylight. As often as not, the gunmen do not even bother cover their faces. Because of their distinctive central Asian facial features, the Hazara make easy targets. The government knows that the assassins, members of the fanatically anti-Shi'a Lashkar-e-Jvangvi, are based in the village of Mastung eighteen miles south of Quetta but does nothing to curb their murderous activity. The year 2012 closed with yet another massacre in the Mastung area; nineteen Shi'a pilgrims headed from Quetta to Iran were killed when their buses were blown up by a remote-controlled bomb on December 30. All in all, more than four hundred Shi'a were murdered in Pakistan in 2012.[1]

The year 2013 opened with an even more deadly atrocity on January 10 when a double suicide bombing at a snooker hall in the Hazara Shi'a district of Quetta killed ninety-two people and wounded scores. In protest, the families of victims refused to bury their remains until the government took action. The administrators of Baluchistan were eventually replaced, but to no avail. A month later, on February 16, at least one hundred persons died, many of them women and children, and over two hundred were wounded when a suicide bomber drove a truck full of explosives into an open market in the Hazara district of Quetta. On March 4 the scene shifted to Karachi, where bombs planted in the Rabia Flower apartment block adjacent to a Shi'a mosque in the neighborhood of 'Abbas Town exploded, killing fifty and wounding two hundred. The Shi'a in Pakistan continue to live in deadly fear, and the government appears unable to prevent the Lashkar-r-Jvanghi from carrying out its murderous Salafist agenda. Pakistan is still reaping the fruit of President Zia ul-Haq's policies that encouraged "Sunnification" of the country with Sa'udi money, as Indian commenter Anita Joshua described it.[2] In neighboring India, such deadly attacks on

Shi'a by the much-larger Sunni community (10 percent of India's population is Sunni, whereas Shi'a make up only about 3 percent) are very rare, but tensions and confrontations between the two often occur, such as the incident in Lucknow on January 17, 2013, when six Shi'a were injured.

Sufis and Ahmadis have also come under attack. Barely a week after the March 25, 2011, Shi'a convoy attack, more than forty Sufis were killed and one hundred wounded by al-Qa'ida suicide bombers at a shrine outside Dera Ghazi Khan in Punjab during a three-day religious festival. At the heart of Pakistan's sectarian problem are its so-called Blasphemy Laws, which make any insult to Islam, especially to the Sunni interpretation of it, punishable by death. On March 2, 2011, the government minister for minorities, Shahbaz Bhatti, a Catholic Christian, was assassinated because of his repeated calls for these laws to be revoked. Secular Muslims and Sufis have also come under attack or been assassinated for their opposition to the Blasphemy Laws.

Domestic politics have also contributed to making Shi'as a target for Sunni attack, and not only by the extremist Salafis who detest them with a visceral vehemence. Like the Alevi of Turkey, Pakistani Shi'a (who make up a comparably large minority) have historically supported the secular Left in domestic politics. The father of Pakistani independence, Muhammad Ali Jinnah, was born a Sevener and later adopted Twelver Shi'ism, even "though he was not a religiously observant man."[3] Since achieving statehood, Pakistan has seen many Shi'a hold prominent political positions, most famously the late prime minister Zulfikar Ali Bhutto (1971–1977), who was overthrown by his fundamentalist Sunni successor Gen. Muhammad Zia ul-Haq, convicted on trumped-up charges, sentenced to life imprisonment, and, later, on General ul-Haq's orders, hanged in 1979. The Shi'a had their revenge when General ul-Haq died nine years later (August 1988) in a mysterious, fiery plane crash, along with senior army officials and then U.S. ambassador Arnold Lewis Raphel. They also enjoyed a brief moment of glory when Bhutto's daughter Benazir, who served two terms as prime minister in the 1990s, returned to power from exile in October 2007, only to be assassinated two months later. The irony was that by then she had adopted an official Sunni identity for obvious political reasons, but this cosmetic change was apparently not enough for the Sunni suicide bomber who murdered her and scores of her followers.

In neighboring Afghanistan, the Shi'a, especially the previously mentioned Hazara tribes of the central and northern part of the country, have also suffered persecution, death, and, as was graphically noted in Khaled Hosseini's best-selling novel *The Kite Runner* (2003), sexual humiliation and exploitation. Closely related to the people of neighboring Tajikistan and Uzbekistan, they claim descent from Genghis Khan's Mongol invaders in the thirteenth century. They have been traditionally looked down upon by the more Aryan Pashtun tribes for their Central Asiatic facial features as well as their Shi'a faith. Under Taliban rule in the 1990s, they were labeled unbelievers and hunted down, threatened with torture to convert to Sunni Islam, and murdered or forced to flee the country if they dared to refuse.[4]

In Iran, Syria, Lebanon, and especially 'Iraq, there have been numerous recent sectarian-motivated suicide and car bombings of Shi'as and Sunnis by each other, and there appears to be no end in sight. The attacks by Sunni insurgents on Shi'a targets in 'Iraq and retaliations by Sunnis against Shi'as (with the Christians and other minorities often caught in the middle) are too numerous to mention and currently ongoing. In Lebanon, street fighting between the two groups in Beirut brought Hizbollah paramilitary forces into direct conflict with the government of then prime minister Sa'ad al-Hariri in May 2009, and there were further outbreaks in anticipation of the release of the UN tribunal's findings on the assassination of Prime Minister Rafiq al-Hariri in 2005; it was feared that the findings would point the finger at some elements within Hizbollah, which they indeed did in 2011. In Syria, a suicide car bomber killed seventeen people outside the Shi'a mosque of Sitt Zaynab on September 27, 2008, and four years later on June 14, 2012, another suicide bomber attempted the same outrage but succeeded only in blowing himself up and wounding fourteen bystanders, though there was some damage to the shrine. In Iran, the execution of the leader of a Sunni militant group called Jundallah (Soldiers of God) on June 20, 2010, brought about the suicide bombing of a Shi'a mosque in the predominantly Sunni city of Zahedan near the confluence of the Afghan-Pakistan borders in the southeastern region of Baluchistan, killing twenty-two worshippers on July 15, the birthday of Imam Husayn and the anniversary of the founding of the Islamic Revolutionary Guard Corps. The perpetrators were strongly condemned by Ayatollah Rafsanjani three days later on state television. During the ten days of 'Ashura' in mid-December, Jundallah struck again, this time killing more than three dozen worshippers and wounding even more outside a Shi'a mosque in the predominantly Sunni Baluchi coastal city of Chabahar directly south of Zahedan near the Pakistan border. Iranian officials blamed "outlaws and American agents" for the deadly attack.

Sunni and Shi'a during the Rise of European Colonialism

Since the establishment of Shi'a rule in Iran under the Safavids in the sixteenth century, the political balance between the two major branches of
Islam has remained relatively unchanged. Apart from Iran, nearly all of the
Islamic world fell under the jurisdiction of Sunni rule—the Ottomans in
the West and the Moghuls in much of the territory inhabited by Muslims
to the east of Iran with their center at Delhi in India. The major exception was what is today Indonesia and Malaysia, which since the sixteenth
century had been ruled first by Portuguese and later Dutch and British
colonial powers. Originally, the region had been a center of Hinduism and
Buddhism, but gradually Islam replaced the older religions through the
peaceful influence of Sunni merchants and traders from India and further
west, making it far and away the most populous area of the world that was
not acquired for Islam by armed conflict. Only the island of Bali remains
predominantly Hindu in religion today, though many other islands of the
eastern Indonesian archipelago are in majority Christian as a result of four
hundred years of European domination. The Spanish colonial masters were
even more effective in spreading Christianity during the same period in
the neighboring Philippines, with the exception of the western half of the
southernmost island of Mindinao and the Julu chain, which are closest to
the Indonesian island of Borneo (the northern part of which is now part
of Malaysia) and predominantly Muslim. The Muslims of western China
and central Asia, the product of the conversion of their Mongol rulers in
the late thirteenth century, were often ruled by independent Muslim states,
though they sometimes came within the sphere of Iran and the Moghuls
until Russian expansion eastward in the nineteenth century brought them
under Orthodox Christian rule or political influence. Likewise, the Sunni
Muslims and substantial Shi'a minority of the Moghul Empire were slowly
absorbed by the growing power of the British in India.

During this period of colonial expansion, however, there were no
changes of consequence in the distribution of Sunni and Shi'a populations.
The Shi'a dominated in Iran, and in Ottoman territories they were the
majority in the southern part of 'Iraq, parts of what is today Lebanon, the
northern Gulf coast, and northern Yemen (Zaydis) in the Arabian Peninsula, where the rule of the distant sultan in Istanbul was almost nonexistent. Other areas of Shi'a minority populations included central Anatolia
(Alevis), northwest Syria ('Alawis and Isma'ilis), parts of Russian Turkestan, and the Indian subcontinent, where most of the world's Isma'ilis were
found. Virtually all of Muslim believers at the beginning of the twentieth

century fell, as they do at least nominally today, within these two main categories: Sunni (80–85 percent) and Shi'a (15–20 percent), the only exception being the million or so Ibadis of Oman (and isolated pockets elsewhere), who are the descendants of the first group to split from the traditional Islamic 'Umma, the Kharijites. But there were other divisions within these two, as we have seen, and even more significant were the localized forces of clan, tribe, race, and, with the collapse of European colonial rule, nationalism and the secular political ideologies of socialism and communism that would have increasing impact on the Islamic world after World War II.

The Final Collapse of the Ottoman Empire and the End of the Sunni Caliphate

In November 1918 the Ottoman Empire surrendered to the forces of the Western Allies. It had been known as the "Sick Man of Europe" for nearly two centuries, and its once-dominant presence in southeastern Europe had all but evaporated, having been replaced by newly independent Christian states in the Balkans with increasingly isolated Muslim minorities (except in the case of Albania, where an independent, predominantly Muslim state had been established in 1913). The famous "Eastern Question"—what to do with Ottoman territories—had now come to a head. Secret treaties between the allies during the war had essentially divided up these lands among the victorious Great Powers, which were so weakened by war that they were able to implement only some of them, and then only briefly. The British and French did succeed in establishing protectorates (League of Nations' Mandates), the former in Palestine, Transjordan, and 'Iraq, and the latter in Syria and Lebanon, respectively, but attempts to dismember the remaining Turkish territories of Eastern Thrace, Constantinople, and Anatolia by Greeks, Armenians, and Italians failed. Had Russia not fallen victim to the Bolshevik Revolution in 1917 following the failure of the Gallipoli Campaign to open up the Bosphorus and provide allied support for the czarist army and state, the map of the Middle East would have undoubtedly been redrawn to the detriment of Islam.

In the end, the Turks were rescued by their hero of Gallipoli, Mustafa Kemal, one of the leaders of the Young Turk Revolution of 1908 who later took the title of Atatürk (Father of the Turkish Nation). From 1920 to 1922 he succeeded in driving out the Greeks from Smyrna (and ultimately all of their historic centers in Anatolia), those Armenians who had survived earlier genocidal massacres from eastern Anatolia, the Italians from Antalya on the southern coast, and the British from Constantinople. An agreement between Atatürk and Lenin provided the Turks with desperately needed arms, allowed the Bolsheviks to concentrate on consolidating their power in Russia, and neutralized any threat to Turkey from its largest traditional enemy. The first Republic of Armenia was caught in the crossfire and divided between Turkey (including the iconic Mount Ararat) and the Soviet Union, which created a rump Soviet Peoples' Republic of Armenia in 1922. In 1923 a new treaty with the Turks to replace the humiliating Versailles capitulation at Sèvres in 1919 was signed at Lausanne in Switzerland, recognizing the new Republic of Turkey. The borders determined then have endured, apart from the annexation of the southern province of Alexandretta (called Hatay by the Turks) from the French-administered mandate of Syria in 1939, a year after Atatürk's death, and the assumption of sovereignty over the crucial Bosphorus and Dardanelles Straits.

One of the first acts of Atatürk's radical transformation of what remained of Ottoman domains in 1924 was to abolish the caliphate, whose powers devolved to the National Assembly of the Turkish Republic. By this single act, nearly thirteen centuries of traditional Sunni Muslim political and religious authority came to an end, with consequences that are still felt today. As we have seen, the original institution had been established on the death of Muhammad in 632, and his first four successors, known as the Righteous (al-rashidun) caliphs (khulafa'), presided over the early expansion of Islam at the expense of the Byzantine and Persian Empires, which had been greatly weakened by two decades of war and, in the case of the Eastern Roman Empire, centuries of religious infighting. But in 661 upon the death of the fourth of these caliphs, 'Ali, the son-in-law and cousin of the Prophet Muhammad and the only caliph recognized by followers who thought that all successors to the Prophet should be chosen from among his direct descendants, Islam was irrevocably split. One group favored a Sunni caliphate in Damascus established by the first Umayyad ruler, Mu'awiya, and his dynastic successors. The Shi'a refused to recognize this caliphate, pledging their allegiance instead to the grandsons of Muhammad and later to Husayn's son and his successors, whom they called imams and to whom they attributed innate spiritual powers.

The Umayyads of Damascus were overthrown in 750 by the Abbasids, who moved the caliphate to Baghdad during the reign of the second ruler of that dynasty. There the caliphate remained, enjoying a century of greatness before entering a gradual decline. The weakening Abbasids were rivaled by another Sunni Umayyad caliphate in Spain until it fell in 1031 and a Shi'a Fatimid dynasty in Egypt and North Africa from 969 to 1171. By the tenth century, the caliphs in Baghdad were rulers in name only, controlled by a succession of central Asian militia-based dynasties until the last Abbasid caliph was murdered in 1258 by the victorious armies of the Mongols. The Mongols were in turn defeated two years later by Sultan Baybars, ruler of the Cairo-based Mamluke dynasty, at the battle of 'Ayn Jalut near Naza-reth, and a surviving member of the Abbasid family was brought to Egypt and given the title of caliph to perpetuate at least a shadow of traditional Muslim authority. When the Mamlukes were defeated in 1517 by the Ot-toman sultan Selim I ("the Grim"), the last of these token caliphs was taken to Istanbul, where he reputedly surrendered his title to Selim and his suc-cessors in perpetuity. The caliphate was held by the Ottomans until it was abolished by Atatürk in 1924.

The title of caliph was immediately claimed by Sharif Husayn of Mecca, the leader of the Arab Revolt in World War I who is remembered primarily by virtue of his association with Lawrence of Arabia, but before he could solidify his claim, his lands, including the holy cities of Mecca and Medina, were overrun by the Sa'udis of al-Najd later in 1924. Hu-sayn died the following year, and in 1926 a conference was convened in Cairo to find a way to reestablish what Atatürk had destroyed. Few Muslim countries sent delegates, and nothing came of their deliberations. Sunni Muslims therefore found themselves for the first time in their history with-out any recognized religious and political authority and no foreseeable hope of one. For a religion that does not recognize any separation between church and state, this created an abnormal and unacceptable vacuum of power that no one has been able fill. A few have tried, like King Faruk of Egypt and the Sa'udi king 'Abd al-'Aziz Ibn Sa'ud, but were unable to gen-erate any support outside their own immediate power bases. This vacuum has encouraged the rise of radicals like the Taliban and al-Qa'ida. Unless the situation is somehow resolved, Sunni Islam will remain unstable and vulnerable to extremism and internecine struggles that affect the entire world, not just countries with Muslim majorities. For Sunnis, there is no adequate substitute for a successor to the Prophet, but there is also no one on the horizon acceptable to four-fifths the world's Muslims, and therein lies the conundrum.

The Rise of Middle Eastern Nationalism and the Creation of the State of Israel

The nineteenth century saw both the decline of the Ottoman Empire and the rapid expansion of European colonialism that eventually enveloped almost the entire Muslim world. The gradual retreat of Islam from Europe had begun in the West in the Middle Ages with the Spanish Reconquista, which ultimately drove the Muslims, as well as the Jews, out of the Iberian Peninsula in successive waves following the conquest of Granada in 1492 well into the sixteenth and seventeenth centuries. The Muslims resettled in North Africa. The Jews settled there as well as Salonica (Thessaloniki) and Istanbul, where they remained a vital thriving presence until the twentieth century; Holland; and the Americas. The discovery of the sea route to India by the Portuguese at the same time led to the gradual submission of the vast Muslim population of Indonesia to Dutch rule beginning in the seventeenth century. British influence in the Indian subcontinent, Ceylon (Sri Lanka), and the Malay Peninsula, which began with the merchants of the East India Company, led to direct imperial political control during the reign of Queen Victoria, bringing what was then the largest concentration of Muslims in the world under the aegis of a Protestant Christian, missionary-oriented European power. In North Africa, the French began their colonial expansion, first in Algeria in the 1830s, followed by Tunisia and Morocco. The British established a strong presence in Egypt in 1882 and later in the Sudan as a safeguard to the newly built Suez Canal and the now much-shorter route to India. They also were gradually adding the pirate, later called trucial, states of the Persian Gulf to their sphere of influence, just as they had in 1839 in southern Yemen with the occupation of the strategic port of Aden at the opposite end of the Red Sea from Suez.

The recently united Italians quickly jumped into the colonial race after 1861 with the acquisition of half Muslim Eritrea in 1882 and entirely Muslim southern Somalia shortly thereafter. The northern region opposite Aden fell to the British and a tiny corner, Djibouti, to the French. In the early years of the twentieth century, the Italians grabbed Libya and immediately began colonizing it with large numbers of previously landless peasants from Sicily and Calabria who by the outbreak of World War II outnumbered the indigenous Muslims. Ethiopia, sandwiched between Eritrea and Italian Somaliland, was overrun and occupied by Mussolini's troops from 1936 to 1941. By the outbreak of World War II, all of Africa's millions of

Muslims had come under the rule of Christian European powers—Britain, France, Spain, Portugal, Italy, and, in tiny "independent" Liberia, a de facto American protectorate.

In Europe by the end of the nineteenth century, nearly all of the Ottoman territories there had been lost to the expanding Austro-Hungarian Empire or newly independent Christian states, while the Black Sea and Caucasus regions of the last Islamic Empire had fallen to the Czarist Russians, who had also recently completed a slow but ultimately successful conquest of the independent Turkish-speaking Muslim principalities of central Asia.

After the fall of the Ottomans in 1918, the victorious British and French were able to establish League of Nations Mandate territories in Syria, Lebanon, Palestine, Transjordan, and 'Iraq in the early 1920s. By the time of the abolition of the caliphate by Kemal Atatürk in 1924, only Sa'udi Arabia, north Yemen, Iran, and Afghanistan remained under independent, traditional Islamic rule. While Turkey was able to resist attempts by Christian powers to carve up its territory, the fiercely secular rule established by Atatürk began ruthlessly to crush the whole framework of the former Muslim religious society there. Islam had reached its lowest point since the conquering tribes of Arabia had swept onto the scene of world history nearly twelve hundred years earlier, and seemed doomed to a future dominated by Western Christian hegemony.

Western imperial domination, however, proved to be short-lived. World War I had severely taxed European finances and its manpower. Colonialism had brought with it the seeds of its own destruction—the forces of nationalism and secular ideologies. In the Middle East, the idea of Arab nationalism, espoused initially by native Christians as a means of enforcing their Arab identity without the unwanted baggage of an Islamic religious association, spread quickly to the Muslim population. The Arab Revolt during World War I had at first rallied around the figure of Sharif Husayn of Mecca, whom many saw as a potential Arab caliph but who, as we have seen, was overthrown by the Wahhabi Sa'udi monarchy at the same time as his Ottoman rival. A new generation of nationalists began to preach a message that stressed a more modern, secular ideal. Typical of this was the Ba'th (Renaissance) Party founded in 1940 in Damascus by two political philosophers, one Muslim and one Christian. The latter, Michel 'Aflaq, became its primary ideologue. The Ba'th movement attracted followers from all segments of the sectarian divisions of Syria, as did the Syrian Nationalist Party, known by its French acronym PPS (Parti populaire syrien). It was founded in 1932 by Antun Sa'ada, a Lebanese-born Greek Orthodox Christian journalist who lived much of his adult life in Brazil, and internationally based on movements like socialism and communism. The Ba'th Party would later come to power in Syria and 'Iraq in the 1960s, and in Egypt the charismatic leader Gamal Abdul Nasser would base his appeal on a combination of religious and secular political ideologies in the form of Arab socialism.

The deeply ingrained allegiance of Muslims to their faith, however, proved strongly resistant to these political movements with their European taint, and many saw them as a thinly disguised form of colonialism. One of the earliest reactions to these attempts to ape Western thought was the Muslim Brotherhood (Ikhwan al-Muslimin), founded by Egyptian ideologue Hasan al-Banna, which almost from its inception excited the antipathy of secular-thinking Muslims who looked to the reforms imposed on Turkish society by Kemal Atatürk as a model which other Islamic countries should follow. Indeed, in many urban areas of Egypt and the Arab East in the 1930s and 1940s a Western-oriented Muslim elite advocated the abolition of the veil and the participation of women in the arts, especially popular music and the rapidly growing local cinema industry based in Cairo. A prominent example of this new trend was the Syrian Druze chanteuse from al-Suwayda known as Asmahan (sister of the famed 'ud player Farid al-Atrash) whose meteoric stage and screen career in Egypt ended in her tragic demise in 1944 at age thirty-two. Such changes had little impact outside the cities, however. In daily life, the veil and strict segregation of the sexes had been something practical only to the small middle- and upper-class segments of Muslim society, but they were never practical in rural areas where whole families lived in one- or two-room dwellings and the women worked in the fields next to the men.

As European imperialism became more and more threatened by overextended lines of supply, the collapse of the global economy in the early 1930s and the rising forces of nationalism both in Europe and the Islamic world, the colonial powers, especially Britain and France, were forced to surrender their authority. 'Iraq became independent in 1932 and Lebanon and Syria twelve years later. Egypt effectively freed itself from direct British control in 1936, and the weak Albanian monarchy established in the early nineteenth century was unable to keep the tide of Arab nationalism at bay, falling to a military coup in 1952 that brought Nasser to power and saw King Faruk sail into exile. In the immediate aftermath of World

War II, India, the Islamic Republic of Pakistan, and Indonesia gained their independence. The next decade and a half saw the French pushed out of North Africa at the same time that the rest of the continent was sending its colonial masters packing. In a short space of time, most of the Muslim world, apart from the Soviet Republics of central Asia, had shed the burden of direct Western Christian control. The one very crucial exception was Palestine, where in 1948 British authority yielded to another foreign presence, the newly proclaimed Zionist state of Israel.

The British Mandate of Palestine, established in 1920, had provided the British with a land link between the Mediterranean and the Persian Gulf and, ultimately, India. For Muslims, it was of vital religious and geopolitical importance. Its capital, Jerusalem, was the third-holiest city of Islam, whose Dome of the Rock housed the site from which the Prophet had begun his ascent to the seven heavens. Of equal importance was the fact that Palestine provided the only a land bridge between the Muslim countries of Egypt and North Africa and the even more populous and powerful centers to the East. If a non-Muslim power were to control this vital piece of territory, the Islamic world would be physically split and the holy site of Jerusalem divided between the new Jewish state and the newly named Kingdom of Jordan (previously Transjordan). This, of course, was exactly what happened in 1948–1949 with the establishment of the state of Israel. For Muslims, the partition of Palestine represented the last gasp of European colonialism, a cruel paradox and an unacceptable development that had to be remedied.

Sunni and Shi'a Response to the Partition of Palestine and U.S. Involvement

What was to become one of the longest-lasting modern political crises of international proportions began at a conference of European Jews in Basle, Switzerland (1897), who subscribed to Zionism, the late-nineteenth-century movement founded by Theodore Herzl. It advocated the return of all Jewish people to the Holy Land and the creation of a Jewish state there, despite the historic presence of the hundreds of thousands of Arabs already living in Ottoman Palestine since the seventh century who were 85 percent Muslim (all Sunni except for a tiny community of Druze, just nine thousand according to the census of 1931) and 15 percent Christian (equal numbers of Greek Orthodox and Catholic Christian Arabs, with very small communities of Armenians, Syriacs, and Protestants). Particularly ironic is the fact that these indigenous inhabitants were very likely the descendants of the original Jewish population, who were converted to Christianity and then later to Islam, intermixed with the various waves of invaders—Byzantine Greeks, Arabs, European Crusaders, Mamlukes, and Turks. They may have also been descended from generations of pilgrims who had been visiting Jerusalem and other Christian holy sites since Emperor Constantine's pious mother, Helena, first identified them in the early fourth century with the help of local residents who for generations had successfully hidden their Christian faith from pagan Roman persecution. The Jews had been finally expelled from Jerusalem and virtually all of Palestine in the early second century by the emperor Hadrian (their temple having been destroyed sixty years earlier by the emperor Titus) and the city of Jerusalem itself leveled and rebuilt with temples dedicated to Roman deities. Gradually, they began to filter back over the centuries, especially during the long period of tolerance ushered in by Muslim rule after 637 AD, interrupted by an intolerant Christian Crusader hiatus from 1099 to 1291, and culminating with Ottoman suzerainty from 1517 to 1918. During this long and relatively peaceful domination from Istanbul, many Jews fleeing persecution in Spain and elsewhere in Europe made their way to Ottoman territories, including Jerusalem and the town of Safad in Galilee, where small communities of mainly elderly Jews who wished to die and be buried in the Holy Land were established and replenished by small but regular influxes of refugees from expulsions and pogroms in Europe.

The new waves of Zionist Jews who began arriving in the late nineteenth and early twentieth centuries were very different from the earlier immigrants in that they were mainly young and imbued with a secular idealism that dictated the establishment of self-sufficient, agriculturally based settlements on land acquired from Palestinian Arabs or, more often, from absentee landlords in Lebanon and elsewhere who were only too happy to accept the lucrative offers of the recent arrivals backed by wealthy supporters in Europe. The reaction by the native inhabitants to this sudden invasion was immediate and almost universally hostile. Although much of the land initially acquired by Zionist "pioneers," as they likened themselves, was undesirable marshland that required considerable effort to reclaim, large tracts of territory of increasing value came under Jewish ownership in the years leading up to World War I.

Both the majority Sunni Muslim population and the large Christian minority living primarily in Jerusalem and smaller towns like Jaffa, Haifa, Acre, Nazareth, and the Bethlehem–Bayt Jala–Bayt Sahur triangle just south of the Holy City felt threatened. Muslim peasants found themselves pushed aside by the Zionist farmers with their modern methods of cultivation and irrigation, and the Christian city-dwellers who formed the backbone of the urban business and banking sector were suddenly faced with equally skilled rivals in these fields. Ottoman authorities for the most part ignored the Jewish influx, or else quietly profited from bribes offered to facilitate land transfers. Some Muslim religious figures began to raise the alarm, as did some local Christian Arab Nationalist leaders, unlike their church leadership which was made up largely of non-Arab heads of Greek Orthodox and Roman Catholic monastic establishments. But violent confrontations were few in number until the Balfour Declaration of 1917 suddenly raised the ante for both Zionists and Palestinians. With the stroke of a pen, the British government had given what had been a fringe movement of European Jewry, rejected by the majority of its own members, a radically enhanced position on the international stage.

When the Balfour Declaration was issued, the outcome of the war in Europe was far from certain. Both sides had fought to a stalemate on the Western Front, and American help had yet to break it. In the east, Russia was down but not out, and the Germans still had to deal with a war on two fronts until the Bolshevik Revolution later that year suddenly changed the picture dramatically. In his rise to power in the early 1930s, Adolf Hitler would claim that the British declaration of support for the establishment of a Jewish state in Palestine was an attempt to subvert the German and Austrian Empires from within by appealing to their own Jewish bankers as well as their large Jewish minorities for whom Zionism held growing attraction. Anti-Semitism was by no means the invention of the Nazis, and many European Jews saw their own state as a means of escaping it. In addition, it was now common knowledge that if the Allies won, the Holy Land would come under British control as part of the terms of the once-secret Sykes-Picot Agreement of 1915. Imperial Britain had a much better record of tolerance when it came to its own Jewish population in modern times than did most other European states, and Prime Minister David Lloyd George was a nonconformist Welshman who knew his Bible and had a personal sympathy for Zionist goals. At the time, the British Israelite movement, which held that the English were one of the ten lost tribes of Israel and called for a return of Jews to Palestine, was still a force to be reckoned with. Another quietly sympathetic backing came from Freemasonry, which was very popular and included in its ranks senior members of the royal family.

After the war ended on November 11, 1918, the British and French set about trying to redistribute the territories of the defeated Ottoman Empire. The British succeeded at least in the Levant, where they were awarded the custodianship of the region including Palestine, Transjordan, and 'Iraq under the terms of the Treaty of Versailles. Zionism had been given a brand new lease of life, and its leaders wasted no time in taking advantage of the British imperial clout that it now enjoyed. But the Palestine Mandate proved to be a far more difficult piece of real estate to manage than the British had imagined. Arab resistance to rising numbers of Jewish immigrants grew stronger in the face of what was perceived as a new colonialist threat, and deadly clashes ensued throughout the 1920s and 1930s, notably in Hebron in 1929.

The Palestinian resistance, led by the then Grand Mufti of Jerusalem Hajj Amin al-Husayni, remained local and entirely Sunni. Shi'a Muslims were unaffected, even those living nearby in South Lebanon. They were the poorest and least organized of the French Mandate's many sectarian communities, and their political concerns, if they had any—and most of them deferred to their tribal leadership for guidance—were directed toward achieving independence from France. The Shi'a majority of 'Iraq was firmly dominated by the powerful Sunni Arab minority, especially after independence from Britain was achieved in 1932 under the rule of King Faysal, whom many individual Shi'a respected since he held the widely accepted pedigree of a direct descendant of Muhammad. For them, any member of the *ahl al-bayt* (the family of the Prophet), even a Sunni, was deserving of special deference. In Iran, the recently established dictator Shah Reza Khan had imposed firm control over the Shi'a mullahs and ayatollahs of Qom after he seized power in 1925. Further to the east in the Indian subcontinent, the British were tenaciously holding on to their increasingly precarious power while the Muslim population channeled its efforts into winning its own state once independence was achieved.

Elsewhere in the Sunni Muslim world, local political authorities held in check any religious fervor that might have at least temporarily supported their Palestinian brothers in a fight against Zionism. It was not until the end of World War II that the very real threat of a Zionist state in Palestine, never promised under the carefully calculated and purposefully vague terms of the Balfour Declaration but now firmly supported by the victorious Americans, began to galvanize both Sunni and Shi'a opposition to the events unfolding in the halls of the newly established United Nations in New York. The failure of this opposition, despite the guarantees of the Balfour Declaration promising that nothing should be done in the establishment of a Jewish home that would diminish the rights of the indigenous peoples already living in Palestine, took some time for the world's Muslims to digest. But once they had, the wheels of justice as they saw them began to grind inexorably toward the dangerous situation the entire world faces today. Until the two seemingly irreconcilable promises made by Arthur James Balfour, 1st Earl of Balfour—that is, to give the Jews access to 8,000 square miles of strategically positioned land in the heart of the Arab world dotted with religious sites emotionally revered by all three Abrahamic faiths without compromising the rights of majority Muslim and Christian Palestinian populations who had lived there without break for many centuries—were resolved, world peace and stability could not be achieved, nor even imagined.

Israel's Initial Victory and Gradual International Isolation

Four factors coincided that allowed for the establishment of an independent Jewish state in Palestine in the wake of the defeat of Nazi Germany. First, the British Empire was on the brink of collapse following six years of exhausting war in both Europe and the Far East. All but reconciled to the loss of the jewel in their crown of possessions, India, and trapped in the middle of hostile confrontations between Arabs and Jews in Palestine with their armed forces stretched beyond their ability to contain them, the British saw no reason to hold on to their mandate in the Holy Land. They happily turned its future over to the United Nations in 1947. Second, buoyed by large numbers of recent immigrants from post-war Europe and with a large supply of recently acquired weapons, the Zionist settlers were well prepared to take on the disorganized Palestinian militias and the ill-equipped armies of their neighboring Arab states. Third, the terrible tragedy of the Jewish Holocaust at the hands of the Nazis and their supporters in Eastern Europe had predisposed world opinion in favor of compensating the survivors with a nation of their own in the Holy Land, even though the native inhabitants had had nothing to do with the massacre of an estimated 6 million Jews in Europe. Fourth, crucial support from the Jewish community in the United States exerted pressure on allies in the UN to support a partition of the Palestine Mandate, allowing for the establishment of the Jewish state. States who wavered, like the Philippines and Haiti, strongly beholden to the United States, as well as the nations in Western

Europe dependent on American financial aid through the Marshall Plan, buckled under American pressure and overcame their initial reservations to the proposed partition. Only Greece, despite its need of the Truman Doctrine to battle a Communist-backed takeover, resisted the pressure, citing concerns of the some 250,000 Greeks living in Arab countries at the time, especially Egypt.

When Israel declared its independence in May 1948, the United States accorded it immediate diplomatic recognition despite strong opposition in the State Department and within both political parties. But President Harry Truman, who was facing an uphill re-election bid in November of that year, had millions of Jewish constituents whose support he needed (as he poignantly remarked at the time) and few Arab ones. Truman had also misquoted the Balfour Declaration as calling for a "Jewish National Homeland" when in fact it had advocated a far less specific "national home for Jewish people." "Home" and "homeland" carry radically different implications.

Three days after the American recognition, which was initially de facto only, the Soviet Union followed suit, upping the ante by becoming the first state to give Israel de jure recognition. The Soviets had very different motives from the United States. Whereas American support was based largely on sympathy for the Jewish victims of the Holocaust and total ignorance of geopolitical realities on the ground, the Soviets were hopeful that the leaders of the new state, many of them Russian-born and firm socialists, would provide them with a base for Communist expansion in the oil-rich Middle East. Many of the early Bolsheviks were from Jewish backgrounds, like Trotsky, and many more had been driven into the Communist fold through opposition to Hitler's National Socialism and other fascist movements steeped in anti-Semitism.

In the war that followed Israel's declaration of independence, only the armies of the Arab Legion in Transjordan, led by their British commander John Glubb Pasha, succeeded in holding on to a small segment of the Palestine Mandate, including the old city of Jerusalem with its major Muslim holy site, the Dome of the Rock, which sat on land revered by the Jews as the site of their second temple. These territories, constituting less than a quarter of the land of the former Palestine Mandate, were annexed by King 'Abdallah once the Israel-Transjordanian Armistice Agreement had been signed in 1949.

In the meantime, an excess of 750,000 Palestinians were forced into exile in neighboring Transjordan, Syria, and Lebanon. Most of them were poor Sunni Muslim peasants, but there were also a substantial number of urban, middle-class Christians and some rural inhabitants of predominantly Christian villages along the Lebanese border. A small number of these refugees were allowed to return over the next few years, but the great majority of them remain cut off from their ancestral lands to this day. In their wake, hundreds of thousands of Jewish inhabitants of Arab countries were encouraged to emigrate to the new Zionist state, creating not only their own refugee problem but dramatically changing the ethnic make up of Israel since virtually all of them were Jews of Spanish, North African, or Middle Eastern descent who practiced a Sephardic form of liturgy (Sephardim) as opposed to the earlier immigrants from Europe, known as Ashkenazim. The Jews of Sephardic origin proudly claim direct descent from the Jewish population displaced from Palestine by Roman persecution and expulsions in the first and second centuries AD. There are Sephardim who regard the Ashkenazim as possibly compromised with a non-Jewish admixture of Turkic blood due to the conversion to Judaism of the ruling elite of the Khazar Empire that ruled much of the Caucasus and beyond in the ninth and tenth centuries. Their descendants joined the already existing Jewish diaspora community in Eastern Europe following the empire's collapse shortly after the destruction of its capital in 969 by the rising forces of the Russians (Rus), who were soon to convert to Christianity in 988.[5]

Initially, Israel enjoyed strong international support outside the Islamic world and even gained a grudging alliance and diplomatic recognition from two major Muslim states: the predominantly Sunni but strongly secular Turkish Republic and Iran, which was ruled by the Pahlevi family who had little use for the ayatollahs who held the allegiance of most of the country's Shi'a majority. Iran had a very long history of favorable relations with and treatment of Jews, dating back to Cyrus the Great who in 539 BC freed the enslaved Jews from their Babylonian captivity and allowed them to return to Jerusalem and rebuild their (second) temple. Many Jews chose to remain in Iran and Mesopotamia; most of those in the latter, some 100,000, left for the new state of Israel in 1948–1949, but the larger community of 150,000 in Iran initially chose to remain there. Their numbers have been drastically reduced to 25,000–40,000 since the establishment of the Shi'a Islamic Republic in 1979, but they remain the largest Jewish community in the Islamic world. Like the larger Christian, mostly Armenian, minority, Iranian Jews are guaranteed seats in the parliament (they were allotted three in the elections of 2012). Most Jews of Persian ancestry now live in either Israel or the United States, mainly in southern California.

Shah Reza Khan was forced to abdicate in 1941 by the British and Americans, who distrusted his pro-German sympathies in the early years of World War II, and he was replaced by his young son Shah Muhammad Reza. Firmly under the thumb of the victorious Allies, especially the British who controlled the country's petroleum industry, he proved eager to supply Israel with its oil requirements, much to the chagrin of his petroleum-rich Arab neighbors who had already begun an economic boycott of the Jewish state. When his democratically elected and highly popular prime minister Mohammed Mosadegh tried to nationalize the oil industry in the early 1950s (the Iranian parliament actually passed the measure with a huge majority), the shah had no choice but to cooperate with the British and Americans in removing him from office. Mosadegh was imprisoned after a famously rigged trial in December 1953, and his supporters were rounded up and also imprisoned if they were lucky enough not to be tortured and killed. From then on, Israel's oil supply flowed uninterrupted from Iran until the shah's overthrow a quarter of a century later.

The conflict between the defeated Palestinians and the victorious Israelis remained a largely local argument apart from the Suez War of 1956, during which the Israeli Army joined the British and French in invading Egypt when Nasser seized control of the vital waterway. Pressure exerted on all parties by an angry President Dwight Eisenhower forced them to withdraw from occupied Egyptian territory, and the situation returned to one of occasional clashes on the ground and verbal exchanges on the floor of the General Assembly of the United Nations.

Three events were to change the dynamic of the hostilities, raising them to a serious international level involving both sides of the Cold War conflict and Muslims everywhere. The first was the 1967 war between Israel and its neighbors launched on June 6 when, citing the need for a "pre-emptive strike," Israel invaded Egypt, Syria, and Jordan. Its forces effectively blocked the Suez Canal to international trade for seven years, seized the water-rich Golan (al-Julan) heights overlooking the Sea of Galilee from the east, and, most crucially, occupied the West Bank of Jordan, including the old city of Jerusalem and its holy Islamic, not to mention Christian, sites. For Muslims everywhere in the world, even in sub-Saharan Africa (whose newly independent peoples were up until this time totally uninvolved in the issue), this was viewed as a catastrophe of unimaginable proportions. Although the Sinai was regained for Egypt in the years following the war launched by President Anwar Sadat in 1973 and the Suez Canal reopened, Jerusalem remained firmly in the hands of the Israelis, who had declared it their "eternal and undivided capital." No country of any importance has recognized this claim, including the United States, despite several attempts by Congress, heavily influenced by the Israel lobby the American Israel Public Affairs Committee (AIPAC), to pass non-binding legislation calling for just that—a move meant to please Jewish voters and their Christian evangelical supporters. The universally accepted position, strongly supported by the Vatican, the Orthodox Church, and the Soviet Union (later Russia), is what was understood at the time of the 1949 Armistice and which still remains, that Jerusalem should be an "international city" administered by the United Nations on behalf of all three Abrahamic faiths, not just the Jews.

The second event that changed everything was the overthrow of Shah Reza of Iran in 1979 by the Shi'a clergy (led by the exiled Ayatollah Khomeini from Paris) he so despised and had for years kept under tight control and the establishment of a Shi'a Islamic state. The triumphal return of the victorious cleric brought an abrupt end to a subdued Iranian governmental support for Israel and, until then, its major source of oil.

The third change was brought about three years later in 1982 when the Israeli Army invaded Lebanon in an attempt to drive out Palestine Liberation Organization (PLO) leader Yasir Arafat from his Beirut and later Tripoli (Lebanon) strongholds. In the end, he sailed reluctantly into exile in Tunisia, but in the meantime the invading Zionists had so angered the heretofore apolitical Shi'a peasantry of southern Lebanon that they rose up in a body, exercising a political force they had never before possessed through an organization that took the name Hizb Allah, or the "Party of God." Strongly backed by the newly ensconced Shi'a religious state in Iran, "Hizbollah" as it came to be known in the West was also embraced as an ally by the 'Alawi-backed Ba'th Party government in Syria. President Hafiz al-Asad (officially a Sunni as Syria's constitution demanded but in reality an 'Alawi, as previously noted) saw the new Shi'a militants as a useful tool for expanding his influence in Lebanon which Syria had never recognized as independent. It wasn't until 2009 that the two countries finally exchanged ambassadors. President Asad had brutally demonstrated his determination to suppress Sunni Islamists who had risen up against his strongly secular Ba'th Party government in February 1982 in the central Syrian city of Hama, long a conservative Sunni stronghold. Thousands of people died, much of the old city was destroyed, and as a lesson to the dissidents, it is said, a ruined mosque was turned into a night club and a brothel. Since then, the majority Sunni population of Syria has nursed a bitter grudge against the 'Alawi-based governments of both Asads, father and son.

Although branded a terrorist organization by the United States after the twin suicide truck bombings that killed 241 U.S. peacekeepers in their barracks at the Beirut International Airport (BIA) and 58 French paratroopers at their headquarters two miles north of BIA in 1983, Hizbollah has always denied direct responsibility for these actions. Its military operations since its founding have been devoted to a single defensive aim—the protection of Lebanon from Israeli invasion—and one offensive goal: the recovery of Jerusalem for Islam from the Zionist enemy. For the first time, the Sunni Palestinians and Shi'a Lebanese found common cause, something the Israelis for all their vaunted military intelligence and professed understanding of the so-called Arab mind failed to prevent, just as a later colossal miscalculation in May 2010—the attack by Jewish commandos in international waters on the peace vessel _Mavi Marmara_, attempting to deliver relief aid to Gaza—would result in a serious breach in the previously good relations with Turkey, their only remaining Muslim ally after the shah's government collapsed. Today, Israel faces hostile neighbors in its own region, growing criticism and at best tepid support in Europe, and a total indifference to its existence elsewhere in the world except possibly India because of its fear of neighboring Pakistan. Only in the United States can Israel count on strong support. But even there cracks are appearing in the façade of unquestioned backing for the goals of Zionism and the actions by a succession of Israeli governments since independence.

Current Divisions within Sunni and Shi'a Islam

Fortunately for Israel, the centuries'-old split in Islam over religious issues that led to a sectarian splintering of the faith has failed to heal itself and has in fact been made even more rigid by political and national rivalries. Although elements within both the Sunni and Shi'a branches have found it in their mutual interest to cooperate on occasion, for most of the time the ancient feuds, mistrust, and hatred have prevailed. In the case of the vast Sunni majority, the lack of a unifying force to replace that of the caliphate abandoned in 1924 has prevented them from realizing even a fraction of their potential to influence world affairs. National identities that in the past paled in comparison to the universal concept of Islam have become as important if not more so since independence was achieved by Muslim countries in the twentieth century. Turks, Algerians, Egyptians, Indonesians,

Bangladeshis, even Kurds, who have no national entity of their own other than a quasi-autonomous region in 'Iraq courtesy of the American-led invasion of 2003, as well as stateless Palestinians see themselves as individual national groups first and foremost no matter how important Islam may be to their greater spiritual identity. The same is true in Shi'a Iran.

Only in Lebanon with its multisectarian national makeup does loyalty to religious community perhaps outweigh attachment to the state, and here, except for the Shi'a, a greater Lebanese nationalism is gradually replacing the narrower religious identity for most of the population. Sunni religious leaders like the shaykh of al-Azhar University in Cairo do enjoy public respect but, unlike the Shi'a ayatollahs in Iran, they exercise no political authority. It is the secular political leaders, however much they may be disliked by large segments of the population, who have the power to make a difference in people's daily lives in the Sunni Muslim world. They may invoke Islam to their benefit, like Libya's Qadhafi did until his overthrow, or Prime Minister Recep Tayyip Erdogan in still-secular Turkey does, but it is the authority of president, party, and secular law that matters, the only exception among Sunni-majority nations being Sa'udi Arabia, where the most conservative form of Shari'a law still prevails. But even there it is the king who wields ultimate power.

Since the establishment of the Islamic Republic in Iran in 1979, the only major Shi'a state has been governed by religious leaders whose fatwas have the weight of enforceable law. The president, Mahmud Ahmadinejad, is a secular politician but answers to the higher authority of the grand ayatollahs. Although seen in the West as an ultraconservative on almost every issue, and disliked for both his provocative statements on the holocaust and Zionism and for his suspicious reelection in 2009 along with the militant suppression of his opposition in the wake of the voting, he is considerably more liberal than his clerical masters. In 'Iraq, where the Shi'a are a majority, and in Lebanon, where they probably form the largest single religious group (though Sunnis dispute this), religious leaders also exert a very strong influence on the secular leadership. In the cases of Mullah Muqtada al-Sadr and Hasan Nasrallah of Hizbollah, they have their own militia and parliamentary bloc. In Lebanon, there is a secular Shi'a party, Amal (Hope), founded by the late Mullah Musa al-Sadr, whose current head is the country's third-most important politician, Speaker of the Parliament Nabih Berri. But he and his followers cooperate on almost every issue with the more militant Nasrallah. Interestingly, it is the Amal supporters in the southern city of al-Nabatiyya who still practice the traditional self-flagellation and blood-letting at the annual 'Ashura' ceremonies that commemorate the death of imam Husayn whereas Hizbollah, following the lead of the late Grand Ayatollah Muhammad Fadlallah (1935–2010), is very critical of the practice, advising their followers to donate blood instead. The traditional authority exercised by the old landowning families like the As'ads of Tyre (Sur), the 'Usayrans of Ba'albak, and the Hamadehs of Hirmal (not to be confused with the prominent Druze family of the same name from Ba'aqlin) has slowly diminished since the appearance of Amal and Hizbollah.

The Druze in Lebanon have their own secular political leadership which has traditionally rested with the Junbalat and Arslan families, each with its own political party, but their spiritual head, known as the shaykh al-'aql, and his council of religious elders (the Masha'ikh al-Din) are very influential in determining the course of internal affairs of their community. The 'Alawis of Syria and the Alevis of Turkey are largely secular in their outlook with little in the way of a religious hierarchy that exercises anything approaching political authority.

The Shi'a, Hizbollah, and Sunnis in Lebanon—A Testing Ground for Muslim Sectarian Rivalry

In only one country in the Muslim world—Lebanon—do Sunnis and Shi'a reside in roughly equal numbers, engaged in daily interaction and bitter conflict compounded by the factor of a third group larger than either one of them (the combined Christian population) plus the added complication of the Druze and much smaller 'Alawi communities. Out of an estimated population of 4.5 million, excluding perhaps as many as 500,000 Palestinian refugees, approximately 2.5 million are either Sunni or Shi'a. Even if the Shi'a are larger in number—as they and some outside sources claim—than the Sunnis (which they strongly deny), the presence of the stateless Palestinians who are entirely Sunni gives the Sunnis inside Lebanon an overall numerical advantage, though not a parliamentary one since the refugees as non-citizens do not enjoy any direct say in the government.[6] The 1.6 million Christians are divided mostly among the four principal groups: Maronite Catholics, Greek Orthodox, Greek Catholics, and Armenians, in that order, with the remaining 400,000 made up of some 350,000 Druze and about 50,000 Alawites. The unwritten National Pact of 1943 at the outset of independence divided political authority among the four largest communities, the Maronites being given the office of Presidency of the

Republic, the Sunnis that of Prime Minister, with the Speaker and Vice Speaker of Parliament going to the Shi'a and Greek Orthodox, respectively. Parliament originally had a Christian edge—six for every five Muslim and Druze deputies—but this changed with the Ta'if Accord of 1989 (which ended the civil war begun in 1975), with an assembly of 128 deputies, 64 of whom were allotted to Christians and 64 to Muslims (27 each Sunni and Shi'a, 8 Druze, and 2 'Alawi, the last previously unrepresented).

From 1976 to 2006 the real power in the country was exercised by the government of Syria, whose army had occupied Lebanon since the early years of the civil war. But the combined effort of Sunnis (whose former prime minister Rafiq al-Hariri was assassinated in Beirut on February 14, 2005), some Christians, and most of the Druze under the leadership of Walid Junbalat and aided by international pressure forced the Syrians to withdraw their armed forces. This alliance, which came to be known as the March 14 Alliance by the date of its first massive rally in 2005, was opposed by the largely Shi'a and Hizbollah Syrian-backed opposition, augmented by Christian, mostly Maronite supporters loyal to former general Michel 'Awn. This second group came to be known as the March 8 Alliance after the date of their first rally in protest of the anticipated Syrian pullout and has continued to act as the surrogates of Syrian influence in the internal affairs of Lebanon.

Although Syria finally agreed to a formal acknowledgment of Lebanese independence and the exchange of ambassadors in 2009, it has strongly backed Hizbollah's insistence on maintaining its own paramilitary wing in order, as claimed by them, to protect Lebanon's southern border from Israeli incursion. The invasion of Israeli military forces in July 2006 brought horrific damage to Shi'a towns and villages in southern Lebanon, the southern suburbs of Beirut, and to the infrastructure of Lebanon as a whole. Nearly every bridge in the country was at least partially destroyed, disrupting traffic and communication for over a year. Many non-Shi'a Lebanese privately blamed Hizbollah for unleashing this massive destruction on undeserving Lebanese civilians, and Israel held the Lebanese government responsible for not disbanding the Hizbollah militia, as called for by UN resolutions, and replacing it with the national armed forces. In the end, Lebanese soldiers were posted to the south for the first time in decades, and Hizbollah went quietly, and quite literally, underground. There is no doubt, however, that it has retained and strengthened its military wing with support from both Syria and Iran.

Despite Hizbollah's support for its allies the 'Alawi community of Tripoli in its ongoing fight with the Sunni majority there (which required Lebanese Army intervention on December 12, 2012, after renewed clashes saw at least seventeen people killed), the Shi'a leadership in Beirut has largely cooperated with President Michel Sulayman and the Lebanese Opposition in order to prevent the Syrian rebellion from seriously destabilizing Lebanon's internal status quo, which is in no one's interest except possibly for President Assad to divert attention away from his desperate problems.

Israel has threatened even greater destruction to the entire country in the event of another war, but this has not resulted in any change in Lebanese government policy. When the then minister of communications, Druze leader Walid Junbalat, tried to take over Hizbollah's private telephone system in spring 2009, armed supporters of the Shi'a group attacked both Druze and Sunni supporters in Beirut and the Druze-dominated mountainous region of al-Shuf, forcing the government to back down and Junbalat to abandon the March 14 Alliance and take an independent stance that included closer ties to his former bitter enemies, Hizbollah leader Hasan Nasrallah and the Syrian government. When the new Syrian ambassador arrived in Beirut, Junbalat was among the first to invite him to a formal reception at his palace in the village of al-Mukhtara, al-Shuf, in June 2009. His closer ties to the March 8 Alliance have not been popular with his Druze constituents, but like most Lebanese, they have had to come to terms with the growing power of Nasrallah and Hizbollah. So has Prime Minister Sa'ad al-Hariri, who was clearly embarrassed by the humiliating defeat of his supporters in May 2009, followed by a first-ever visit to President Assad in Damascus, whom in the past he publicly held responsible for his father's assassination in 2005.

With the results of the international tribunal set up to investigate Rafiq al-Hariri's murder expected to be announced at any time, Nasrallah denounced what he predicted would be the results: the blaming of Shi'a and, specifically, Hizbollah involvement. When one of the three figures originally detained by the Lebanese government as a suspect in the case was released and returned to Lebanon in September 2010, Hizbollah met him at the airport, located in the heavily Shi'a southern suburbs of Beirut, and took him under their protection, defying the government to do anything to stop them. Tensions reached new heights on January 13, 2011, when the ten Hizbollah members of parliament resigned over Prime Minister Hariri's refusal to disavow the tribunal, bringing down the government and ushering in a new one a few days later led by former prime minister Najib Miqati of Tripoli, with Hizbollah and Syrian support. Nasrallah has always claimed that Hariri's assassination was the work of Mossad, the Israeli secret service, in an effort to intensify the enmity between Shiʿa and Sunni in Lebanon and elsewhere in the Middle East.

Israel and the United States immediately claimed that the fall of the Saʿad Hariri government was the result of a "Hizbollah coup," whereas in fact it had been nothing more than a successful parliamentary maneuver by the Shiʿa bloc, assisted by the defecting government coalition partner, Walid Junbalat's predominantly Druze Progressive Socialist Party (PSP), or as Michael Young in the Beirut *Daily Star* described it, "a coup, but a constitutional coup within the confines of state institutions."[7] It took prime minister designate Miqati five months to form a government, which the Hariri opposition claimed was "made in Syria" and reflected both its Hizbollah and Christian backers loyal to Michel ʿAwn, not to mention Junbalat's PSP, which was rewarded for its "treachery" with three cabinet posts. No Sunni MPs from Beirut were included in the new government, and many observers predicted it would be short-lived, especially in light of Syria's internal disruptions and the threat of governmental collapse facing President Bashshar al-Asad. As a concession to wounded Sunni pride, however, an additional cabinet post beyond that which they would normally have expected was awarded to them at the expense of the Shiʿa entitlement, but this did nothing to change who was really in power. It was also not enough to prevent ousted Prime Minister Hariri from taking up residence in Paris for fear of assassination by Hizbollah or Syria if he remained in Lebanon.

The much-anticipated results of the tribunal were finally delivered to the Lebanese state prosecutor on June 30, 2011, and did indeed indict four Hizbollah members, two of them in senior positions. Mustafa Badr al-Din, Hizbollah's military commander, stood accused of planning the assassination, and Salim al-Ayyash, a high-ranking party official, was charged with carrying out the operation. The government was given thirty days to arrest the subjects. Predictably, Hasan Nasrallah, speaking the next day on the Hizbollah television channel, al-Manar, dismissed the indictments as "illegitimate" and charged the tribunal with acting in the interests of the United States and Israel in an attempt to drive a wedge between the Sunni and Shiʿa communities in Lebanon, a tactic he predicted would not succeed. He also vowed never to release the four Hizbollah members the tribunal wanted to bring to justice, "never in thirty days, thirty weeks, thirty months, thirty years, or three-hundred years." The following day, the March 14 opposition members in parliament called on the new Sunni prime minister to announce his government's commitment to the implementation of the tribunal's indictments or resign.

Clearly, the Sunni-Shi'a divide in Lebanon could not be wider. The majorities of each group live separately from one another. On the western slope of Mount Lebanon from Beirut north to the Syrian border, 90 percent of Muslims are Sunni, with Shi'a found only in a dozen or so villages in the hills behind Jubayl (Byblos) and a few more in the Batrun and Kura districts. In the city of Tripoli and the northern districts of al-Diniyya and the 'Akkar, there are few if any Shi'a, but there are a substantial number (about fifty thousand) of their 'Alawi allies. In Tripoli itself, armed confrontations along the fault line in the poor, old city areas of Bab al-Tabanneh (Sunni) and Jabal Muhsin ('Alawi) have been frequent and ongoing, especially in late May and early June 2012 with at least twenty-five deaths and scores of wounded. This time, though, the sectarian fighting spread to rural areas of the 'Akkar, where kidnappings became rife on roads connecting Sunni and 'Alawi villages, much like what happened during the worst days of the Lebanese Civil War 1975–1990. Fighting re-erupted six months later in December 2012, resulting in at least seventeen deaths before the Lebanese army was called in to halt the conflict.

Across the mountain in the Biqa' Valley, Sunni and Shi'a are found in about equal numbers but rarely in the same settlements, with the exception of the city of Ba'albak. In Beirut, they live in different parts of town for the most part, but where the two meet near the central Martyr's Square, fighting has been frequent and bloody, as in Tripoli. In the coastal region south of Beirut, Sunnis control as far as the city of Sidon (Saida), a Sunni stronghold dominated from the eastern hills overlooking the city by a ring of Greek-Catholic Christian villages. South of Saida, the Shi'a form the vast majority of the population, apart from the modest number of Christian inhabitants of a dozen or so Maronite and Greek Orthodox small towns and villages. The only Sunni presence that can be found is in the town of Tyre (Sur), where there is also a small Christian minority

Despite pleas from the religious leadership—Sunni, Shi'a, and Druze—for reconciliation and an end to hostilities, tensions have continued to rise. If open civil struggle were ever to break out again in Lebanon, the main protagonists this time would be the Sunnis and Shi'as, with both Christians and Druze, as well as the Palestinian refugees—all of them privately well-armed—on the sidelines, at least initially. The question then would be if either Syria or Israel would intervene. Hizbollah has always promised that it would never fight fellow Lebanese, but after the eruption of violence on May 17, 2009, many non-Shi'a question this, and there is no doubt that Hizbollah is the strongest military force in the country. Although the Lebanese Army is stronger than at any time in the past, especially after its successful defeat of an uprising at the Palestinian refugee camp of Nahr al-Barid on the northern border with Syria in 2007, it has many Shi'a soldiers and officers in its ranks; there is doubt where their loyalty would lie if forced to choose in a contest with Hizbollah. The chief of the Lebanese Armed Forces is Brig. Gen. Jean Qahwaji, a Maronite Christian (as usual since independence) from the exclusively Maronite village of 'Ayn Ibil in the southern Shi'a heartland overlooking the Israeli border, appointed in August 2008 to replace the former chief, Michel Sulayman (from the town of 'Amsheet[8] near Byblos), who had been elected president of the republic three months earlier in May after six months of parliamentary wrangling. He has strong ties to and close relations with the Shi'a population he grew up surrounded by, perhaps a consideration behind his selection.

The Sunni-Shi'a Divide in 'Iraq, Bahrain, Yemen, Libya, and Syria—The Arab Spring and Its Sectarian Undertones

In 'Iraq and Bahrain, where the Sunni-Shi'a conflict has also often turned violent, the situation is very different from that of Lebanon. Both 'Iraq and Bahrain have a long history of Sunnis dominating Shi'a and recent attempts to finally alter this injustice have had different results: In 'Iraq, the American-led invasion in 2003 allowed the Shi'a majority to gain political power for the first time in the Muslim history of the region. In Bahrain, attempts to overthrow the ruling Sunni elite by the majority Shi'a population have so far failed. Most recently, it was the force of the uprisings against political dictatorship across the Arab world which began in Tunisia early in 2011, quickly followed by Egypt and dubbed the "Arab Spring" by the media, which spurred the Shi'a of Bahrain to attempt, once again, to wrest control of their tiny island kingdom from the al-Thani ruling family and its governing elite drawn from the minority Sunni population.

In the first two instances, Tunisia and Egypt, success came quickly for the protesters. And in both cases the population was entirely Sunni (except for the 10 percent Christian minority in Egypt) so that no sectarian differences among the Muslim population complicated the change. Libya likewise has no indigenous Shi'a population, but other factors stalled the ultimately successful efforts to end Col. Mu'ammar Qadhafi's forty-plus-year reign. In 'Iraq, the Shi'a majority had already taken control of the government through its own version of the democratic process, so there was no need or support for a popular uprising. In the case of Yemen and Syria, minority Muslim groups and tribal factions were instrumental in the prevention of changes called for by those opposing the long-established dictatorships in Yemen for over a year and in Syria until now.

'Iraq

'Iraq is the home of the Shi'a movement and location of four of its holiest sites: the tombs and mosque shrines of 'Ali in al-Najaf; Husayn in Kar-bala'; the Kathimayn mosque/shrine in the Kathimiyya district of Baghdad on the western bank of the Tigris, burial place of Musa al-Kathim and his grandson Muhammad al-Taqi, the seventh and ninth imams; and the golden-domed al-'Askariyya Mosque in Samarra, a predominantly Sunni city north of Baghdad, the final resting place of the tenth and eleventh imams, Musa al-Hadi and his son Hasan al-'Askari. The Samarra' shrine is also associated with the twelfth imam, Muhammad al-Mahdi, who is thought to have gone into hiding and subsequent occultation from a cave beneath a cellar in the mosque from which he will emerge as the mahdi to bring in the Last Days. The near-destruction of al-'Askariyya Mosque was in the massive February 2006 bombing carried out by al-Qa'ida extremists and resulted in one of the bloodiest Sunni-Shi'a confrontations in recent history but not an all-out civil war, which was the apparent intention of the Sunni attackers. Major work to rebuild the shrine began almost immediately, bringing Sunnis and Shi'as together in a cooperative effort to restore the mosque to its former golden glory.[9] The only major Shi'a shrine outside 'Iraq is at Mashshad in northeastern Iran, which contains the tomb of the eighth imam, 'Ali Rida (Reza) Ibn Musa al-Kathim.

The majority Shi'a population of 'Iraq has been ruled by a minority Sunni Arab establishment from day one. The Umayyad and Abbasid caliphates were both ruthless in their attempts to suppress their Shi'a subjects. Following the Mongol invasion and overthrow of the last Abbasid caliph in 1258, which turned Baghdad and much of the populous and fertile Tigris and Euphrates Valley into an uninhabited wasteland, a variety of Turkish tribes held sway until the coming of the Sunni Ottomans in 1534, who

established a rather tenuous authority until their collapse following World
War I. In spite of centuries of oppression, the Shi'a still made up the majority of the Arab population—probably two-thirds or more—but the British
rulers who succeeded the Ottomans under a League of Nations Mandate
established in 1921 continued to favor the Sunni ruling elite. After 1920
they created a kingdom ruled by Faysal I, younger brother of the Sharif
Husayn of Mecca, who although a Sunni was universally acknowledged as
a direct descendant of the Prophet Muhammad and therefore more acceptable to the Shi'a majority, with their love for the family of 'Ali, than someone from the local Sunni minority. The king and his successors nevertheless tended to favor their Sunni co-religionists, whose numbers had been
considerably augmented by the addition to the new country of 'Iraq by the
mountainous region north and west of Mosul, largely Sunni Kurd with
a smaller number of Turkomen Christians and Yazidis. The Turkomen,
who according to the last reliable sectarian-based census of 1957 (revised
1958) make up 9 percent of 'Iraqis, are an ethnic and linguistic minority
with strong ties to Turkey. They are religiously divided roughly fifty-fifty
between Sunnis and Shi'a of both the Twelver and extremist ghulat sects.

No 'Iraqi census since independence has reported figures to the actual
number of Sunnis and Shi'a in the country while detailing all other sectarian
and linguistic divisions. The rough census of religious groups conducted by
the British in 1921 showed a total population of 2,850,000, of whom just
over half (1,490,000) were Shi'a. Sunnis amounted to 1,150,000, some 30
percent of whom were Kurds; 88,000 Jews (mostly in Baghdad); 79,000
Christians (largely in Mosul and the north); and 43,000 others, principally Yazidis in the north and Mandaeans (Sabaeans) in the south.[10] The
Turkoman minority is spread across northern 'Iraq, not just Ninevah (Mosul) *liwa* (province) but also in the neighboring *liwat* (provinces) of Irbil,
Kirkuk, and Salah al-Din.

Following the overthrow of the monarchy in 1958, 'Iraq was ruled by
a succession of revolutionary secular governments led by Sunnis, the last of
whom, Saddam Husayn, was particularly intolerant of his Shi'a subjects.
Throughout this period, the religious divisions remained roughly the same,
apart from the departure of all but about one hundred Jews following the
establishment of Israel in 1948. It was thought by those proposing the 2003
American-led invasion that toppled Saddam that both the Shi'a and the
Kurds would welcome the foreign troops as liberators, but, as history has
shown, this was a simplistic misreading of a very complicated reality. The

resultant internal bloodletting led to tens of thousands of 'Iraqi deaths and the displacement of large numbers of people from their traditional homes, notably a substantial number of the million-strong Christian minority to neighboring Syria and Jordan and further abroad to escape persecution by Sunni extremists. Both the Shi'a and the Kurds have profited politically from the events following 2003—the Shi'a by achieving power in Baghdad through a parliament that reflects their larger numbers, and the Kurds by being allowed to establish an autonomous region in the north where Shi'a governmental authority carries little weight. They have no love for their fellow Sunni Arabs who dominate the region from Baghdad north to Mosul, having suffered as much as the Shi'a at their hands since Ottoman times and most recently under Saddam. The Kurds are happy with the autonomy they have achieved since the invasion and have managed to bury their own deep tribal divisions for the moment, concentrating on gaining control over the oil-rich city of Kirkuk, which they consider their capital but which is also home to large numbers of Arabs and Turkomens. In the meantime, the ancient city of Irbil (Arbela) serves as their administrative center.

The Shi'a have their own internal divisions, some favoring close ties to Iran, others following a more nationalist 'Iraqi agenda. It would be an error to assume that 'Iraqi Shi'a would automatically side with the conservative religious government of their large eastern neighbor, especially since many of their brothers and fathers died fighting Iran in the 1980s. The failure of the U.S.-backed coalition that drove the 'Iraqis out of Kuwait in the first Gulf War in 1991 exposed the Shi'a to even further restrictions and persecutions by the secular Sunni/Ba'thi government of Saddam Husayn. Having risen up against him after his defeat by the coalition forces in anticipation of an invasion that would drive him from power, 'Iraq's Shi'a were ruthlessly crushed and brutally punished, not only individually but collectively. This was seen in Saddam's ecologically disastrous draining of the lower Tigris and Euphrates wetlands which drove tens of thousands of the Shi'a "Marsh Arabs"—made famous by Wilfred Thesiger's book of that title—from their ancient homes. Their bitter resentment of the Saddam regime was one of the leading factors that encouraged the United States to invade 'Iraq in 2003. The George W. Bush administration had been assured on the basis of highly erroneous intelligence from the CIA and others, including the pro-Israeli Jewish neocons in the government such as Richard Perle, Douglas Feith, and Paul Wolfowitz—who passed on totally fabricated lies from their highly suspect exiled 'Iraqi Shi'a crooked politician crony, Ahmad Chalabi (wanted at the time in Jordan for financial chicanery)—that U.S. forces would be greeted by "Iraqis in the street throwing flowers" at their feet.

In the end, Chalabi proved to be wrong, useless, and worse than an embarrassment. Fortunately for him, his calumnies and false promises were overshadowed by the massive accumulation of rancid egg on the faces of President Bush, Vice President Dick Cheney, and Secretary of Defense Donald Rumsfeld when it was revealed to all and sundry that there were no weapons of mass destruction in Saddam's arsenal, which had been the justification for the ill-advised invasion in the first place. But the genie was out of the bottle. The Shi'a majority was now free to take power through leaders like Muqtada al-Sadr, who had no love for the Americans and were certainly not busy plucking flowers to throw in their direction.[11] In the years that followed Saddam's fall, arrest, and execution, two Shi'a-controlled governments have cemented their authority over all of the country except for Kurdistan and the disputed, vastly oil-rich city of Kirkuk with its volatile mix of Kurd, Turkoman, and lowland Arab, and its own Sunni/Shi'a divisions. Neighboring Iran's influence has gradually permeated the new Shi'a leadership while the former Sunni rulers have been relegated to the sidelines.

Any government in 'Iraq in the near future will certainly be dominated by one form of Shi'a leadership or another, with Sunnis left with little choice but to cooperate or remount the insurgency that gained them little during the early years of occupation by America and its allies. Tensions have risen markedly since then Sunni vice president Tariq al-Hashimi fled to the autonomous Kurdish region at the end of 2011, and later to Turkey, to avoid arrest after Shi'a prime minister Nuri al-Maliki issued a warrant charging him with running death squads responsible for assassinations and bombings. Interpol put out a "red" notice for his arrest, but both Turkey and Sa'udi Arabia indicated that they would refuse any extradition requests. President al-Maliki accused Turkey of being a hostile state with a sectarian agenda, not a charge likely to endear him to Prime Minister Erdogan. In the meantime, sectarian killings have continued to mar Sunni-Shi'a relations. On December 5, 2011, at the conclusion of 'Ashura', thirty-two Shi'a pilgrims were killed and seventy-eight wounded near the city of Hilla in the vicinity of the ruins of ancient Babylon. A week later, multiple bomb blasts killed 57 and wounded 180 in Shi'a neighborhoods of Baghdad. On January 6, 2012, more than seventy Shi'a were killed and scores more wounded in attacks on pilgrims in al-Nasriyya in the south of the country and in Sadr City, the Shi'a suburb of Baghdad. A week later, thirty-one Shi'a, including sixteen security police, were blown up in an attack on a funeral procession in Sadr City, and sixty-five more were wounded. On June 13, 2012, no fewer than sixteen bomb attacks, mostly directed at Shi'a pilgrims, chiefly those headed for the shrine of imam Musa al-Kathim (Kazem) in the Kathimiyya district of north Baghdad but also in Karbala', killed at least seventy-two and wounded more than two hundred. These confrontations plus the collapse of Sunni participation in the government had distracted attention away from the ongoing dispute between Baghdad and the Kurdish region. Mass protests by 'Iraqi Sunnis in early 2013 are evidence of their continued frustration and even desperation. More dangerously, suicide attacks on Shi'a targets such as a marketplace in Baghdad on February 7, 2013, which killed at least twenty-one and wounded 120, have resumed. Six weeks later, on March 29, as they were leaving Friday prayers, twenty-two worshippers died and over 140 were wounded in suicide bomb attacks on four Shi'a mosques, three in Baghdad and the other in Kirkuk. The attacks, attributed to al-Qa'ida, were clearly aimed at eroding Shi'a support for Nuri al-Maliki and spreading fear among the Shi'a majority that their own Shi'a-dominated government could no longer protect them. It was perhaps no coincidence that the attacks occurred on Western Good Friday, observed by 'Iraq's uniate Chaldaean and Syriac Catholics who make up more than 80 percent of the country's Christian minority, the message being "you could be next." Apparent retaliation for March 29 was not long in coming. On April 1 a gasoline tanker plowed into the police headquarters in the Sunni city of Tikrit, halfway between Baghdad and Mosul, home to the late dictator Saddam Husayn and his extended clan, killing nine.

The current autonomous rule in 'Iraqi Kurdistan is very tenuous and probably untenable without U.S. (and covert Israeli) support. Neither Turkey nor Iran is happy with the prospect of even a quasi-autonomous Kurdish state in the region given their own large, restless Kurdish minorities. In Turkey, an ongoing armed military insurgency led by the Kurdistan Workers' Party (Partiya Karkerên Kurdistan, or PKK), an illegal political party, aims at establishing a Kurdish state or, failing that, seriously disrupting life in southeastern Anatolia where Kurds are the majority and where Turkey's main source of oil and gas is located. The smaller population of Kurds in Syria is also concentrated in the region where these vital resources are found, al-Jazira province on its northeastern border with 'Iraq and Turkey, making any designs for a Kurdish state equally unpopular with the 'Alawi-backed government, and undoubtedly any future administration in Damascus. During the uprisings in Syria since the spring of 2011, the Kurds were among those who demonstrated for reform, notably in the northeastern city of Qamishli, demanding citizenship for those thousands of their number who had entered Syria from Turkey and 'Iraq over the years, especially recently, but were not allowed nationality by the government.

Of 'Iraq's estimated population of 33 million, probably 58 percent are Shi'a, mostly Arab but with some Kurds and Turkomen (particularly at Tal 'Afar west of Mosul) and Shi'a Turkoman-majority towns in Kirkuk and Salah al-Din provinces like Tuz Kharmato, the target of no fewer than nine major suicide bombing attacks in the decade since the Sunni-led insurgency that followed the overthrow of Saddam Husayn began in 2003. An estimated 38 percent are Sunni, two-thirds of whom are Arab and the remainder Kurd; and 3 percent are Christians, Yazidis, and others, a figure that includes many thousands from these smaller minorities that have fled the country to escape persecution, some permanently. These smaller groups of 'Iraqis, especially the Christians, were protected from militant Sunni fundamentalists by Saddam's dictatorship, and one long-serving minister and leading member of the Ba'thi inner circle was Tariq 'Aziz, a Chaldaean Catholic from the north of the country, now facing the death penalty despite pleas from the Vatican. Under Saddam, there were no bombings of Christian churches or kidnappings and murders of bishops, as there have been since the Bush invasion.[12] Probably half of 'Iraqi Christians have either fled the country altogether or retreated from cities like Baghdad, Basra, and Ramadi to their ancestral villages in the north under the protection of autonomous Kurdish administration. The major change in the Sunni-Shi'a distribution that has taken place since 2003 is the movement of Sunnis from Shi'a neighborhoods, especially in Baghdad but also in Basra. During the secular rule of the Ba'th party under Saddam Husayn, there was considerable intermingling between the two communities, both socially and by marriage. For those families of mixed parentage, the resurgence of ancient hatred has had devastating effects as they face the problem of where to live and how to raise their children.

Bahrain, Yemen, Libya, and Syria

The unrest in Bahrain, very similar to the unsettled situation in 'Iraq since independence, is the result of a majority Shi'a population being governed by a Sunni royal family aided by a small minority of Sunni elite. More than two-thirds of Bahrainis are Shi'a, and although the country is one of the more liberal Gulf States (alcohol is openly served in hotels), they form a carefully orchestrated minority (eighteen out of forty) in the country's showcase parliament elected at the end of October 2010 (all of whom resigned following the 2011 uprising). Throughout the months preceding the election, hundreds of Shi'a activists were arrested for conspiring against the government and promoting terrorism. Hostilities broke out again in February 2011 when Shi'a demonstrators, apparently inspired by the successful uprisings in Tunisia and Egypt a few weeks earlier, were ruthlessly put down by the Sunni authorities, leaving at least five dead and many more wounded. Whereas the uprisings in Tunisia and Egypt that quickly toppled the existing regimes had no sectarian Muslim component—virtually all Tunisian and Egyptian Muslims are Sunni—the Bahraini revolt was sharply divided along Sunni and Shi'a sectarian lines.

The other uprisings in Yemen, Libya, and Syria were more complicated. In Yemen, the demonstrations added yet another dimension to the ongoing civil conflict between the long-established secular government of President 'Ali 'Abdallah Saleh and the Fiver (Zaydi) Shi'a rebels in the north of the country, known as Huthis after their former leader, Husayn Badr al-Din al-Huthi, killed in 2004. Rather ironically, Saleh, president of North Yemen since 1978 and a united (with the previously independent south) Yemen since 1990 until his resignation in early 2012, is himself of Zaydi Shi'a origin but has been largely rejected by them, including his own tribe. On June 5 Saleh fled to Sa'udi Arabia after being seriously wounded in an attack on his palace, leaving Yemen in political confusion. Continued Sunni-Zaydi Shi'a civil war complicated by tribal rivalries and the presence of a strong al-Qa'ida network in the south made matters worse. Saleh's return some weeks later, clearly suffering from severe burns, did little to stem to ongoing hostilities. After being granted immunity from prosecution by parliament on January 20, 2012, Saleh went to the United States for further treatment of his burns and in February announced he was stepping down as president.

He was succeeded by his vice president, 'Abd al-Rabb 'Mansur Hadi, who on February 27 was elected president in an uncontested poll with 98.5 percent of the vote. The country remains unstable as a group that calls itself "Al-Qa'ida in the Arabian Peninsula" has managed to entrench itself in predominantly Sunni areas, in some of which it became the local ruling authority. On May 21, 2012, a suicide bomber in a Yemeni Army uniform blew himself up at a military parade rehearsal intended to celebrate the anniversary of the unification of North and South Yemen the following day, killing upward of one hundred predominantly Shi'a soldiers and injuring twice as many. Al-Qa'ida in the Arabian Peninsula claimed responsibility, calling it an act of revenge for American drone attacks on the areas of the country they control. In a separate but possibly related incident the next day, a member of Yemen's tiny remaining Jewish community was shot and killed in Sana'a. On June 18 the general commanding an army unit charged with largely successful attempts to drive al-Qa'ida out of the regions it controlled in the south and east of the country was blown up by a Somali suicide bomber in the port of Aden. Drone attacks on September 30, 2011, killed the American-born (of Yemeni parents) and educated imam Anwar al-'Awlaqi, head of Yemen's al-Qa'ida affiliate, and two weeks later his sixteen-year-old Denver-born son, 'Abd al-Rahman. Since these and subsequent drone attacks, the power of al-Qa'ida in southeastern Yemen has declined significantly. In the meantime, the Zaydi Huthi rebels in the far north of the country have continued their armed opposition to the central government.

Whereas Libya has no Shi'a population of any consequence, it does have a 20 percent Berber linguistic and ethnic minority, many of whom adhere to the Ibadi sect, the dominant faith of Oman, concentrated in the northwest of the country. The city of Zawiya, near the border with Tunisia, which was an early center of the rebellion, has a significant Ibadi and Berber component. Leader for life Mu'ammar Qadhafi, overthrown during a popular uprising in August 2011 and killed two months later, had few friends among Sunni leaders elsewhere in the Muslim world and was loathed by Shi'a everywhere for allegedly murdering the prominent Lebanese imam Musa al-Sadr during his visit to Libya in 1978.

Born in Qom, Iran, the son of parents from Sur (Tyre) in southern Lebanon, al-Sadr took up the cause of the country's downtrodden Shi'a minority in the early 1970s, founding the Amal party in 1974, still a significant force in Lebanese politics, led by the Speaker of the Lebanese Parliament Nabih Berri. Sadr was on an official visit to Libya when he disappeared. According to official Libyan sources, he left Libya for Italy, but the Italian government has no record of his ever having arrived. A former Libyan diplomat later claimed that Qadhafi personally ordered Sadr's murder for reasons unknown. Though no information that would shed light on Sadr's mysterious disappearance has emerged in the wake of Qadhafi's overthrow and violent demise, the Libyan dictator was known to harbor hatred for Muslim sectarians and given to simplistic (some would say crackpot) pronouncements on how to solve the region's problems. He famously suggested, at the height of the Lebanese Civil War in the early 1980s, that the way to resolve the conflict was obvious—Lebanon's Christians should convert to (Sunni) Islam, as if that were a reasonable option for an entrenched minority that had firmly resisted the forces of Islam for centuries against all odds.

In Syria, the situation was similar to that in Bahrain, where a strongly entrenched minority controlled the government, the army, and internal security forces. Although the Sunni majority would dearly love to throw the ruling Alawites out, they face a bitterly determined enemy who is not willing to relinquish power easily, as the bloody street confrontations in Dar'a and many other cities in March and April 2011 and the ever-expanding conflict since then have clearly demonstrated.[13] President Asad has as much to fear from his own entrenched old-guard Alawite elite as he does from Sunni protesters should he be perceived to be yielding to rebel demands. They and thousands of ordinary Alawites could face terrible retributions if militant Sunnis were to triumph. The *New York Times* carried a page-one article about demonstrations in Syria where protesters allegedly chanted "Christians to Beirut and the Alawites to the coffin."[14] All minorities are fearful of a militant Sunni takeover, but none more so than President Asad's sectarian Shi'a power base.

As large demonstrations continued to rock the country, a major, openly sectarian-based confrontation between opposition Sunnis and pro-Asad 'Alawis occurred in the city of Homs in mid-July 2011. The city, Syria's third largest, was at that time about 70 percent Sunni, 20 percent 'Alawi, and 10 percent Christian. Although it remained quiet but tense after the fighting died down, Syrian activists for peaceful change expressed fears that such episodes of violence based on age-old communal mistrust and hatred "undermine the revolution and serve the interests of its enemies who want to turn it into a civil war."[15] Clashes between pro-government and opposition forces have continued since. As is often the case, the smallest community, made up of mostly Greek and Syriac-Orthodox Christians, was caught in the crossfire, resulting in the total evacuation of all its 80,000–85,000 members who fled either to Damascus or nearby Lebanon in March 2012.[16]

In nearby Hama, forty kilometers to the north, the absence of any sizeable 'Alawi minority and a tradition of antigovernment sentiment since the bloody events of 1982 allowed the ultra-conservative Sunni population to push security forces out of the city center in June. But on the eve of the holy month of Ramadan (July 31), army tanks smashed their way back in through improvised barricades, inflicting an untold number of casualties in the process—150 dead according to one estimate. Despite international criticism, the EU ban on importing Syrian oil, the unprecedented imposition of economic sanctions by the Arab League on November 27, 2011, Turkey's suspension three days later of all financial credit dealings, and ongoing domestic protests, President Asad continued to hold on to power.

Crucial for him in being able to ignore increasing diplomatic pressure were the support of both Russia and China in the UN Security Council. Russia was especially worried about losing its only Mediterranean naval base at Tartus just north of the Lebanese border, as well as its lucrative arms sales to the Asad regime. It was also deeply concerned for the future of Syria's large Orthodox Christian minority should a radical Sunni government gain power. The two permanent members of the Security Council cast a rare double veto on October 5, 2011, to block a U.S.-sponsored resolution condemning Syria for "its oppression of antigovernment forces," a tactic reemployed four months later on February 4, 2012, much to the disappointment and irritation of Secretary of State Hillary Clinton and other Western diplomatic figures. Finally, on February 17, Clinton and her allies asked for and got an overwhelming, but nonbinding, condemnation of Asad's crackdown on dissidents in the General Assembly with a vote of 137 to 12. Once again, Russia and China were among the dissenters, along with other predictable opponents of anything the United States wanted: Bolivia, Cuba, Venezuela, and Zimbabwe. Twin bomb blasts in Damascus on March 17 that killed twenty-seven and wounded another ninety-seven were a further indication, if any were needed, that the situation was spiraling out of control. In a desperate attempt to bring Asad to heel, the UN proposed sending a special envoy, former UN secretary-general Kofi Annan, to Damascus to persuade the Syrian president to accept UN observers and a six-point peace plan of Annan's devising. The plan was endorsed on April 1 by representatives of nations making up the "Friends of Syria" who were meeting in Istanbul at the invitation of Prime Minister Erdogan. The Arab League had already endorsed the plan the previous day. The Syrian president, under strong pressure from Russia—which saw the plan as a way to assuage international criticism of its support for the Asad regime—agreed to the conditions, and a shaky ceasefire was put in place on April 10. The results of Annan's plan were to prove less than satisfactory, and by early June it appeared to be on the verge of collapse. In early August Annan announced that he was resigning his commission at the end of the month. On August 16 the United Nations announced that it would appoint a new peace envoy, the seventy-eight-year-old former Algerian foreign minister Lakhdar Brahimi, who has worked off and on with the UN in the Arab world since 1994 and is known as a fair and strong-minded negotiator.

In Bahrain, sporadic demonstrations continued throughout February and March 2011, and, fearing Iranian intervention on behalf of the local Shi'a majority, the Sunni ruling family called on Sa'udi Arabia and neighboring Gulf States for support. On March 14 two thousand troops—twelve hundred of them Sa'udi and eight hundred from the United Arab Emirates (UAE)—marched across the King Fahd Causeway into Bahrain under the auspices of the Gulf Cooperation Council in order "to protect oil and financial institutions." Sa'udi authorities promised that this support was "open-ended," reflecting their fear that the Bahraini Sunni elite would ultimately be unable to contain the Shi'a uprising. Local opposition leaders called the intervention an invasion, and the threat of an Iranian response caused political ripples as far away as Washington since, among other reasons, Bahrain is the base for the U.S. Fifth Fleet. The first official statement from the Iranian Foreign Ministry stated ominously that "the presence of foreign troops [in Bahrain] was unacceptable." Two days later, armed troops dispersed opposition demonstrators gathered at the Pearl (Lu'lu') Traffic Circle in the capital city Manama and surrounding Shi'a suburbs and villages. The monument that gave the Pearl Traffic Circle its name was destroyed and opposition to the Sunni ruling class crushed. By the first week of June, the uprising was deemed to be over, martial law was lifted, and the Sa'udi and Emirate troops were withdrawn, but not without leaving a lasting rancor among the majority Shi'a population of the island and deep public anger at Sunni/Wahhabi repressive measures among the Shi'a populations of Iran, 'Iraq, and Lebanon.

Unwilling to be swayed by pressure from the outside, especially Iran and 'Iraq but also from the United States, a Sunni-dominated military court in Manama convicted twenty-one activists on June 22 of conspiring to overthrow the government, sentencing eight of them to life imprisonment and the others to terms of up to fifteen years. All but one of those convicted were Shiʻa, the sole exception, a self-declared "secular" Sunni who received a relatively light sentence of five years in prison. A week before, the Bahraini crown prince had reassured President Obama in person that his father's government was committed to "dialogue and reconciliation."[17] After months of relative calm, protests re-erupted on February 14, 2012, the first anniversary of the initial series of demonstrations. Protests continued, mostly in Shiʻa villages outside the capital Manama, and international attention was drawn to a hunger strike by the Shiʻa activist ʻAbd al-Hadi al-Khawaja and a threat to cancel the Formula One race in Bahrain for the second year running. This time, however, the Sunni government was better prepared. The race went ahead without incident, and al-Khawajaʼs hunger strike finally ended on May 29 after 110 days, with no further concessions to the island's Shiʻa demands forthcoming. Continued sporadic protests by the Shiʻa majority have had no lasting effect on continued Sunni hegemony.

During the Pahlevi rule of Shah Reza Khan and his son, Iran openly supported local Shiʻa opposition to the ruling al-Thani family, and the Islamic Republic of the ayatollahs has also used the disgruntled majority as a means of extending its influence from the tiny island nation onto the nearby oil-rich Saʻudi mainland which is home to the kingdom's Twelver Shiʻa minority. Largely confined to the Eastern province, they are carefully overseen by their Wahhabi masters, who deeply distrust them not only for their Shiʻa beliefs but because they are seen as potential supporters of any Iranian designs on the vast oil reserves of the region. Although there have been frequent and recent protests in Bahrain against dominance by the Sunni majority, the Shiʻa in Saʻudi Arabia have so far remained largely politically docile, knowing that any uprising against the government in Riyadh would bring immediate and unforgiving retaliation. It is not surprising that the Sunni crackdown on Shiʻa activists in Bahrain would have an impact on the other side of the causeway linking the island with the Saʻudi mainland. There have been reports of crackdowns on Shiʻa clerics, the closure of mosques in the Eastern province, and of restrictions placed on Shiʻas wishing to visit sites holy to them in Medina, where there is a small but historic minority Shiʻa presence known as the Nakhawila.

3

The Future of Militant Islam

The extreme interpretation of Islam that drove the perpetrators of the 9/11 attacks is almost exclusively the invention of Muslims schooled in Wahhabi/Salafi Sunni doctrines that are famously intolerant of any other view of their religion. It considers moderate and secular Sunnis, all Shi'a and other sectarians, and, of course, members of all non-Islamic faiths, or no faith at all, to be infidels. As such, they may justly be killed in the fight to impose true Islam as they see it on the entire world. Nearly all the Twin Tower terrorists held Sa'udi nationality; support for al-Qa'ida is strongest in the Wahhabi-dominated kingdom, the southern and eastern Sunni portions of neighboring Yemen, the anarchic failed state of Somalia across the Gulf of Aden, in the tribal regions of northwest Pakistan, and across the porous mountainous border into Afghanistan. Although the Taliban movement shares many of the ideas of al-Qa'ida, the two should not be seen as one and the same. The former has a strongly Afghan or Pakistani nationalist and Pashtun tribal outlook, whereas al-Qa'ida has a very international agenda aimed at driving any and all Western influence out of Dar al-Islam, especially Sa'udi Arabia, and spreading its extreme ideas of Islam among Muslim minorities in Europe and North America.

The Shi'a have absolutely nothing in common with nor any links to such radical Sunni Islamists. There are certainly elements within Shi'ism that harbor expansionist, proselytizing ambitions, but their goals are strictly limited to attacking Israel and American interests. The suicide truck bombings at Beirut International Airport on October 23, 1983, which killed 241 U.S. peacekeepers and (two miles north) 58 French paratroopers, must be seen in the context of the Israeli invasion of Lebanon the year before and the U.S Navy's bombing of towns, villages, and other sites in the foothills east of Beirut that sheltered Palestinian and Lebanese forces opposed to foreign military presence, especially Israel and the United States. The Shi'a-backed political paramilitary groups that mushroomed after the

97

Israeli invasion of 1982 attacked the U.S. Marine base in retaliation for the Israeli invasion of Lebanon and widespread civilian massacres such as that perpetrated at the suburban Beirut refugee camps of Sabra and Shatila by pro-Israeli Christian Maronite militias.

Since 1983 most activities of the military wing of Hizbollah have been directed against the Israeli military forces occupying southern Lebanon until they finally withdrew in 2000, and targets in Israeli proper. Hizbollah has always asserted that these attacks have been in direct response to Israeli provocations, especially in 2006, but they do not deny that their ultimate ambition is to drive the armed might of the Israel Defense Force (IDF) out of Palestine and regain Jerusalem for Islam, goals spelled out in their 1985 manifesto. In this they are supported by the vast majority of other Shi'a and the Sunni Palestinians who have borne the brunt of Israeli expansion and occupation. It is one of the few areas of common ground where all Muslims can meet and agree, and one where Israel and the United States find themselves facing a formidable enemy. Israel has marshaled every means at its disposal to combat this threat, from carpet bombings of Gaza throughout January 2010 and political assassinations as far afield as Oslo and Dubai to the building of "security walls" and Jewish settlements on land seized illegally from its Palestinian owners. But so far, they have served only to push back a final day of reckoning that could have fatal consequences for all concerned.

More than half a century ago, the late Jewish-American historian and political scientist Alfred Lilienthal (1913–2008) wrote a book widely condemned by Zionists, titled *What Price Israel?* Although branded as something of an eccentric at the time, Dr. Lilienthal would feel quite vindicated, but also frightened, to see how some of his predictions have begun to manifest themselves, in particular his fears that a Jewish state would endanger and ultimately isolate Jews elsewhere, including the United States. Opposition to the establishment of the state of Israel has always existed in the United States, some of the strongest voices coming from the Jewish community itself, notably from ultra-Orthodox Jewish leaders who are awaiting the promised Messiah to bring about the restoration of Jewish rule in the Holy Land. The recently established and cleverly named J Street group (there is no J Street in Washington between I and K, and the area between I and K Streets is the center for the lobbyist offices) has been highly critical of many Israeli policies. Most Jews, however, have always given unwavering political and economic support for the Zionist state.

The Muslim population in the United States, by contrast, has had little influence in the American corridors of power despite a recent wave of immigration that has seen their numbers rise to a number approaching if not equal to the American Jewish population. They have only two representatives in Congress—African American converts from Indiana (André Carson, who has represented the 7th district/Indianapolis since 2008, a seat which his grandmother Julia Carson held for many years before him) and Minnesota (Keith Ellison, from the state's 5th district/Minneapolis, since 2007). Both won reelection in 2012 with substantial majorities—63 percent and 75 percent, respectively—even though Muslims form a small minority of their constituents. Americans of Christian Arab descent have been more successful in achieving high national office (e.g., Ray Lahood and Darrell Issa), but they have been in the United States far longer, their ancestors having emigrated from Lebanon, Syria, and Palestine for economic and religious reasons as early as the 1880s. Until recently, they have been one of the few sources of support for a more balanced U.S. foreign policy approach to the Middle East, and some have been particularly outspoken. Metropolitan Philip Saliba of the Antiochian Orthodox Church of North America, whose patriarch has his seat in Damascus, is among them, along with one of his more famous parishioners, Helen Thomas (originally Tannus). Thomas was the longtime doyenne of the White House Press Corps until an ill-advised but obviously heartfelt remark condemning Israel for its occupation of Palestinian Arab territories ("Tell them to get the hell out of Palestine") was broadcast nationwide in May 2010, causing her to lose her job as a result of the ensuing uproar from people who found the comments offensive. The nonagenarian Thomas refused to disappear quietly and has continued to speak out in the media on the issue of Palestine, most recently in an interview with David Hochman for *Playboy* (April 2011).

The Sunni Muslim population of the United States comes from all over the Islamic world but the first to reach America came as early as the 1880s as immigrants from Greater Syria. Initially, they were a very small part of a much larger wave of Christians from the region who settled in lower Manhattan and Brooklyn before gradually expanding throughout the country. The first known purpose-built American mosque in continuous use was erected in Cedar Rapids, Iowa, of all places, in the early 1930s. The even less likely small town of Ross, North Dakota, disputes this claim, since their mosque was built in 1927, but it soon after fell into disuse and disrepair. Today, there are more than fifteen hundred active places of Muslim worship in the United States. America's Sunni community includes a growing number of converts from Christian backgrounds, especially among African Americans, many of whose ancestors were slaves brought from predominantly Muslim West African regions like Senegal, Gambia, and Guinea. The smaller Shi'a population is divided among Iranians who are largely refugees from the strict Islamist regime imposed by Ayatollah Khomeini in 1979 and generally opposed to conservative, traditionalist views, and more recent immigrants from Lebanon and 'Iraq who tend to have stronger religious associations.[1]

By and large, both groups have tried to blend in with the communities where they have settled but, by the simple act of building houses of worship, have called unwanted attention to themselves from extremist Christian groups, especially after 9/11. Even Arab Christians with names like Usama, Jihad, and Abdallah have found themselves threatened by individuals or organizations who think anyone with a Muslim or Arab background is a supporter of al-Qa'ida. The most militant are those who call themselves Christian Zionists, perhaps as many as 20 million American Evangelicals who believe that the end of the world is nigh and that in order to bring about the second coming of Christ, according to their unique interpretation of the Book of Revelation, the Jews must return to Palestine. Their vocal support for the state of Israel, though welcome in Zionist Jewish circles, is tempered by the fact that these Evangelicals believe that this return will be accompanied by the conversion of Jews to Christianity. As distasteful as this is to Israeli leaders, the political and financial support Christian Zionists offer has been grudgingly welcomed in a world in which friends of the Jewish state are becoming fewer and opposition to Israeli treatment of Palestinians is rising, even in the United States, particularly in intellectual circles. Most prominent among the Christian Zionist zealots is the Rev. John Hagee of San Antonio, Texas, whose vociferous hate messages against Muslims and Roman Catholics forced Republican 2008 presidential candidate Sen. John McCain to repudiate the pastor's endorsement. Not all Evangelical preachers, however, follow the Christian Zionist line. Some, like the Rev. Ted Pike, director of the National Prayer Network, a self-described "Christian/Conservative watchdog organization" based in a suburb of Portland, Oregon, have gone on record supporting the very conservative Orthodox Jewish view that the modern state of Israel is the flawed creation of nonobservant Jews, atheists, and Bolsheviks, in clear violation of God's plan to bring about the return of the Jews in diaspora to an Israel created by the Messiah as part of the End Days scenario.[2]

Because of the traditionally strong support for Israel given by the United States, Muslims across the board are reluctant to accept American efforts to interpose themselves in the issue of Palestine as a fair broker. They see nothing fair about the occupation of a land inhabited for centuries by an overwhelming Muslim majority and the dispossession of a large portion of its people. They deeply resent the treatment of Palestinians under Israeli military rule and chafe at foreign Jewish control over their Muslim holy sites in Jerusalem. Attempts by the international community to achieve peace through diplomatic means have come to naught as far as they are concerned, and they are fearful of extremists within Israel itself, many of them from America, who want to expel the Israeli Arab citizens (some 20 percent of the population and 30 percent of Israelis under the age of ten) and "re-settle" them, along with the Arab population of the West Bank, in neighboring Arab countries, especially Jordan, and, worst of all, to build a third Jewish Temple in Jerusalem, which would require removing the Dome of the Rock and al-Aqsa mosques. It should not come as a surprise that many Muslims have been driven to extremes, both religiously and politically, by these prospects.

To date, this extremism has not succeeded in attracting many supporters from among the 4 million to 6 million Muslims in the United States, but it has won many converts elsewhere in the world, notably in England (as witnessed by the July 2007 attack by Sunni militants on the London transport system) and Spain (where an al-Qa'ida-sponsored attack on a commuter train caused scores of deaths three years earlier). Inroads by Muslim militant extremism have been more successful in conservative countries of the Islamic world, like Sa'udi Arabia, Afghanistan, and Pakistan. The dismantling of the secular Ba'thist government of 'Iraq by the Americans in 2003 raised up a strong Sunni insurgency there in response to a resultant rise to power of the Shi'a majority, and even previously nonviolent Muslim societies like Indonesia have seen a rise in militant Islam over the last decade.

Most Americans have failed to comprehend the reasons for the depth of Muslim resentment over the creation of a Jewish state on what is perceived to be Arab soil and the ensuing desecration and destruction of many mosques and churches, but most of all for the occupation of Jerusalem. This resentment has been further fueled by the wars in 'Iraq and Afghanistan, which have resulted in Muslim civilian deaths many times over the number of Americans (and others) lost in the attacks on September 11, 2001. Muslims have also been angered by cartoon caricatures of the Prophet published in Denmark and threats by an ignorant Pentecostal preacher in Florida to burn copies of the Qur'an, which actually occurred in early 2011 when a copy of the book was "tried and found guilty" by his tiny congregation of a few dozen followers of fomenting hatred and violence. Similarly, the outrage in Egypt and elsewhere in the Muslim world in response to the mockery of the Prophet Muhammad in the YouTube video produced by a Coptic Christian immigrant to California in the weeks leading up to the Benghazi terrorist attack on September 11, 2012, was indicative of the widespread belief among many devout Muslims that the American government, not just isolated individuals, was behind the efforts to defame their religious beliefs.

A growing number of Americans do understand, however, that Muslim anger is not going to disappear by ignoring it. Unless it is dealt with and assuaged, whether that means accepting the right of Muslims to build mosques wherever they have a legal right to do so or by actively pressuring Israel to make substantive efforts to facilitate the "two-state" solution in Palestine, an endless succession of violent reactions to what are seen as Western provocations cannot only be guaranteed, it can increasingly include the specter of a nuclear component.

During the latter days of the Cold War, the West appeared to turn a blind eye to Sunni Pakistan's acquisition of atomic weapons as a political foil to counteract India's close friendly relations with the Soviet Union. India had nuclear capabilities, and, of course, so did Russia and China, so why, it was argued, should Pakistan, then a solid Western ally, be denied? Now that the Soviet threat is gone and India is a good friend to the West, Pakistan is threatened from within by its own Taliban insurgency and a strong Sunni Islamist presence in the military and especially the intelligence agencies, but it is too late to redress the damages already done. In the aftermath of the successful elimination of Usama bin Ladin by U.S. Special Forces on May 2, 2011, at his very visible hideout in Abbottabad, Pakistan, virtually in view of the country's principal military academy, relations between the two ostensible allies have soured. Pakistan's internal situation has deteriorated dramatically, and anti-U.S. feelings, both among the public and within the military, always present, have risen to a disturbing level, especially as evidenced by the sentencing of the medical doctor who helped the CIA locate bin Laden to thirty-three years in prison for "treason" by a regional tribal court in late May 2012. Support for the Taliban, both within Pakistan and in Afghanistan by elements inside Pakistan's highest intelligence agency, the Inter-Services Intelligence (ISI), and the highest echelons of military leadership, has been an open secret for years, vehemently denied by the Pakistanis, but it was made apparent with the killing of bin Laden. Both the military and civilian leadership have been deeply embarrassed by these and other revelations of collusion with Islamist militants, and the future of continued U.S.-Pakistani cooperation, especially in terms of military aid, is under serious threat.

The prospect of Pakistan's nuclear weapons falling into the hands of Islamic militants is an appalling possibility. Equally disturbing for many is the threat of Shi'a Iran also acquiring the capability of building an atomic weapon. Although insistent that their nuclear program is entirely for peaceful purposes, Iran cannot be completely trusted to keep to its word now or in the future, and it is unlikely that its primary target would be its Sunni neighbors. The announcement by Iran in early 2010 that it has its own source of uranium ore has further weakened the ability of the United States and its allies to make the sanctions they have imposed effective in preventing the further expansion of Iranian nuclear ambitions and thus has made a military option to halt its enrichment program that much more likely. There is no doubt that these sanctions have severely crippled the Iranian economy, but whether this will stop the government from pursuing its nuclear energy goals remains doubtful.[3] So much in the way of national honor and pride is at stake that it would take a successful popular uprising to stall progress in this direction.

The cooperation between some elements in both Pakistan and Iran to destabilize Afghanistan and undermine American and North Atlantic Treaty Organization (NATO) military efforts there has shown that Sunnis and Shi'as can work together, just as Hizbollah has actively cooperated with the militantly Sunni Hamas government of Gaza. As the popular Arab proverb says, "My enemy's enemy is my friend," perhaps only until the immediate threat from the enemy has passed, but "my friend" nevertheless when the chips are down. How then are Israel and the United States to deal with the unsettling possibility of such cooperation?

Israel, which has neither confirmed nor denied possessing nuclear weapons but is thought to have had its own arsenal of as many as three hundred bombs for several decades, has threatened to use military force to destroy Iran's nuclear facilities. Prime Minister Benjamin Netanyahu made this point very clear when he famously drew a red line on a crudely drawn diagram while addressing the UN General Assembly on September 27,

2012, to indicate how far he was willing to let this perceived "existential threat" to Israel proceed and which he expected President Obama (or as he clearly hoped at the time, a president-elect Mitt Romney) would adopt as his own. Estimates by both Israeli and American sources as to when Iran might be able to successfully build a nuclear weapon, let alone achieve the means to deliver it, vary considerably, from as early as June 2013, the date projected by Netanyahu in his speech, to a year or years down the road. The United States and NATO have expressed deep concern over Iran's program to produce nuclear power but have stopped short of making overt military threats and stressed the need for stronger diplomatic pressures and economic sanctions. An invasion of Iran by American forces is not a realistic option given the country's size, both in area and population, and the almost certain lack of support if not outright opposition from U.S. allies. It is also increasingly unlikely that the top U.S. military leadership, already with their forces still committed on the ground in ʻIraq and Afghanistan and the deep unpopularity of both wars at home, would even consider becoming involved in yet another unwinnable war, and they would make this sentiment well-known to any sitting U.S. president, no matter how frenetically Israel's right-wing friends on both sides of the aisle and in both houses of Congress would dance to Jerusalem's tune.

Iran's leadership has promised serious retaliation for any Israeli attack, which in any event could not destroy but only temporarily halt Iran's nuclear progress, and no country wants to see a regional nuclear war unfold that could seriously disrupt international oil supplies for a very long time as well as unleashing a massive Muslim backlash against the West. Never mind that most Iranians are Shiʻa; the world's Sunni majority would feel obliged to close ranks in support of its Muslim brothers and sisters however heterodox their beliefs. Even strict Wahhabi/Salafis would be forced, at the very least, to pay lip service to Shiʻa resistance. The U.S. positions in Afghanistan, ʻIraq, and Pakistan would be permanently undermined with disastrous consequences for its military presence in the region. The royal families of Saʻudi Arabia and the Gulf States could easily be overthrown in the wake of such an upheaval, to be replaced by populist revolutionary governments that could endanger the industrial world's oil supplies even further, at least in the short run but certainly long enough to make life very uncomfortable for millions of people in West and developing countries around the world. Would Israel undertake such a rogue operation? Is its famous Masada mentality—national suicide, as occurred in 31 BC when nearly one thousand Jewish men, women, and children leaped to their deaths from this 1,300-foot-high desert fortress overlooking the Dead Sea rather than submit to the victorious Roman army—so ingrained that it would consider steps that could lead to its own destruction?

There are many who believe that it could happen and that Iran would not only fail to yield in the face of such a prospect but might even welcome it as an opportunity to achieve what some observers believe is its own long-term goal of a revived Persian Empire dominating the Middle East and its vast oil wealth. The ancient grandeur of Persia is as deeply ingrained in the modern Iranian national consciousness as its more recent Shiʿa Muslim affiliation, and the ayatollahs would not hesitate to use the loyalty of the 100–150 million Shiʿa outside Iran both in neighboring countries and elsewhere to help expand their authority.

Where would Israel fit into such a picture, assuming it survived the consequences of its nuclear attack on Iran, and would the United States risk coming to its aid with a by now certainly hostile Europe in the way? NATO would not be of much use if most of its member governments proved unwilling to stick their necks out for a tiny but heavily armed outpost of European culture in a sea of Islam that for them has long been more trouble than it is worth. Just as the rulers of late Medieval Europe at last tired of the incessant demands of the ever-threatened Crusader principalities of Outremer, so may the United States and especially Europe grow weary of constantly having to respond to Israel's demands. As the last of the Holocaust survivors die and the enormity of Hitler's crimes fade from international memory despite the memorials to it, what other options does Israel have on the table to ensure its survival?

The obvious answer is twofold: first, to capitalize on the divisions within Islam while they still can—and there is suspicion in some quarters that they are doing just that, especially in Lebanon—and second, to come to a final settlement with the Palestinians as soon as possible, which they, or at least the right-wing government of Netanyahu, appear to be trying to avoid at all costs. In the first case, if Hasan Nasrallah's unsubstantiated (and very dubious) accusations that Israel plotted Rafiq Hariri's assassination in 2005 in order to further divide Shiʿa and Sunni in Lebanon are correct, then this policy may have been in the works for some time. A pronouncement by Ismaʿil Haniya, leader of Hamas in Gaza, on December 1, 2010, indicated that he and Hamas could be persuaded to accept a peaceful solution if it were approved by a vote of Palestinians around the world. Perhaps he thinks privately that such an event would never happen or that if it did a majority of those polled would not approve, but the opening is there, one that must be giving Hizbollah pause.

If Israel delays compromise and a formal conclusion to hostilities with the Palestinians on the basis of a two-state solution, it will be overtaken by demographics—its own stagnant population growth contrasted with rapidly increasing numbers of Palestinians both inside the pre-1967 boundaries of the country and in the occupied territories of Gaza and the West Bank. Partial ethnic cleansing, like that which took place during the 1967 war when a further 300,000 Palestinians were driven into exile in Jordan, would not be tolerated by the international community. Gone are the days when Prime Minister Golda Meir could pretend that "there is no such thing as a Palestinian," although former Speaker of the House of Representatives Newt Gingrich made such a risible claim during his failed race for the 2012 Republican presidential nomination when he stated that the Palestinians were "an invented people," no doubt in the vain hope of attracting sufficient Jewish and Christian Zionist voters to win the nomination. No one understands the Palestinian demographic threat better than former Israeli prime minister Ehud Olmert. Addressing the annual Herzliya conference in January 2008, he described the perils it foreshadowed: "For 60 years, we fought with unparalleled courage in order to avoid living in a reality of binationalism, and to insure that Israel exists as a Jewish and a democratic state with a Jewish majority. We must . . . understand that such a reality is being created, and in a very short while it will be beyond our control."[4]

The growing division, moreover, within Israel itself between secular and Orthodox (Haredim) Jewish citizens promises long-term consequences that will further weaken the country's ability to take action, especially since the Orthodox element, which is the only portion of the Jewish population that is growing, does not contribute either to the economy (in fact they are a serious drain on it) or even more important, to the military. Increasingly, the young, educated, secular Israeli Jews, who form the majority of those their country depends on for its defense, are quietly leaving for a new life in Europe and the United States, where they don't have to risk their lives protecting illegal settlements on the West Bank. Most Askhenazi Israelis who have, or can claim, a European passport and a number have returned to places like Germany and Poland, as Helen Thomas bluntly suggested they should, to live and work, something that would have been unheard of a generation ago.

Israel and the U.S. vs. an Independent Palestinian State

With Sunnis and Shi'as currently at each other's throats in Lebanon, 'Iraq, and Bahrain, and a Sunni majority in Syria attempting to overthrow its quasi-Shi'a 'Alawite leadership, at first by peaceful (and later not-so-peaceful) means since February 2011, a final settlement in Palestine that recognizes an Arab state there with its capital in East Jerusalem would prevent, or at least stave off indefinitely, the threat of a "one-state" solution that would end the Zionist dream forever. The adamant refusal of the Palestinian Authority leaders to continue the negotiations with Israel that the United States has continually sponsored unless the expansion of Jewish settlements on the West Bank, and especially in East Jerusalem, is stopped is based not only on a belief in the righteousness of their demands but also a conviction that in the long run, time is on their side. As both parties to the conflict know, the Palestinians have an ace up their sleeve—a unilateral Declaration of Independence. If this were to happen, the Israelis would cry foul and immediately withdraw from negotiations, should any happen to be going on at the time. The United States would reject the idea outright, but the vast majority of the world's countries would rally to their support, and within hours many would accord de facto if not de jure recognition of a Palestinian state. Who outside of Europe would refuse? Probably Canada and Australia would follow Washington's lead. No others of any political consequence come to mind.

Already six South American countries—including Brazil and Argentina, which have significant Jewish populations—have recognized a Palestinian state with pre-1967 boundaries, much to Israel's chagrin. In Europe, there would be strong support among left-leaning political parties and groups and overall sympathy from many others. Support in many NATO countries over the issue would bring strong political divisions in these countries to the fore and could bring down some governments—a prospect that neither Israel nor the United States would like to see.

There were in fact rumors that Russia and Spain were both contemplating such proceedings. On a visit to the West Bank in January 2011, President Dmitry Medvedev reiterated Russia's support for an independent Palestine with East Jerusalem as its capital in a statement at Jericho, originally voiced by the Soviet Union in 1988 after Yasser Arafat proclaimed Palestine's independence in Algiers in that year, but stopped short of a formal recognition. On January 25, 2011, Ireland raised the status of the Palestinian diplomatic mission to the rank of embassy, just as France and

Spain had done earlier and which many other European countries are doing now despite strong Israeli condemnation. Turkey, NATO's only Muslim member state, with a currently pro-religious government determined to curb the power of its strong secular elite in both the military and the political establishment, could play a crucial role any Palestinian move. Relations with Israel have been frigid ever since the Mavi Marmara attack. Attempts by Israel to heal the rift have gone nowhere since its leaders refuse to apologize for its actions, and Turkey has made it crystal clear that it will accept nothing less.[5] Once Israel made it clear that no apology was forthcoming, Turkey, partly in response to a UN panel report on the May 31, 2010, flotilla incident, expelled the Israeli ambassador to Ankara and downgraded its diplomatic mission to the lowest possible level on September 2, 2011. All cooperative military missions and related activities were also suspended.

On May 13, 2011, after two years of fruitless negotiations, special envoy to the Middle East George Mitchell resigned. Six days later, President Obama in a policy speech at the State Department called for a peace settlement based on pre-1967 borders, a proposal anathema to radical Zionists and their American supporters. It was immediately rejected by Prime Minister Netanyahu in a speech before a joint session of Congress on May 24, even though it was consistent with the official American policy since the Israeli military occupation of the West Bank and their annexation of East Jerusalem and the Golan Heights in 1967, an act considered illegal under international law. A prominent Israeli peace commentator, Uri Avnery, described the scene as "all rather disgusting—There they were, the members of the highest legislative bodies in the world's only super power, flying up and down like a bunch of yo-yo's."[6] The following day, in a show of Sunni solidarity with Hamas, the military government of Egypt opened its border with Gaza.

Six weeks earlier (April 6), forty prominent Israeli leaders from the Left and including former heads of the army and security services and the son of Israeli Prime Minister Yitzak Rabin, slain by a radical Zionist activist in 1996, proposed an "Israeli Peace Plan, eerily evocative of Sa'udi King 'Abdallah's all-but forgotten peace proposal in 2002, calling for a two-state solution, Israeli withdrawal from the West Bank and the Golan Heights and East Jerusalem, except for the Jewish quarter and the adjacent Western ('Wailing') Wall, and compensation paid to Palestinian refugees. Not surprisingly it was rejected by the "Greater Israel" Zionists whom Prime

Minister Netanyahu relied upon for his support and for his re-election bid in January 2013, but it does demonstrate the strength of the forces opposed to Likud that such a document could have even circulated."[7] The surprising collapse of the Likud/Israeli Beitnahu party alliance support in the January 22, 2013, parliamentary elections (from forty-three seats in the Knesset to just thirty-one) and the rise of a new centrist secular party, Yesh Atid, confirmed this. Netanyahu was finally able to form a coalition government on March 15, confirmed in parliament three days later, which included both Yesh Atid and the pro-settlement expansion Israel Home party, plus Hatunah, another centrist party recently formed by former prime minister Tzipi Livni, but for the first time in over ten years it did not include any of the ultra-orthodox parties like Shas. Livni was made justice minister and put in charge of resuming peace talks with the Palestinians but is not likely to get much support from Netanyahu and his political and spiritual ally Naftali Bennett, head of Israel Home.

On September 23, 2011, Palestinian Authority president Mahmud 'Abbas formally submitted a request to the UN Security Council for full membership in the international body, a move which Israel and the United States were able to delay and ultimately defeat when the council's admissions committee was unable to make a unanimous recommendation. In the meantime, the full membership of UNESCO, the UN's Economic, Scientific, and Cultural Organization, voted overwhelmingly (107–14, with fifty-two abstentions) in favor of full Palestinian membership on October 31, 2011, following an earlier recommendation by its executive board on October 5 that it do so. Apparently caught off-guard by this end run around the Security Council, both the United States and Israel cancelled their contributions to UNESCO, and the Jewish state reacted further by announcing yet more housing projects in illegal settlements on the West Bank, to the chagrin of Germany which had been one of the fourteen "no" votes in the balloting. Since the United States contributes 22 percent of the UNESCO budget, many of the agency's projects had to be put on hold, reduced, or even cancelled. Israel's allies in the U.S. Congress, led by then-chairwoman of the House Foreign Affairs Committee, Florida Republican Ileana Ros-Lehtinen, further moved to punish the Palestinian Authority by demanding that the United States end its $600 million in annual aid, even though Israeli military leaders like Gen. Itzan Elon, commander of the Judea and Samaria Divisions, said that such a step would lead to instability and insecurity for both Palestinians and Israelis, condemning at the same time "increasing violence by radical Israeli settlers, which he called 'Jewish terrorism.'"[8]

Undeterred by its failure to gain full UN membership through the Security Council in November 2011, the Palestinian Authority announced a second bid in September 2012, this time through a vote in the General Assembly to join the UN as a nonmember observer state, the same status as that held by the Vatican. Despite strong opposition from Israel and the United States, the vote on November 29 was even more lopsided than the UNESCO vote a year earlier: 138 for, nine against, with forty-one members abstaining. Those countries who voted yes included France, Spain, Italy, and many other NATO members. The only European country voting no was the Czech Republic. Other no voters included the United States and Canada and of course Israel; the remaining nos were Panama and four sparsely populated Pacific Island mini-states heavily dependent on the United States for financial support. Those abstaining included Great Britain, Australia, and, most significantly, Germany, which came as a major shock to Israel who had relied on German financial and political support ever since its founding, due in large part to German guilt over the Holocaust. Angela Merkel, after a meeting with Netanyahu a few days later, was adamant: "We have agreed only that we do not agree," she said in a statement to the press. Obviously, the world order, as far as Israel was concerned, had changed seismically.

The Jewish state reacted predictably by announcing more settlements in the area east of Jerusalem, most significantly for the first time in the sensitive E-1 area, which provides the only link between the northern and southern areas of the West Bank. It also announced it was withholding $100 million in monthly tax revenue that it collects on the Palestinian Authority's behalf indefinitely, a serious blow to the West Bank's cash-strapped economy. Prime Minister Netanyahu reluctantly backpedalled in January 2013 when he ordered one-month's transfer to be authorized. In the meantime, international condemnation was quick and universal. Five European nations—Great Britain, France, Spain, Sweden, and Denmark—summoned the Israeli ambassadors to their countries to protest these punitive measures, while the Obama administration, now strengthened by its convincing win in the November 6 elections, condemned Israel's settlement plans on December 3, urging Israeli leaders to reconsider their unilateral decisions. In a strongly worded editorial on December 4, the *New York Times* argued that "expanding settlements hurts Israel's long-term security interests."[9]

Prime Minister Netanyahu nevertheless defended himself and his country from international criticism on December 6, steadfastly refusing to change his settlement policy. In response to Israeli intransigence, the UN Security Council, on December 19 and in a vote of 14–1 (with only the United States opposing and no abstentions) strongly condemned Israel for its recent settlement expansion plans. All permanent members (aside from the United States) plus Germany and India voted in favor, and, in an unusual move, all made public statements after the vote. Speaking on behalf of the council's four European members, the British ambassador told reporters that the group "strongly opposes" Israel's announced plans, especially those in the area known as E-1 which threaten the contiguity of a potential Palestinian state with Eastern Jerusalem as its shared capital with Israel. Both Russia and China expressed their condemnation and concern, with Russia calling for an immediate meeting of the ministers of the so-called Middle-East Quartet (United Nations, United States, European Union, and Russia). The tripartite group known as IBSA (India, Brazil, and South Africa) said in an additional statement that Israel's settlements not only must be stopped but also dismantled. The UN secretary-general termed the settlement plan as "a violation of international law and an obstacle to peace" which would result in a "near fatal blow to the very fragile Middle East peace process."[10] U.S. State Department spokeswoman Victoria Nuland said only that Israel's construction plans "run counter to the cause of peace."[11]

Israel's ambassador to the UN predictably dismissed the Security Council move, but it was becoming more and more clear that Israel and the United States were painting themselves into a very awkward, if not dangerous and above all unnecessary, international political corner.[12]

Despite the Palestinian success in achieving recognition by the UN as a state, albeit a nonmember and an observer, the response in the Palestinian Authority and in most of the Muslim, both Sunni and Shi'a, world was nothing short of euphoric, apart from Gaza where the Hamas response was muted to say the least, but they clearly recognized, if grudgingly, that al-Fatah had scored a significant victory. As an indication of this, on January 4, 2013, Hamas allowed the previously banned Fatah opposition to hold a large public rally in Gaza City to mark the forty-eighth anniversary of the founding of the PLO, the first time they had been allowed to do so since the Hamas government was elected in 2007. The following day, President Mahmud 'Abbas announced that henceforth the Palestinian National

Authority would be known as The State of Palestine, and that name would appear on all official documents, including passports. Although they had gained nothing materially, and in the short run lost access to tax revenues, the Palestinians in the long term had brought Israel face to face with the prospect that the International Criminal Court could now consider investigating alleged Israeli war crimes against them, something they have been trying to initiate for years but could not because they lacked the status of a "state" that they had now acquired.

Mahmud 'Abbas's first official visit after the vote was to Pope Benedict XVI on December 17 at the Vatican, with whose former solitary ranks as a nonmember observer state the Palestinians were now joined. Pope Benedict XVI "welcomed the [passage of the] resolution," calling for both the resumption of "negotiations between the parties in good faith and according due respect to the rights of both," and renewed the Holy See's "call for an internationally guaranteed special status for Jerusalem, which Israel rejects."[13] The Pope's message could not have been more clear. In the wake of the Palestinian success, Israel had become even more isolated internationally than ever before.[14]

The Future of U.S.-Israeli Relations in the Face of Rising Sunni and Shi'a Anger Worldwide

The possibility of both Israel and the United States failing to find a way out of the corner they have painted themselves into since 1967 has not been lost on Washington. For the past fifty years or more, the American public has been told that the political aims and ambitions of Israel are the same as those of the United States in the region and the world, and that a strong and secure future of Israel is in America's foreign policy interests. Whenever Israel's policies have come into question in the UN Security Council, the United States has used its veto to prevent any binding resolution that would give international credibility to the critics of Zionist policies throughout the world. In most instances, the United States has been the only permanent member of the Security Council using its veto to protect Israel's unpopular policies, especially its illegal settlements on occupied Palestinian territory in Jerusalem and the West Bank. On February 18, 2011, a Security Council resolution proposed by the Palestinian delegation calling for condemnation of these settlements was vetoed by the American ambassador despite strong support from all other members of the council, including Germany, whose prime minister, Angela Merkel, reportedly rebuked her Israeli counterpart, Benjamin Netanyahu, when he telephoned to protest Germany's vote—the first time that has ever happened.

Chinks in the increasingly isolated American armor of solidarity with Israel, despite its official opposition to such issues as illegal settlements (often populated by militant American Jews), are beginning to appear as more and more people in government, and especially in the U.S. military, begin to question the wisdom of this previously unchallengeable view. In September 2011 former secretary of defense Robert Gates and former president Bill Clinton came out with public statements criticizing Israel in terms that would have been unthinkable a year earlier. On September 6 Gates referred to Israel as "an ungrateful ally" and that for all its military aid and diplomatic assistance, the United States "has received nothing in return. . . . Every American needs to know this."[15] Two weeks later on September 22, Clinton, speaking at his Global Initiative Conference in New York, accused Israel Prime Minister Netanyahu of not being interested in peace. "[He] lost interest in the Peace Process as soon as two basic Israeli demands seemed to come into reach: a viable Palestinian leadership and the possibility of normalizing ties with the Arab World."[16] Strong as these criticisms may appear, however, it is worth noting that they came from public figures who were beyond the reach of AIPAC political retribution.

The one seemingly unassailable bastion of support for Israel remains the U.S. Congress, many of whose members rely on AIPAC and other Jewish sources of support to fund their campaigns. Those who fail to toe the line face serious re-election challenges. The mid-term elections on November 2, 2010, brought the Republicans back into control of the House of Representatives, and they retained that control after the general election on November 6, 2012, albeit with a seven-seat fewer majority (Democrats went from 194 to 201; Republicans declined to 234). The Republicans retained control of the House largely due to gerrymandering by Republican-controlled state legislatures. Democrats won 50.5 percent of the total popular vote for House races. Many of the new members elected in 2010 were vocal in their support for Israel. But many others from the "Tea Party" movement were equally forceful in their demands for budget cuts, including foreign aid across the board, which would include Israel, the major beneficiary for the past fifty years or more of such largesse. Shortly after he was elected in November 2010, Sen. Rand Paul of Kentucky referred specifically to the massive annual American foreign aid to Israel, saying that "we can no longer afford it."[17]

The quiet but expanding sea change of perception regarding America and its relations with Israel, especially at the highest echelons of power, has yet to alter official government policy, but it has many people thinking long-term about what it means for the future of the United States. It hasn't as yet trickled down to public opinion—most polls show that nearly two-thirds of Americans support the Israeli cause over that of the Palestinians. But this division differs radically when broken down by education and political and religious affiliation. Among conservative Evangelical Christians, especially those without a university education or those whose college had a strict Evangelical orientation, the support for Israel is nearly universal. For Catholics, mainstream Protestant Christians, and nonbelievers, especially those with secular university degrees, the split is 50–50, or slightly in favor of Palestinians. Among Arab Americans, both Christian and Muslim support for Palestine is almost universal; among African Americans it is the reverse of the national average. Most surprisingly, criticism of Israel by American Jews is increasing, and support for Zionism is in decline, particularly among those under the age of forty.[18] Sooner, rather than later, the United States will have to decide if the continued existence of Israel as a Zionist, Jewish-by-definition state is in its long-term interests, and if Jews, especially those outside the confines of the former British Mandate of Palestine, are safer because of the "national home" proposed by Lord Balfour in 1917.

If no peaceful solution to the Palestine Question is reached within twenty years, if not sooner, the final decision will have had been made by a coming together of forces and events beyond anyone's control. Whether it is an Israeli nuclear attack on Iran or a nuclear retaliation by Iran backed by a nuclear Pakistan with not inconceivable Turkish support, the consequences for Jews everywhere, and by extension, the governments of Europe and the United States, will be life changing, possibly catastrophic. The devastating forest fire in northern Israel in the autumn of 2010 demonstrated just how unprepared Israel is to deal with any kind of domestic disaster. It may have one of the world's best defense systems to prevent an attack from outside, but if an attack were to succeed in gaining a foothold, the forces available on the ground to confront and control the damage appear to be surprisingly limited. But the chief threats to Israel, as perceived by political commentator Fareed Zakaria, remain "those from new technologies—rockets, biological weapons—and demography."[19] To these can be added the threat of more mass confrontations between peaceful protesters from neighboring Arab countries descending on border posts and military positions, such as those of May 15, 2011, and daring the Israeli soldiers manning them to fire. Such tactics are now under consideration by both Sunni and Shiʻa Muslim leadership in Lebanon and Syria, encouraged by the newly, if tenuously, united governments of Fatah and Hamas in the West Bank and Gaza, strengthened by the Israeli-Hamas exchange of rocket fire in October 2012. To what lengths would the Israeli military go to prevent a peaceful "walkover" of their borders? The massacre of thousands of unarmed demonstrators would undoubtedly have a massive impact on world opinion, and lead to more chaos in the region.

In another example of what can be achieved by nonviolent protest, 1,800 Palestinian political prisoners (out 4,500 in Israeli jails) staged a hunger strike, following the example of Khader Adnan, an activist who was arrested on December 17, 2011, under Israel's infamous "administrative detention" laws, which allowed for arrest and indefinite detention without trial or appeal for anyone suspected of "anti-Israel" activity. Although hunger strikes had been attempted before by individual prisoners, never had so many done so at one time or gained so much international publicity. Finally on May 14, 2012, in a deal brokered by Palestinian Authority president Mahmud Abbas, the prisoners ended their strike in return for Israel agreeing to place a six-month limitation of "administrative detention" and improving conditions for prisoners overall. Khader Adnan was released. Well-known Palestinian Christian nationalist and PLO spokeswoman Hanan ʻAshrawi applauded the actions of the prisoners, saying that "the hunger strikers' courage is magnificently inspiring and their selflessness deeply humbling. They have truly demonstrated that nonviolent resistance is an essential tool in our struggle for freedom."[20] Peaceful resistance in the face of an enemy determined to break your will using all means at their disposal is never an easy path, but if pursued by enough people it can and does work, especially in the age of social networking. Not even Prime Minister Netanyahu and the most militant Greater Israel Zionists can stand up over time to the pressures of concerted and focused peaceful efforts by the Palestinians to achieve their legitimate goals, backed by the overwhelming support of world opinion outside an increasingly divided American Congress, the vast majority of whose constituents are primarily concerned with domestic, chiefly economic, issues. Why send billions of dollars abroad, they ask, when millions at home are desperately worried about making their next mortgage payment and putting food on the table?

Conclusion

In the wake of a catastrophic threat to Israel's existence, whether brought on by an attack on Iran and a counter-attack against Israel or mass murders on Israel's borders, the world's attention may well be forced to consider the consequences of a bloody civil conflict between the two rival forces of victorious Islam, Sunni and Shi'a, that could well break out for what's left of a severely weakened, isolated, or even obliterated Zionist state. A peaceful solution is within Israel's grasp if it is able to control the extremists in its own society. Were that to happen, there would doubtless be radical Muslim elements that would refuse to accept it, but their fight would then be with their own co-religionists and not with Israel or the United States. Whether Israel opts for half its cake and survival, or a stubborn refusal to make any compromise thus risking another Masada that could involve the entire world, the Sunni-Shi'a divide will continue to fester for the foreseeable future, with or without the convenient punching bag of the "Zionist entity." As we have seen, violent Shi'a (Qarmatians) have in the past desecrated and destroyed the holy of holies in Mecca, and the extreme Wahhabi Sunnis have done the same to the most sacred Shi'a shrines in Karbala' and al-Najaf. If the common enemy, Zionism, were no longer a unifying rally cry, the refrain of *Allahu Akbar* might well resonate for different ambitions and heretofore unanticipated goals.

Today's Twelver Shi'a are a relatively small minority of the world's Muslims, not much in excess of 15 percent at the most, but they are concentrated in the very heart of the Islamic world. The tinderboxes of Sunni-Shi'a confrontation, both actual and potential, are Lebanon, Syria, 'Iraq, Iran, and the Gulf, especially Bahrain and eastern Sa'udi Arabia. This region, described by King 'Abdallah II of Jordan as "the Shi'a Crescent" in 2004, contains heavily armed military and paramilitary forces in Lebanon,

117

Syria, 'Iraq, and Iran and close to 100 million followers who subscribe to a belief in the appearance of Mahdi who could usher in the End Days at any time. Another 100 million or more Shi'a live in relatively close proximity to the Gulf through central Asia, Afghanistan, Pakistan, and India. What are the possible scenarios that could play out over the next decade should open conflict erupt, either between the Muslim world and Israel or between militant Shi'ism and the Sunnis on the borders of and within the Shi'a Crescent? Two come to mind, one that would bring Shi'a Iran to dominance in the region and another that would result in Sunni Turkish hegemony.

In the first case, it is becoming clearer by the day that a large number of Israelis, possibly the majority, are backing off from any nuclear confrontation with Iran. In late May 2011 the recently retired head of Mossad, Meir Dagan, warned that any such action would be "stupid" and would unleash the forces of war in the region which Israel has no strategy or ability to contain. Another former head of Mossad, Zvi Zamir, agreed, and the former chief of IDF Intelligence, Shlomo Gazit, went on record that "an Israeli attack on Iran's nuclear reactors would lead to the liquidation of Israel."[1] Would the United States willingly be drawn into war if such an attack, which all signs indicate it opposes, were launched? Not if the American military had anything to say about it and the president were able to resist pressures for Israel's allies in Congress. All that the president would need to do would be to remind Congress of what Prime Minister Netanyahu said in his speech before the joint session of both houses on May 24, 2011: "You do not need to send American troops to Israel. We defend ourselves."

Iran has shown no signs of slowing down its nuclear program, and the climate in Israel, despite hawkish noises from Netanyahu, Ehud Barak, and other right-wing politicians in response to Dagan's outspoken criticism. But if an Israeli preemptive attack did happen, Iran would emerge as an even stronger leader in the region, and in the words of Maj. Gen. Shlomo Gazit, "Israel will cease to exist."[2] American military positions in Bahrain and the Gulf would be severely compromised, shipment of oil through the Gulf to a thirsty world would stop, and unimaginable forces would be unleashed that no amount of Sa'udi and Emirates money could contain.

In the second scenario, we have the growing power of Turkey, now the world's eighteenth-wealthiest industrial nation with vast agricultural resources, not to mention the largest army in the region.[3] The government of Prime Minister Erdogan was reelected on June 12, 2011, to a third term and has shown increasing interest in expanding its influence in the Arab world that the Ottomans controlled for centuries. If Israel is persuaded not to attack Iran, it will be in no small part due to the realization that it has more to fear in the long run from its one-time ally than it does from the enemy to the east whose power and potential threat it has greatly exaggerated for domestic and American political consumption. In its long history, Iran has rarely attacked anyone since its wars with the ancient Greeks nearly 2,500 years ago, with the exception of proxy attacks by Hizbollah. Rather the contrary—it has been the victim of attack, most recently in the 1980s by Saddam Husayn. Turkey, on the other hand, has a long history of aggression, and as its economic power continues to grow so does the temptation to expand, especially into the Turkish-speaking regions to its east in the Caucasus and central Asia where its roots lie.

But whether a regional war is begun by Israel in Iran or sense prevails and compromise resulting in the creation of a Palestinian state is achieved, one thing is for certain: the growing power of Turkey and Iran are bound to bring them into eventual conflict over territory and resources. This would amount to a modern revival of the old Ottoman-Safavid rivalry that dominated regional politics in the seventeenth and eighteenth centuries, between the torchbearers of the Sunni caliphate—the sultans in Istanbul—and the champions of the Shi'a opponents of that hated caliphate, the Iranians. At stake would be the Arab Fertile Crescent and the oil-rich Arabian Peninsula, both of which, apart from the eastern region bordering the Persian Gulf, were less than one hundred years ago subject to Ottoman Turkish rule. It is clear that Iran has ambitions in the rest of the peninsula, which Turkey never controlled and which have large Shi'a populations. Those who have the most to lose in such a confrontation would be the weak, phenomenally wealthy Sa'udi Kingdom and the princely states of Kuwait, Bahrain, Qatar, and the UAE. Might not a deal between the two major powers of the region, especially as Israel declines or in another scenario is destroyed, sound the death knell for these artificial states for which the rest of the Muslim World has no deep attachment? Puritan Wahhabi rule over the Holy Cities of Mecca and Medina has never been popular among most Muslims, both Sunni and especially Shi'a. The latter have never forgiven the massacre of Shi'a pilgrims by Sa'udi police during the Hajj in 1987–1988 and deeply resent the small number of Shi'as that the Sa'udi government allows to fulfill their once-in-a-lifetime obligation every year. Is a deal being struck behind closed doors in Ankara and Teheran? Are oil-rich shaykhs facing extinction? The answer to the first question is that we don't know for sure but it shouldn't come as a surprise if we find out it is. The answer to the second question is yes, but the more important question is when?

The idea of a Shi'a crescent attracted a lot of attention, especially among American neoconservatives, when it was first suggested nearly a decade ago. But how much of a real threat is it? Apart from Iran, which is large, wealthy, and overwhelmingly Shi'a in its population, government, and mystique, the other component regions are less secure in their Shi'a orientation. 'Iraq is the only Arab country with a Shi'a majority and a Shi'a-dominated government, but unlike Iran its political administration is largely secular. The religious element is split between a respected leadership headed by Grand Ayatollah Sistani of Karbala' (an Iranian, but independent of Iran's mujtahid establishment) and the radical spokesman for the poor, urban element of the Shi'a population, Muqtada al-Sadr. Many 'Iraqi Shi'a are wary of any closer ties with Iran than already exist. The war between the two countries under Saddam in the 1980s brought Shi'a into conflict with Shi'a, and the personal scars of lost fathers, husbands, and sons remain on both sides. There is also, unlike in Iran, a large and vocal Sunni presence that until recently ruled the country through a long succession of sultans, kings, and dictators. 'Iraqi Sunnis are very distrustful of Iran and its political motives in the region. Oil-rich Azerbayjan is in majority Shi'a, but Turkish-speaking and on very bad terms with Iran, which it claims occupies the southern half of Azeri territory. Iran has been very critical of Azerbayjan's close ties with the United States and its relative tolerance toward Israel. Their mutual border is frequently closed to commercial traffic.

The situation in Bahrain has cooled, but for how long? It is the only Gulf country with a Shi'a majority, but when combined with the majority Shi'a population on the Sa'udi mainland just opposite in al-Hasa Province and minority Shi'a populations in Kuwait and some parts of the UAE it still has the potential to disrupt the oil-rich region. The Shi'a of Yemen pose no threat to anyone due both to their isolation and also the allegiance of most to the Zaydi branch, which does not have close ties with Iran. The real danger comes from the Sunni southeastern part of the country (the former British Protectorate of Aden), where a power vacuum has allowed al-Qa'ida to gain a foothold along with similar entrenchments across the Straits of Mandab in Somalia.

The Shi'a of Pakistan are a majority only in the extreme northeastern region of the country (originally a part of Kashmir occupied after the partition of India in 1947–1948), but they, along with the population of the adjacent Wakhan Corridor of Afghanistan, are almost entirely Nizari Isma'ilis and not closely allied to the Twelver population to the south in Punjab and Sind (Karachi). As mentioned earlier, they are the most moderate of all Shi'a in their religious beliefs and deeply loyal to their leader, the forty-ninth Isma'ili imam, Prince Karim Aga Khan IV. And all Shi'a in Pakistan are under siege, as are the Sunni Sufis, from the increasing power of militant forces of Salafi groups like the Taliban who are strongly supported by the Wahhabi religious establishment in Sa'udi Arabia. In Afghanistan, the minority Shi'a of the central and northern part of the country are increasingly isolated and under threat from a resurgent Taliban. The political support the latter receives from Iran, despite their deep religious differences, in order to wage a proxy war against America makes any support by Iran for the weak Shi'a population there, especially the persecuted Hazara tribes, unlikely.

The weakest links in the Shi'a Crescent, however, lie to the west, in Syria and, by association, Hizbollah in Lebanon. The ongoing upheaval in Syria, which has resulted at the time of this writing in tens of thousands of deaths, has attracted international attention and strong indications from not only the United States and Europe but also Turkey and the Sunni states of the Arab Peninsula that regime change is necessary. The serious escalation of violence in May 2012 culminated in the horrific massacre on May 25 at Hawla, a Sunni village surrounded by 'Alawi settlements thirty-four kilometers west of Homs, killing 108 civilians including forty-nine children, and another at the nearby Sunni village of al-Qubayr on June 6 saw nearly as many casualties. These massacres completely overshadowed the regime's attempt to deflect attention from the uprising by staging sham parliamentary elections on May 7. No sooner had the newly elected house met on May 24 than the news of the Hawla outrage broke, leaving the future of the Annan ceasefire in serious doubt. The Security Council unanimously condemned the murders, and following the Hawla incident eleven nations, including the United States, the United Kingdom, France, and Turkey, expelled Syrian diplomats as punishment. The United States, Sa'udi Arabia, and Qatar had withdrawn their ambassadors months earlier, so the Asad regime was left even more dependent on Russia, and to a lesser extent China, for support.

By July Annan's mission was in a shambles and in early August, as noted earlier, he announced his resignation, effective August 31. His replacement, the former Algerian foreign minister and longtime diplomat Lakhdar Brahimi, was equally unsuccessful in bringing the fighting to a halt. Instead, the conflict escalated with the increase in the number of rebel forces, including foreign fighters from all over the Sunni world, notably Qatar, Saʿudi Arabia, ʿIraq, and Chechniya, and the introduction of al-Qaʿida-linked jihadist groups into the equation, notably the Jabhat al-Nusra li-Ahl al-Sham (the Support Group for the People of Syria), whose stated aim is to replace the Asad regime with an Islamic state under Shariʿa law. On the other side, Shiʿa volunteers from ʿIraq, Lebanon, and Iran strengthened the pro-regime resistance. On July 18 a bold strike by the opposition forces in Damascus targeting the military leadership killed Defense Minister Dawud Rajha, the most influential Christian (Greek Orthodox) in the Asad power structure, and two other senior figures: Rajha's deputy, Asif Shawkat (Asad's brother-in-law), and senior military adviser Maj. Gen. Hassan Turkmani, a leading Sunni in the otherwise Alawite-dominated government elite. Asad's youngest brother, Maher, commander of the Republican Guard and head of Internal Security, was severely wounded. On the same day, a UN resolution threatening Syria with sanctions was vetoed yet again by Russia and China. By late July the fighting had spread to Damascus and Aleppo, and the latter reached a standoff with neither side able to claim victory. In the meantime, much of the ancient city and its monuments, including the old covered *suq*, or central market, and its neighboring medieval mosque, had been heavily damaged. The fighting for Syria's largest city and northern commercial hub has continued unabated well into 2013.

Two factors prevented the rebel forces from succeeding in overthrowing the regime: the lack of a central leadership and the strong resistance by ʿAlawi, Christian, Druze, and some Kurd minorities (30 percent of Syria's total population) to the perceived belief that rebel success would lead to the establishment of a fundamentalist Sunni state along the lines of that in Egypt in the wake of the Arab Spring. The United States and Western European states were unable to agree on any plan to facilitate the overthrow of President Asad, although they all agreed in principle that this was desirable. In mid-November 2012 the Syrian opposition factions based in Doha, Qatar, signed a unity agreement in hopes of attracting foreign aid and military assistance, and while France, Turkey, and the United States recognized the new leadership, the United States put in its own caveat, refusing to recognize the Jabhat al-Nusra front as part of the junta of rebel forces.

In its attempt to bring Lebanon into the fray, President Asad issued arrest warrants for former Lebanese prime minister Saʿad Hariri and a member of his future parliamentary bloc on December 11. Two days later, Hariri ratcheted up the war of words, calling Asad "a monster" and rejecting the legitimacy of the warrants, which Interpol also refused to honor. The use of the word "monster" was a particularly personal slap at Asad since the Arabic word *wahish* ("beast" or "monster") was originally the Asad family name, changed in 1927 by his grandfather to the more attractive *asad,* one of the many Arabic words for "lion." The epithet "dog" (*kalb*), frequently hurled at the president by his opponents, also had personal resonance since the Asad family comes from the *Banu Kalb* or *Kalbiyya,* the most influential of four leading Alawite tribes. In the meantime, the regime's mishandling of the resistance, notably the pointless provocation of the already hostile government of Prime Minister Erdogan by the shooting down of a Turkish fighter jet off the coast of Latakia in late June, and continued slaughter of civilians in botched air strikes against rebel targets led the Russians to begin to reconsider their unqualified support. On December 6, 2012, Secretary of State Hillary Clinton met with her Russian counterpart, Sergei Lavrov, in Dublin to discuss possible solutions to the stalemate. On December 13 the Russian foreign ministry acknowledged that the Asad regime's ability to defeat the rebels was "in doubt." In May 2013, however, the Russians indicated renewed support for the Asad regimes by confirming that they would supply the government with S-300 anti-aircraft missiles, which could seriously compromise any possible "no-fly" zone that might be imposed to protect the rebel forces by nations supporting them.

The question was not if Asad would have to go but when and how. There were fears that he might use Syria's reserve of chemical weapons in a desperate attempt to stay in power, and there were also fears that a new government, which would inevitably be Sunni-dominated, might take serious retaliatory steps against the Alawites and other minorities who had relied on the Asad government for support. In an op-ed piece for the *New York Times* on November 16, 2012, Simon Adams stated the obvious: "Assad's war crimes have put his fellow Alawites at risk of being massacred."[4] In an editorial entitled "Syria Endgame" in the Beirut *Daily Star* on December 14, 2012, Russia was held responsible for ending matters quickly and cleanly, not only for the sake of Syria and its neighbors but for its own interest in the region. "Russia needs to accelerate its efforts to convince Assad that the game is over. A failure to do so would hurt Russia in a post-Assad Syria even more, since it will be for the loss of life and destruction that take place from now on, following Thursday's [December 13] admission that the tide had turned."[5]

With the fall of the Shi'a Crescent's weakest link, and its only one with a border with Lebanon, Hizbollah would lose its conduit of arms and supplies from Iran. Faced with this prospect, there were fears that it might try to stage a military coup to take over all of Lebanon with very unpleasant consequences. In the meantime, Hassan Nasrallah and his followers continued to reject the mounting evidence that the 'Alawi-dominated regime in Syria was doomed. Following the October 22, 2012, assassination of the Sunni head of Lebanese Intelligence, the Sunni-led Opposition delegates boycotted parliament in protest over what they saw as a deliberate Hizbollah provocation. In response, the Shi'a leadership refused to negotiate with the Opposition about setting the legal parameters for Lebanon's next parliamentary elections, scheduled for June 2013. It seemed clear that Hizbollah would prefer to have no elections at all, especially if Asad and his regime were to fall in the interim period. Should they attempt a military coup, the Lebanese Shi'a leadership, despite its military strength, would face a nearly impossible and bloody task trying to impose, let alone maintain, its rule over the 75 percent of the country dominated by Sunni, Christian, and Druze majorities in their respective regional strongholds. Strong criticism of the Shi'a organization's military wing has come from both Sunni and Christian Maronite leaders. When Hizbollah gratuitously offered to defend Lebanon's offshore gas and oil rights against Israel by force, former Sunni prime minister Fu'ad Sanyura (Siniora) bitterly criticized their leader, Hasan Nasrallah, for infringing on the rights of the Lebanese state to defend itself, saying such a move would confiscate the state's role and involve the country in an external conflict. The following day, the newly appointed Maronite Patriarch, soon-to-be cardinal Bishara Butrus al-Ra'i, reiterated the church's position that only the Lebanese state should be responsible for arms.[6] During the month of August 2011, which coincided with Ramadan, opposition to Shi'a and especially Hizbollah support for Bashshar al-Asad's beleaguered dictatorship rose to new heights, especially among Lebanon's Sunnis, who strongly resented the massacre of their co-religionists by the Ba'thi regime. They were particularly bitter that the same Syrian Sunni civilians who welcomed tens of thousands of Lebanese Shi'a refugees during the Israeli invasion of Lebanon's south in 2006 were now becoming victims of Shi'a aggression and, to make matters even more hurtful, during the most sacred month of the Islamic calendar.

Even Iran, although it is the center of Shi'a political and religious power, is not without its own internal problems. Many Westerners view the country through the outspoken views of its president, Mahmud Ahmadinejad, but, as mentioned, he is not nearly as conservative as the final power brokers in the country, the ruling ayatollahs, especially the Supreme Leader 'Ali Khamenei. In May and June of 2011 a private rift between the two faces of political leadership in Iran became very public, with the president being openly criticized by the religious forces and his personal allies in government being arrested, including the deputy foreign minister. In another instance, the president sacked the country's minister of intelligence, only to be publicly embarrassed when the Supreme Leader reinstated him. Privately, it was thought that Ahmadinejad was becoming too powerful and assuming a kind of religious mantle for himself with his frequent references to the imminent return of the mahdi. He was also under suspicion of trying to strengthen the office of the presidency, deliberately made relatively weak by the ayatollahs, who remain very distrustful of secular authority and popular elections. On June 27, 2011, Iran's parliament summoned the president for questioning.

The conflict went quiet for several months but resurfaced in mid-September 2011 when the president announced with great fanfare, in advance of his annual visit to the UN in New York, that the two American "hikers" held under arrest and sentenced to eight years in prison would be released on bail. In a very public rebuke to Ahmadinejad, the Iranian courts declared that the president had no right to release them and that it was up to them to review the appeal for bail. Perhaps as a sop to Ahmadinejad, the courts released the two on September 21 on the eve of his New York trip.

In an even more curious twist, on October 11 the United States claimed that it had uncovered a plot by the Quds (Jerusalem) Brigade of the Iranian military forces to sponsor an assassination attempt on the Sa'udi Ambassador to the United States, 'Adil al-Jubayr, at a popular bistro in Washington with the assistance of a Mexican drug cartel in total conflict with all previously known Iranian methods to advance its regional goals. However that accusation—instantly and vehemently denied by an Ahmadinejad spokesman—plays out, it remains clear that conservative religious forces are very much in control, and ultra-conservative groups in Iran were gearing up for parliamentary elections in 2012 in hopes of ousting supporters of the president in advance of presidential elections a year later. As it turned out, their efforts were rewarded. Ahmadinejad supporters in parliament were reduced to one-quarter. In the first round of elections on March 2, the conservative parties won an outright majority, and in the run-off elections on

May 4 of the sixty-five seats still in play, the reformist parties supporting Ahmadinejad took only thirteen, with forty-one going to the conservatives and eleven to independents. Of the 290 seats in the new parliament (*majlis*), 182, or nearly two-thirds, were held by conservatives; seventy-five by Reformists (barely one-quarter); nineteen by independents; and fourteen by minorities (five Armenian, four Assyrian/Chaldaean Catholic, three Jews, and two Zoroastrians).

Some Western observers are of a mind that despite the president's quirky beliefs, he represents the best chance for a diplomatic settlement of concerns over Iran's quest for nuclear power; but if the Supreme Leader has his way, there may not even be an office of president to contest. In late October 2011 Ayatollah Ali Khamenei "told an academic gathering . . . that 'changing Iran into a parliamentary system' in which voters no longer elected a president would not be a problem."[7] The March–May 2012 parliamentary elections in Iran confirmed the Supreme Leader's claim of mass support. Ahmadinejad's future after the June 2013 presidential elections— in which his designated political heir was refused by the Guardian Council on May 21 to stand—remained in question.

Should an internal upheaval in the future overthrow the current Shi'a theocracy in Iran, replacing it with a secular government of an unknown political dimension, the entire course of relationships in the region could be drastically changed. Without the ayatollahs in control, giving leadership to the millions of Shi'a outside Iran, the real or imagined strength and threat of a Shi'a Crescent would diminish overnight. Iran would remain a key player in regional politics by virtue of its wealth and size, but one without the religious mission that currently defines it. Such a development does not appear likely in the near future, but ultimately the Iranian population, especially that of the cities, will tire of the severe restrictions on their personal life and the economic pain of sanctions from abroad, and an uprising like the Arab Spring may well bring down the Shi'a Islamic state structure. Until then, the West and the rest of the Islamic world will have to contend with the current reality.

In Turkey, the rigidly secular state put in place by Atatürk over the opposition of the Sunni religious establishment by sheer force of his charismatic personality in the 1920s and 1930s has been gradually undercut by the government of Prime Minister Erdogan. A religious Muslim, he and his Justice and Development party have trod their way very carefully through a maze of Turkish politics, gradually undercutting the secular elite of both the upper echelons of urban society and the military. The secular parties have been unable to win even 40 percent of the vote in recent elections, and the strongly conservative rural population is very much behind Erdogan's party. Having been reelected to a third consecutive term—a first in Turkish history—in the general elections of June 12, 2011, with nearly 50 percent of the popular vote (49.83 percent, up three percentage points over the previous election), the prime minister quickly moved to consolidate his party's gains, and secular Turks feared he might begin to implement more conservative social policies that would further restrict personal freedoms, such as use of the social internet and the consumption of alcohol.[8] Despite the Qur'anic prohibition on its use, Turkey is a major producer, domestic consumer, and exporter of both wines and spirits, especially the popular local drink (and favorite of Atatürk) *raki*, an anise-flavored alcoholic drink that is a close cousin of the Arab '*araq* and the Greek *ouzo*. Already Erdogan's government has imposed a government agency to control it, and the price has more than doubled due to taxation aimed at reducing consumption.

The country's large Shi'a Alevi and ethnic Kurdish minorities, each forming between 15 percent and 20 percent of Turkey's population, are suspicious of Erdogan's intentions. Although most of the Kurds are fellow Sunnis, they have a long history of fighting for their autonomy, if not independence, from Ankara, and there have been bloody conflicts with the government and the army over the past decades, which Erdogan's party has done little to defuse. The Alevis, as mentioned earlier, are on the whole very secular in outlook and strongly supportive of the Atatürk legacy. As Twelver Shi'a, they are very much at odds with the very religious Sunni element within the Justice and Development Party. Very aware of these concerns, Erdogan has gone out of his way to address them. On November 23, 2011, he publicly apologized for the "Dersim Massacres" of Alevi Kurds in the final years of the Atatürk era (1936–1939). The very small Christian communities, mostly Armenians in Istanbul, Syriacs in the southeast of the country, and Arabic-speaking Greek Orthodox in and around Antioch, about 130,000 in total, have benefited by Erdogan's recent efforts to conform to the demands of the EU, one of which is that Turkey's longstanding restrictions affecting Christian and other minorities be lifted.

Most significant, though not specifically mentioned, is the Greek Orthodox Church, whose primus inter pares ("First among Equals"), the Ecumenical Patriarch of Constantinople, Bartholomew I, resides in Istanbul.

He is viewed by the Turks as an uncomfortable reminder of the Byzantine Empire and its imperial capital, which they finally captured in 1453 and still hold despite many attempts to dislodge them, most recently during and in the immediate aftermath of World War I. Although his local constituency of some 2,500 ethnic Greeks has been dwindling for years, the Patriarch is strongly supported by Orthodox countries neighboring Turkey, especially Greece and Bulgaria, and now Russia and Ukraine in the post-Soviet era. The United States also has large communities of Orthodox Christians today, numbering anywhere from 5 to 10 million, largely Greek, Russian/Ukrainian, Armenian, Serbian, and Lebanese, whose roots in America go back well into the nineteenth century. More recent arrivals have come from Egypt (Coptic) and 'Iraq (Syriac and Assyro-Chaldean). Bartholomew I enjoys high international visibility (especially for his championing of environmental issues) and has been careful to be publicly supportive of the Turkish government. He and his allies have been working to reopen the only remaining Greek Orthodox seminary in the country on the Princes' Islands of Halki in the Sea of Marmara, closed in 1971 during a time of confrontation with Greece over Cyprus. Both the EU and the United States have put considerable pressure on Turkey, and in 2010 the Patriarch expressed the belief that the seminary would open in 2011. To date that has not occurred, but unofficial sources inside Erdogan's party have confirmed that this is likely to happen as part of Turkey's bid to join the EU.

Despite the distrust of the secular elite, Erdogan's government has continued to advance its policies: first, to undercut the power of the military; second, to move for a new constitution to replace the one imposed after a military coup in 1982; and third, to expand Turkey's influence in the region. In the first case, there has been visible success in reducing the influence of the country's highly secular-oriented military. On July 29, 2011, four generals and the leaders of all three of Turkey's military branches resigned as a group, by sending in early retirement notices, thus appearing to relinquish their historic role as "sole protector of the republic" and ceding preeminence to the prime minister.[9] This acquiescence on the part of the military, which has carried out three coups since 1960, demonstrated the power of Erdogan and his party. In the second case, a move to write a new constitution is already causing fear of further challenges to democracy, the secular state, the courts, and religious and ethnic minorities.

As for his third policy goal, the prime minister has wasted no time in making his influence felt in the region. He had already laid Turkey's demands on the line to Israel regarding the Mavi Marmara incident, namely an official apology, compensation for the victims' families, and a lifting of the Gaza embargo, which Prime Minister Netanyahu has been unwilling (or unable, for domestic political reasons) to accept. On August 17, 2010, he refused outright, despite pressures from the United States to make an apology, essentially rejecting the possibility of restoring cordial relations between Israel and Turkey in the near term at least, consequences be damned. Having managed to sabotage its relationship with one of the two principal Sunni powers in the region, Israel succeeded in endangering its ties with the other, Egypt, in mid-August 2011, when in response to an attack on its territory near the southern port of Eilat by terrorists allegedly from Gaza infiltrating the region via Egypt, the Israeli military chased the perpetrators back into Sinai, violating the country's sovereignty and in the process killing three Egyptian security personnel who happened to be in the way. The response from Egypt's new military government, no longer as willing to support U.S. policy in the region as the overthrown president Husni Mubarak had been for three decades, was strongly critical. Although this time—unlike after the Mavi Marmara incident—a spokesman for the Israeli government, Defense Minister Ehud Barak, made an immediate apology of sorts (Israel "deeply regrets" the Egyptian loss of life), protesters in Cairo waving Palestinian flags called for the expulsion of the Israeli ambassador.[10]

During President Obama's state visit to Israel at the end of March 2013 (his first as president), he clearly put pressure on Netanyahu to resolve the three-year diplomatic standoff with Turkey. The Israeli prime minister, having narrowly won reelection in January and formed a shaky coalition a few days before Obama's arrival, obviously felt politically safe to do so. On March 24, he telephoned Turkish prime minister Erdogan and, in a twenty-minute conversation, apologized for the loss of Turkish lives in the May 2010 Gaza-bound Peace Flotilla incident resulting from the actions of Israeli commandos; he also offered to make financial restitution to the families of those murdered. Erdogan agreed to restore diplomatic relations with Israel, but clearly there is no love lost between either party, and it is far from certain if they will ever become as cordial as they were prior to the Mavi Marmara attack.

With Israel's ties to two of its three regional partners collapsing, Washington is becoming increasingly worried. In early December 2011 then secretary of defense Leon Panetta essentially told Israel to "reach out and mend fences," rather than pursue policies that have "seen Israel's isolation from its traditional security partners in the region grow." With regard to the stalled Peace Process, Panetta said bluntly that Israel needs to "get to the damn table" with the Palestinians, unusually strong language from Israel's very valuable ally.[11]

Tired of Syria's unsuccessful months-long crackdown on its internal dissidents, Turkey's foreign minister, Ahmet Davutoglu, issued a warning to President Bashshar al-Asad on August 15, 2011, to end his government's brutal measures "immediately and unconditionally, warning that unspecified steps would be taken otherwise,"[12] a threat that Turks do not issue without having the muscle to back it up, though as yet they have been reluctant to do so. Having for several months allowed an umbrella political opposition group known as the Syrian National Council to operate in Turkey, Erdogan has also provided shelter to the commander and dozens of members of the Free Syrian Army, consisting of defectors from the Syrian Armed Forces, to plan and carry out attacks inside Syria from a base in southern Turkey. Three days after Erdogan's threat, U.S. Secretary of State Hillary Clinton, supported by the British, French, and German governments, issued a called for President Asad to "step aside," but with no accompanying threat as to what would happen if he didn't and no call for anyone specific to replace him. Predictably, President Asad rejected the demand. Two weeks later, on September 2, 2011, the EU banned all oil imports from Syria in order to cut the Asad regime's funding for the ongoing crackdown on dissent. Seven weeks later, on October 24, the United States withdrew its ambassador to Damascus, citing fears for his safety; the Syrians recalled their ambassador in a tit for tat, but such pressures had little impact. To date all efforts to pressure the Syrian regime have only succeeded in pushing President Asad into a corner from which, increasingly, there appears to be little escape. In a little-noted twist, 'Iraq's Shi'a prime minister, Nuri al-Maliki, perhaps in anticipation of what his American overseers might do, and also perhaps in response to pressure from his other minder, Iran, announced his support for President Asad on August 12, 2011, calling for the Syrian protesters "not to sabotage the state."[13] A few days later, he issued an even stronger statement, accusing the protesters of advancing the cause of Israel, claiming "the Zionists and Israel are the first and biggest beneficiaries of this whole process."[14] This appeal stood in stark contrast to his earlier strong support for the Shi'a protesters in Bahrain when they rose up against their minority Sunni rulers earlier in the year. A few days later, however, the Iranian foreign minister, obviously worried about the deteriorating situation in Syria, called on the regime to temper its crackdown on dissidents, and on November 11, 2011, the Arab League suspended Syria over the issue of brutality toward demonstrators. The Sunni minority in 'Iraq strongly supports the Syrian demonstrators, who are entirely Sunni from all appearances, and the Speaker of the 'Iraqi Parliament (identified in the *New York Times* on August 13 as a Sunni even though his name, al-Najafi, would indicate Shi'a roots) said that the Asad regime was "suppressing the freedoms of the Syrian people."[15] With the Turkish government taking the side of the protesters, and with apparent backing from leaders of the EU and the United States, Erdogan was clearly moving to advance his country's influence and interests in Syria, which less than a century ago was under Ottoman rule and had been since 1516.

Turkey has never been happy with the loss of territory imposed on it after the Ottoman Empire was dismembered following World War I. It did manage to re-acquire the district of Antakya (Antioch) in 1939 and has never given up its claim to Aleppo and other parts of Syria, as well as Mosul and much of northern 'Iraq. This includes the oil-rich region of Kirkuk, which has a substantial Turkish-speaking population mentioned earlier but also a much larger population of Kurds, who are currently enjoying autonomy and are as decidedly uninterested in the prospect of Turkish rule as they were with direct Arab control from Baghdad. There is, however, a long history of Pan-Turkism that advocated the unification of all Turkish-speaking populations of central Asia with the "fatherland" (*vatan*). It was strongly endorsed by the leaders of the Young Turk Revolution of 1908, including Atatürk and his more powerful rival at the time, Isma'il Enver Pasha, who, true to his beliefs, died trying to raise up the population of what is today Tajikistan in August 1922. Shortly after his death, the Bolsheviks put an end to anti-Communist activity in the area, and the movement was quashed in the short-run, though it definitely remained on the back burner in Turkish politics.

Today, Turkey is definitely the strongest player in the region. Its population is equal to Iran's and its economy is, as noted earlier, the eighteenth largest in the world. Although oil and gas reserves are limited, it has huge coal deposits, hydroelectric power from dams on the Tigris and Euphrates rivers, a more than self-sufficient agricultural base, expanding industrial production, and a sound road and rail infrastructure. Thanks to more than half a century of NATO membership, its military capabilities are without

peer, with the possible exception of Israel, but the number of its troops on
the ground far exceeds that of the Jewish state. It has hopes of joining the
European Common Market, which may not be realized in the near future,
but at least one obstacle has been removed now that there is civilian control
of the military.

The problem with the establishment of any pan-Turkish, Sunni "commonwealth" is that only one of its neighbors, Syria, has a majority Sunni
population, and it is currently in the throes of a conflict between that
majority and a minority Shi'a 'Alawi government. Two of the three countries
on its eastern border are Christian—Armenia and Georgia, both fearful of
any Turkish expansion in their direction—as well as the Shi'a powerhouse
Iran, and north of it Azerbayjan and the Russian province of Daghestan,
both Turkish-speaking but with heavily Shi'a majorities. The nearest Sunni
Turkish population is in Chechniya on the northern slopes of the Caucasus
beyond Georgia, which is firmly under Russian military control. The Turkish-speaking population of central Asia lies beyond the Caspian, divided
among former Soviet republics, notably Turkmenistan, Uzbekistan, Tajikistan, and Kazakhstan. The latter has a large Russian Orthodox population
as well as its own regional ambitions. Still, the potential is there to create
a "Sunni Crescent" that, with Pakistan to the east and Sa'udi Arabia to the
south, would geographically contain its Shi'a counterpart.

In another move to expand Turkey's influence on its southern flank,
given only tiny notice buried on page 9 of the *New York Times*, the prime
minister announced on August 19, 2011, that Turkey was establishing an
embassy in Somalia, where no major country had maintained a diplomatic
presence for years, in order "to draw attention to the famine sweeping the
country" as well as build a road from the airport to the center of Mogadishu, "dig wells to improve water supply and build schools and houses."[16]
Obviously, the Turks would not be going in without sufficient manpower
to protect their investment of resources in such a dangerously lawless environment. With such a visible establishment in a failed state in which only
al-Qa'ida and a beleaguered UN-armed peacekeeping force had heretofore managed to maintain a presence, Turkey would definitely be making
a statement about its foreign policy intentions in a remote corner of the
Sunni Arab world where no one else had for years dared to take risks.

There is little doubt that a Middle Eastern, mainly Sunni "commonwealth" with Turkey dominating the other players is something that has interested Erdogan for a long time. How he can achieve it is another matter.

Both Pakistan, which is in desperate need of some stabilizing influence in its increasingly fractured society, and Sa'udi Arabia, which lives in fear of threats from the most radical of its own ultra-conservative Wahhabi extremists, would welcome support from an increasingly powerful fellow-Sunni state. Any opposition from conservative religious elements in both countries will have lessened since three successive Erdogan victories have eroded the strong secular nature of Turkish society.

Having elected an Egyptian parliament in October 2011 dominated by the Muslim Brotherhood (dissolved by the ruling military council by order of the Mubarak-appointed Supreme Court on June 14, 2012, for alleged election "irregularities") and a Muslim Brother, Muhammad Mursi, as president on June 17, 2012, in a closely contested run-off election with former old-guard prime minister Ahmad Shafiq, though with his powers severely restricted by order of the military, Egypt might well be willing to join Turkey in a closer alliance. In such a scenario, Iran, 'Iraq, Hizbollah, and Hamas as well as Israel would feel, in a sense, surrounded. Perhaps in a bid to challenge Turkey's role in Egypt, Mahmud Ahmadinejad flew to Cairo in January 2013, the first time an Iranian sitting president had paid a state visit to Egypt since Shah Reza had fled there following the Islamic Revolution of 1979 that overthrew him. Although Ahmadinejad was courteously received by President Muhammad Mursi, his visit did not proceed without incident. While touring the Mosque of al-Hasan in the old city, a major Shi'a religious center during the Fatimid era, several Salafi extremists threw shoes at him, a sign of profound disrespect in Muslim society, as President George W. Bush learned to his discomfort on a visit to 'Iraq in December 2008. Following Turkey's near-severing of diplomatic ties with Israel, Erdogan visited Egypt to strengthen diplomatic and military ties with the post-Mubarak regime and announced that it had plans to increase Turkish naval presence in the eastern Mediterranean to stop "Israeli bullying," as Foreign Minister Davutoglu described it, with the ultimate aim of ending Israel's blockade of Gaza. These recent moves have underlined the obvious efforts of the Turkish government to expand its influence in the region.

One extremely important unanswered question is what impact the reportedly extensive oil and natural gas reserves recently discovered in the eastern Mediterranean will have, not only on Turkey's ambitions but on the economies of Cyprus, Israel, Lebanon, Syria, and, of course, Turkey itself. On March 30, 2013, Israel began production of natural gas from its first off-shore well. In addition, the expansion of U.S. gas and shale oil production may make the world's one remaining superpower an energy exporter once again. This could have an immense impact on the U.S. economy by reducing its reliance on Middle Eastern energy suppliers, and dramatically alter the importance of both Israel and the oil-rich Arabian kingdoms and principalities to U.S. diplomatic goals.

President Obama has already indicated that China and the Far East are priority number one in his second term. With the Middle East being potentially moved to the back burner, the Sunni-Shi'a rivalry might be allowed to play out its multiple conflicts in a less internationally charged environment. Regional leaders may already be jockeying for power with this possibility in mind.

Shortly after Mursi's election, he moved quickly to consolidate his power. On November 22, 2012, he issued a decree granting himself broad powers above any court as guardian of the revolution. Despite popular protests and street riots, he pushed forward with a referendum on a new constitution, which was approved with a comfortable majority on December 16, 2012, in apparently free and fair elections. Clearly Mursi, his Muslim Brethren, and Salafist supporters had won the day, at least for now.

How far Turkey is willing to go in establishing a "commonwealth" of Sunni nations in order to counter the influence of the "Shi'a Crescent" and the ambitions of a Greater Israel boils down to educated guesses. The one thing that the author has learned from observing the Middle East for more than fifty years is that there are few certainties. What can be said without much fear of contradiction is that nothing will change the Sunni-Shi'a divide any time soon. So long as Israel under its present administration continues to reject any peaceful solution to its problems with the Palestinians, except on its own narrow, uncompromising terms, both sides of the Muslim divide will focus on what each perceives to be its common enemy. As shown earlier in this conclusion, this need not be the case. It is up to the United States to make it clear to its self-proclaimed "sole democratic ally" in the Middle East that a solution must be reached. Then, and only then, will the hundreds of millions of Sunnis and Shi'as turn their attention back to each other, as they had done for centuries prior to the events of 1948, and allow the West time to catch its breath and, one hopes, prepare for whatever new and problematic developments lie down the road in this politically troubled and historically volatile region.

Appendix 1

The Traditional Islamic Calendar

The Islamic calendar is based on twelve lunar months of 28–29 days, for a total of 354–355 days annually, meaning that these months fall 11–12 days earlier each year according to the Western calendar. The Muslim year one corresponds to 622 AD and marks the flight of Muhammad and his followers to Yathrib from Mecca to escape persecution. All historical dates since then are designated AH (after Hijra) according to Muslim reckoning.

The most important months are the fasting month of Ramadan, the pilgrimage month of Dhu al-Hijjah, and the first month of the Muslim year, al-Muharram, the first ten days of which are observed as 'Ashura', in which Shi'a Muslims commemorate the suffering and death of their third imam, Husayn. The two principal feasts are that of 'Id al-Fitr, the three-day feast that ends the fasting month of Ramadan, and the 'Id al-Adha, the feast of sacrifice that follows the month of Pilgrimage, also three days, during which all Muslims slaughter a clean (*halal*) animal such as a sheep, goat, cow, or camel, as opposed to one that is forbidden (*haram*), namely the pig, to celebrate the sacrifice of Abraham (Ibrahim) who killed a ram instead of his son at God's command. In Islam, as noted earlier, the son in question is not Isaac but Ishmael (Isma'il), the son of his wife's servant Hagar, which is why Christians often referred to Muslims in earlier times as Ishmaelites. They also referred to Islam as "Hagarism," after Isma'il's mother (medieval Armenian sources speak of Muslims as Hagaratsik— the descendants of Hagar). In 1977 two British scholars, Patricia Crone and Michael Cook, published a controversial study titled "Hagarism: The Making of the Islamic World," which viewed early Islamic development, based on seventh-century Armenian, Greek (including the treatise *On Heresies* by St. John of Damascus), Syriac, and other contemporary sources, as an outgrowth of Messianic Judaism.

Other minor feasts include the Prophet's birthday. For strict Muslims, no other birthdays, including one's own, are allowed to be celebrated, such commemorations being considered modern Christian aberrations. All Muslim feasts are calculated according to the observation of the new moon, and it is a matter of sectarian pride when the new moon is sighted—the Shi'a usually failing to see the new moon at the end of the month until one day after the Sunnis so as to prolong the fast of Ramadan and thus appear more righteous. The Druze, who do not follow the outward observance of the Five Pillars, having their own seven requirements of faith, celebrate only the Feast of al-Adha, without the pilgrimage that precedes it. They do not observe either the fasting month of Ramadan or the Feast that breaks the fast (al-Fitr), though individual Druze are free to do so if they choose.

Muslims take great pride in the rigors of the Ramadan fast, which requires abstinence from food, drink, and sexual activity from dawn to dusk. This can be particularly demanding when it falls in the hot months and lengthy days of summer as it currently does. Such abstinence, however, is not entirely peculiar to Islam and appears to have its roots in Eastern Christianity, whose adherents, both Orthodox and Catholic, follow a strict regime of fasting, abstaining from all food and drink from midnight to noon, during the forty days of Great Lent that precedes Easter. And whereas Muslims are allowed to eat whatever they chose every day during Ramadan when they break the fast with the evening meal of *iftar*—which despite early Islamic practice has become a massive banquet of every imaginable delicacy followed by a huge intake of sweets that are customarily consumed only during this month—Eastern Christians are subject to strict dietary restrictions throughout Advent (the forty days before Christmas), Great Lent, and other fasting days, including most Wednesdays and Fridays. In multi-confessional Lebanon, the price of meat and chicken escalates during Ramadan and drops during Advent and Lent, whereas that of fish and shellfish soars during those lengthy Christian fasting periods.

Ramadan was originally intended by the Prophet to be a month of spiritual regeneration as well as fasting, which he traditionally broke with a few dates. While the more pious Muslims still follow his example, the majority takes Ramadan as an excuse for excessive feasting and as a rule gains weight during the process. One important event during the holy month is the so-called Night of Power (Laylat al-Qadr), which occurs on an odd-numbered day during the last ten days of the month and commemorates the actual first revelation of Qur'anic scripture. Believers stay up the whole night praying, believing that God will pay particular attention to their requests on this auspicious date.

A curious modern-day Ramadan practice that the author has observed in Lebanon is the abstinence from alcohol, specifically during this month. The Qur'an proscribes the consumption of *khamr*, or date wine, to all Muslims at all times, probably because of the excessive consumption of this mildly alcoholic beverage during the poetry festivals of pre-Islamic Arabia that led to widespread drunkenness and lapses of morality. A popular Islamic saying states that "wine is the vessel of sin" (*al-khamr jima' al-ithm*). Pure alcohol by process of distillation is an invention of later Islamic society, and the word (*al-kuhul*) is Arabic. Any form of alcoholic drink, not just date wine, is regarded by all Islamic schools of law as prohibited—a fact that is frequently ignored by many Muslims, both Sunni and Shi'a, throughout the Islamic World—but for some reason those who do consume it have come to think that if they give it up during Ramadan they will be excused for imbibing the rest of the year! Shops and restaurants that usually sell or serve alcohol, even those run by and catering to Christians, are often pressured to take it off their shelves and menus during this period as a sign of respect to the sensibilities of their Muslim neighbors. Similarly, Christians living in Muslim areas as a rule do not publicly consume food or drink during daylight hours. The social pressure on Muslims to conform to the Ramadan fast is very strong, though many in fact do not (but almost always in secret), and children under the age of puberty, the aged, the sick, and travelers are normally exempted.

By and large, the mainstream Shi'a observe the traditional Sunni feasts and fasts, though the extremist ghulat sects generally do not, with some exceptions like the Druze (who celebrate only the 'Id al-Adha) and the 'Alawi (who observe a number of Muslim, Christian, and even pagan Persian holidays). The principal Shi'a feast, 'Ashura', which Sunnis tend to ignore or celebrate for other reasons (chiefly the safe passage of Moses and the children of Israel through the Red Sea), is the ten-day celebration commemorating the martyrdom of 'Husayn, his family, and followers near Karbala' in 680. The high point is the "passion play" (*ta'ziya*) reenacting the massacre, which is preceded by processions of frenzied followers clad in mourning black crying out the names of Husayn, Hasan, and their father 'Ali, using his original name, Haydar. The latter was given to the baby by his mother before the prophet, on seeing his cousin for the first time, bestowed on him the title of "exalted" (*'ali*). At the same time, the worshippers curse the names of the first three caliphs, Abu Bakr, 'Umar, and 'Uthman. In many Shi'a population centers, the ceremony is accompanied by flagellation and deliberate ceremonial shedding of blood by men and boys, even infants. The author witnessed the 'Ashura' celebrations in al-Nabatiyya, south Lebanon, in June 1993, where the flagellants made small incisions on their foreheads and then began their procession around the site of the passion play, constantly striking the wound to make it bleed profusely, all the while shouting the names of Haydar and Husayn. On that occasion, numerous Red Cross volunteers and ambulances were very much in evidence. For Sunnis, 'Ashura' is celebrated, if at all, with two days of fasting in remembrance of the deliverance of the Jews from Pharaoh by Moses (Musa), and also as the day when the Ark of Noah (Nuh) came to rest on dry land, an observance which Muhammad, according to tradition, is said to have initiated.

Other exclusively Shi'a religious celebrations include the *arba'in*, or "forty," which takes place every year on the fortieth day after 'Ashura'. Remembrance services forty days after the death of a family member are common for both Muslims and Eastern Christians after their death, but this Shi 'a observance not only commemorates the killing of the third imam but in particular the suffering and death of many of Husayn's household from thirst and exposure, especially the women and children who were compelled to travel across the desert from Karbala' to Damascus after their capture by the caliph Yazid's forces following the martyrdom of Husayn. In addition to the Prophet's birthday, the Shi'a also celebrate that of the twelfth imam, Muhammad al-Mahdi, on the fifteenth day of the month of *Sha'ban*, as well as the *'Id al-Ghadir* on the eighteenth day of *Dhu al-Hijjah*, which marks what Shi'a believe to be an announcement of the imamate of 'Ali by the prophet Muhammad before a large assembly of Muslims. According to the Hadith of the "Pond" or "Pool" (*ghadir*) of Khumm, Muhammad told his followers that whomever's master/client (*mawla*) I am, so is he also 'Ali's. Sunnis do not deny the veracity of this Hadith, but for Shi'a it is a festive occasion for reaffirming their belief in Islam and exchanging gifts. Extremist Sunnis ignore it completely, recognizing only the two central Muslim festivals, the 'Id al-Fitr at the end of the fasting month of Ramadan and the 'Id al-Adha, which concludes the annual pilgrimage to Mecca and Medina as worthy of celebration.

Appendix 2

Chronology

568–70   Birth of the Prophet Muhammad

610   Revelations of the Qur'an begin at Mecca, and continue up until the prophet's death.

613   Muhammad begins preaching his new religion and his few early followers start to pray in public.

614–17   Small numbers of early Muslims flee persecution in Mecca to the protection of the Christian Ethiopian emperor in Axum.

622   Muhammad and most of his followers flee to al-Madina to escape efforts by the pagan establishment in Mecca to stamp out the new religion. This "flight" (al-Hijra) marks the beginning of the Islamic Calendar.

630   Muhammad returns to Mecca in triumph.

632   Muhammad dies and is buried at al-Madina. Abu Bakr is elected successor, or caliph (khalifa).

634   Abu Bakr dies after restoring Muslim rule over the Arabian Peninsula during the al-Riddah (secession) wars.

636   Muslim wars of conquest begin. Battles of Yarmuk and al-Qadisiyyah.

637   Jerusalem is taken following the Muslim victory over the Byzantines at the battle of Yarmuk, and soon all of Greater Syria is under Muslim sway. 'Iraq and Iran are overrun following the decisive battle of al-Qadisiyya. Egypt soon follows.

644   'Umar is assassinated, succeeded by 'Uthman.

656   'Uthman is in turn assassinated, succeeded by Muhammad's cousin and son-in-law 'Ali.

657   Battle of Siffin.

658   The dissident Kharijites defect from the main body (umma) of Islam following the Battle of Siffin and are in turn defeated by 'Ali at the Battle of Nahwaran.

661   'Ali is assassinated by a Kharijite survivor of Nahwaran and is suc-
       ceeded by Mu'awiya, governor of Syria, who moves the caliphal
       capital from al-Madina to Damascus where an Umayyad dynasty
       is established. Supporters of 'Ali dispute Mu'awiya's claim to suc-
       cession, giving their allegiance to 'Ali's descendants through his
       wife, Fatima, Muhammad's only surviving child, and their two
       sons, Hasan and Husayn, known as imams.

680   Mu'awiya dies and is succeeded by his son Yazid I. 'Ali's second
       son, Husayn, leads a small band of seventy-two followers to Kufa
       in 'Iraq to lay claim to the caliphate, but he and all his compan-
       ions are killed by a thousand-man army loyal to Yazid on Octo-
       ber 10. This date marks the defining break between the main-
       stream Sunnis loyal to the Umayyad dynasty and the breakaway
       Shi'a. The event is commemorated every year by the Shi'a during
       the first ten days of the Islamic month of Muharram, known as
       'Ashura'.

712   The first split in Shi'a ranks occurs following the death of the
       fourth imam. Those who rejected the succession of the fifth
       imam, Muhammad al-Baqir, in favor of his brother Zayd are
       known today as Zaydis or "Fivers." Shortly thereafter, they es-
       tablish a dynasty in Yemen which survives until 1962. Muslim
       armies cross from Morocco into Spain at Gibraltar.

732   Muslim armies continue to expand both eastward into Central
       Asia and the western Indian subcontinent (Sind, now Pakistan)
       and westward across North Africa into Spain and over the Pyre-
       nees into France but are stopped at a battle near Poitiers in central
       France by an army led by Charles Martel, father of Charlemagne.

750   The Umayyad dynasty in Damascus is overthrown by the 'Ab-
       basids who move the capital from Damascus to Baghdad.

756   A second Umayyad dynasty is established in Cordoba, Spain, by
       'Abd al-Rahman I, the only member of his family who managed
       to escape massacre by the 'Abbasids.

765   A second major split in Shi'a Islam develops following the death
       of the sixth imam, Ja'far al-Sadiq. Those loyal to his eldest son
       and heir, Isma'il, but who predeceased his father, gave their sup-
       port to Isma'il's son, Muhammad as the true seventh imam, as
       opposed to Musa al-Kadzim, Ja'far's third surviving son whom
       the majority, who came to be known as "Twelvers" (ithn'ashari),

accept as the imam. Those who support the succession of Isma'il's son and heirs are referred to as Isma'ilis or "Seveners." The Isma'ili line of succession remains unbroken. The current imam—the forty-ninth—is the Agha Khan Karim, born in 1936.

786–809   The reign of caliph Harun al-Rashid marks the golden age of 'Abbasid rule in Baghdad.

869–889   The Zanji rebellion in southern 'Iraq where Shi'a form the majority threatens the stability of the 'Abbasid caliphate.

873   In the midst of the Zanji rebellion, the last imam of the Twelver Shi'a disappears at age five, and according to them enters into a state of occultation from which he will return at the End of Time as the mahdi, or precursor-redeemer expected by all Muslims, both Sunni and Shi'a, to bring in the Day of Judgment. In the meantime, he is the Hidden Imam whose return is expected at any moment.

909   An Isma'ili dynasty, known as the Fatimids, is established in Tunis, gradually extending its authority over much of North Africa.

922   An early Sufi mystic, Mansur al-Hallaj, is crucified in Baghdad for his beliefs. They are later embraced by the great Sunni theologian, al-Ghazali (1058–1111).

930   An Isma'ili dynasty known as the Qarmatians, based in Bahrain and eastern Arabia, sacks Mecca, slaughtering as many as twenty thousand Sunni pilgrims and absconding with the sacred Black Stone housed in Islam's holiest site, al-Ka'ba (the focus of the annual Meccan pilgrimage—later ransomed), and threaten to march on Baghdad.

945–1055   The Zaydi Shi'a Buwayhid Dynasty takes control of 'Iraq and Iran from the nominal rule of the nowpowerful 'Abbasid caliphate but does not impose its faith on the majority Sunni population.

969   Egypt falls to the Fatimids, who establish their capital at Cairo.

1009   The Church of the Holy Sepulcher in Jerusalem is destroyed at the order of Fatimid Caliph al-Hakim bi-'Amr-Allah.

1017   Caliph al-Hakim declares himself to be the embodiment of the Godhead and demands obeisance from his subjects.

1021   Caliph al-Hakim disappears mysteriously in the desert outside Cairo. His followers, persecuted by al-Hakim's son and successor, al-Zahir, flee to the Lebanese mountains where they entrench themselves as the Druze sect.

1031	Umayyad Caliphate in Spain ends, replaced by a succession of North African dynasties that lasted until Granada fell to the Spanish in 1492.
1054	A schism between the Catholic West and Orthodox East leads to the weakening of the Byzantine Empire in its fight to survive Muslim conquest.
1071	Seljuk Turks defeat a Byzantine army at Manzikert in Armenia, opening up all of Anatolia to Turkish Muslim occupation.
1095	Pope Urban II proclaims a Crusade to liberate Jerusalem from Muslim rule in response to an appeal by the Byzantine emperor Alexius Comnenus for aid against the advancing Seljuks.
1099	Crusader armies recapture Jerusalem from Islamic control, establishing a Western Christian presence in the region that lasts for two hundred years.
1144	Muslims reconquer the County of Edessa, one of the four Crusader principalities established after 1099, resulting in 1146 in the Second Crusade, which fails to achieve anything.
1171	Sunni Kurdish military leader Salah al-Din al-Ayyubi (Saladin) ends Fatimid rule in Egypt and establishes his own Ayyubi dynasty.
1187	Saladin defeats Crusader armies at the Battle of Hattin, leading to the reconquest of Jerusalem for Islam a few months later. The Third Crusade, launched in 1189 to reconquer Jerusalem, fails in its goal but reestablishes its presence in Acre on the Palestinian coast, where the Crusaders are left with a very narrow band of territory that is increasingly threatened.
1204	The army of the Fourth Crusade conquers and plunders Constantinople, establishing a short-lived Latin Empire (1204–1261) that leaves the Byzantine Empire terminally weakened and vulnerable to Turkish conquest.
1207– 1263	The greatest of all Sufi figures, Jalal al-Din al-Rumi, establishes a religious order based in Konya, central Anatolia, where it continues to attract devotees.
1250	The last Ayyubid ruler of Egypt is overthrown and replaced by a dynasty of Mamluk sultans.
1258	The last 'Abbasid caliph of Baghdad is killed in the wake of the Mongol capture and destruction of Baghdad. The Mamluk sultans in Cairo claim to be the heirs to the 'Abbasid caliphate.

1260	Advancing Mongol armies are turned back by the Mamluk sultan Baybars at the Battle of 'Ayn Jalut near Nazareth in Palestine.
1268	Antioch is retaken by Baybars for Islam and virtually destroyed.
1291	Acre, the last bastion of Crusader presence in mainland Syria, is retaken by Baybars's successor.
1331	The Ottoman (Osmanli) Turks capture Nicaea (Iznik) and establish their capital at nearby Bursa, threatening the rapidly shrinking Byzantine domain.
1365	Ottomans cross into Europe, taking the city of Adrianople (Edirne) and advancing into the heart of the Balkans. Constantinople is now surrounded by Ottoman forces.
1389	Ottoman Sultan Bayezid I defeats Serbian forces at the Battle of Kosovo, bringing most of the Balkans under Muslim control.
1396	A Crusade launched, largely by Hungarians, to recover the loss of territory to the Ottomans is thoroughly defeated at the Battle of Nicopolis in Bulgaria. Muslim control of the Balkans is secured.
1430	Thessaloniki (Salonica) falls to the Ottomans.
1453	Constantinople falls to Ottoman sultan Mehmet II. The Byzantine Empire ceases to exist with the fall of Trebizond eight years later.
1492	The last Muslim ruler of Granada is forced from Spain by King Ferdinand and Queen Isabella. In the same year, which saw Christopher Columbus's first voyage to the New World, Muslims and Jews who refuse conversion are expelled from the Iberian Peninsula. The Muslims relocate to North Africa while most of the Jews move to the Ottoman Empire, which welcomed them, settling principally in Thessaloniki, where they remain a large presence until they are deported to concentration camps and annihilated by the Germans after their invasion of Greece in 1941. No more than five thousand Jews remain in Greece today.
1501	A new Shi'a dynasty, the Safavids—the first since the Fall of the Fatimids in 1171—comes to power in Iran under Isma'il I. One of his first acts is to impose the Shi'a faith of the country which up until then had been staunchly Sunni. During the reign of Shah 'Abbas I (1587–1629), Safavid rule stretches from 'Iraq to Pakistan and well into Central Asia.
1516	The Ottoman Sultan Selim I ("The Grim") defeats the last Mamluk ruler of Egypt and brings Syria and Egypt under Ottoman sway.

1520–1566	Sultan Selim's son, Sulayman "the Magnificent," brings in the golden age of Ottoman power and prestige.
1526	Sulayman defeats the Hungarians at the Battle of Mohacs and advances toward Vienna.
1529	Sulayman's siege of Vienna ends in failure, thus reducing Ottoman pressure of the heart of Christian Europe.
1571	At the Battle of Lepanto, in the Gulf of Corinth, Catholic naval forces under Don Juan of Austria defeat the Ottoman fleet, but no permanent damage is done to Ottoman control of the Balkans.
1617–1633	Fakhr al-Din II, a Druze from the princely Ma'an family, establishes a large autonomous region within the Ottoman Empire encompassing what is today Lebanon and much of Syria and Palestine. Thought to have converted to Maronite Christianity, he invited Jesuit priests from Italy and France to establish schools and printing presses throughout the region. Sultan Murad IV was finally able to engineer his capture, and he was taken to Istanbul where he and three of his sons were convicted of "apostasy" and executed. He is widely regarded by Druze and Christians as the Father of Modern Lebanon.
1683	The Second Ottoman Siege of Vienna also fails, after which the empire's power and presence in Europe begin to decline rapidly.
1711	At the Battle of 'Ayn Dara in central Lebanon, the Ma'anid faction of the Druze defeat their Yasbaki rivals, most of whom flee to southern Syria. There they establish a second Druze presence in what comes to be known as the Jabal al-Duruz, or the Druze Mountain, now the southernmost province of Syria, al-Suwayda, where they make up 90 percent of the population. The remaining Yazbakis in Lebanon are a minority, attached to the Arslan family, while the descendants of the Ma'anids form the majority Junbalat faction.
1740	A strict form of Sunni Islam named after its founder, Muhammad Ibn 'abd al-Wahhab, takes root in the central Najd region of the Arabian Peninsula under the protection of the ruling shaykh, Muhammad Ibn Sa'ud. The Wahhabis were, and are, strongly anti-Shi'a, and in 1802 they raid and raze the Shi'a shrines of 'Ali and Husayn in 'Iraq, killing many Shi'a faithful in the process.
1832	Greece achieves its independence from the Ottoman Empire after a struggle which began in 1821. European assistance was

instrumental in their success, and a Bavarian king is imposed on the Greeks as the price of their aid. Ottoman power in the Balkans continues to decline.

1830   The French invade and occupy Algeria. The leader of the Muslim opposition, Prince Abdel Kader al-Jaza'iri, successfully resists French occupation until finally surrendering in 1847. He accepts exile and spends most of the rest of his life in Damascus, where he was instrumental in saving many Christian lives during the Massacres of 1860 in Lebanon by Druzes and in Damascus by Sunnis. The French solidify their colonial presence, later expanding their control to Tunisia and Morocco. Using the 1860 massacres as a pretext, the French under Napoleon II send troops to Beirut and force the government in Istanbul to accept an autonomous region of Mount Lebanon with a Maronite Christian majority and Christian (but not Maronite) governor, which lasted until the outbreak of war in 1914.

1856   The Tanzimat reforms imposed on the Ottomans by Western Powers grant increased rights to non-Muslim communities in the empire.

1877   The last Muslim Mogul ruler of India is replaced by Queen Victoria, who is crowned Empress of India as the British take control of the entire subcontinent, following the transfer of power from the East India Company to the Crown in the wake of the 1857 Mutiny.

1882   The British occupy Egypt, extending their control south into the Sudan in 1898.

1908   The Young Turk Revolution overthrows the sitting sultan and makes his successor a nominal ruler.

1911–
1913   The Balkan Wars between the Ottomans and their enemies drive Turkey out of all but a small corner of the Balkans. Albania gains its independence and Italy occupies Libya and the Dodecanese Islands.

1914   The Ottoman Empire enters World War I on the side of Germany.

1915   The defeat of the British and their allies at Gallipoli by the Turks under a rising leader, Mustafa Kemal, later called Atatürk, prevents them from establishing a direct route of contact with the Russians, thus saving Istanbul for Islam and paving the way for the Bolshevik Revolution two years later. In the same year, the

British and French begin secret negotiations to partition the Ottoman Empire between them once victory is achieved.

1916   Sykes-Picot Agreement is signed by Britain and France, without assent of the Russians, to divide the Arab provinces of the Ottoman Empire (outside the Arabian Peninsula) into British and French spheres of influence.

1917   Britain publishes the Balfour Declaration, which calls for the establishment of a "homeland" for the Jews in Palestine.

1918   The Ottoman Empire surrenders to the Allied Powers at Mudros on October 30. British and French troops occupy Istanbul from 1919–1922.

1919   At the Peace Conference in Versailles, the Treaty of Sèvres signed by Turkey and the victorious Allies gives much of the former Ottoman territories in Asia to Britain and France. The Greeks take the opportunity to occupy Smyrna (Izmir) and its surrounding countryside.

1920   The British establish a League of Nations Mandate in Palestine and open the country to Jewish-Zionist immigration and settlement.

1920   The French establish a League of Nations Mandate in Syria and Lebanon.

1920   The British install Prince Faysal, son of Sharif Husayn of Mecca who had led the Arab resistance to the Turks during World War I, as king of the newly established British League of Nations Mandate over 'Iraq. His brother 'Abdallah is made king of Transjordan. Husayn remains in Mecca but is overthrown four years later by the Wahhabi princes of the Najd in the interior of the Arabian Peninsula under 'Abd al-'Aziz Ibn Sa'ud.

1922   Ataturk expels the Greeks from Smyrna and establishes a secular Turkish Republic.

1923   The Treaty of Lausanne replaces the Treaty of Sèvres and recognizes Turkish sovereignty over the strategic straits linking the Black Sea to the Mediterranean.

1928   Egyptian school teacher Hasan al-Banna establishes the Society of Muslim Brothers (*Ikhwan al-Muslimin*).

1929   Fierce confrontations between Zionist settlers and Palestinian Arabs break out in Hebron, a city sacred to both as the burial site of Abraham. Sixty-seven Jews are killed.

1932   Antun Sa'ada founds the Syrian Social Nationalist Party.

1939   The British publish a White Paper calling for a strict limit to Jewish immigration to Palestine, but World War II intervenes to prevent its implementation.

1940   Michel 'Aflaq cofounds and leads the secular Renaissance (al-Bath) Party, which establishes a strong political presence in Syria and 'Iraq.

1947   Weakened by the War, Britain announces it is terminating the Palestinian Mandate and turns its fate over to the League of Nations' successor, the United Nations, which calls for the partition of the territory between Arabs and Jews.

1947–   The Arabs reject the partition plan, which gives a majority of
1949   the land to the Jews, who comprise only a third of the population. In the ensuing conflict, the Jews occupy all but about a fifth of the territory of the former mandate, declaring the independence of the State of Israel on May 1, 1948. Most of the remaining part of Palestine, including East Jerusalem, now called the West Bank, is annexed by King 'Abdallah of Transjordan to form a new state called Jordan. The Gaza Strip is occupied by Egypt.

1964   The Palestinian Liberation Organization (PLO) is established and leads the opposition to Israel's occupation of Gaza, the West Bank and East Jerusalem.

1967   Israel invades Jordan, Syria, and Egypt in what is known as the Six-Day War. Jordan's Palestinian territories are occupied by Israel, as are the Golan Heights in southeastern Syria and the Sinai Peninsula of Egypt. The Suez Canal is closed.

1973   The Egyptians launch a surprise attack in what is known as the Ramadan/Yom Kippur War and manage to secure the east bank of the Suez Canal and reopen it to international traffic. Eventually, the Sinai Peninsula is restored to Egyptian control.

1979   The shah of Iran is overthrown in a coup led by forces loyal to the exiled Grand Ayatollah Khomeini, and a Shi'a Islamic Republic is proclaimed.

1982   Israel invades Lebanon and remains in control of much of the solidly Shi'a southern part of the country, until they leave in the face of strong popular opposition led by Hizbollah forces in 2000.

1985   Hizbollah publishes its manifesto, calling for the expulsion of Israeli forces from Lebanon and ultimately Palestine.

1990   'Iraq invades Kuwait but is driven out by a coalition of American forces and their allies six months later. They fail to continue the war into 'Iraq, and Saddam Husayn remains in power, persecuting his Shi'a and Kurdish subjects, whom he suspected of disloyalty.

1993   The Oslo Accords grant a measure of autonomy to what is called the Palestine Authority in parts of Gaza and the West Bank.

1995   The assassination of Prime Minister Itzhak Rabin by a Yemeni right-wing Jewish fanatic brings the Peace Process to a standstill.

2001   Terrorists loyal to al-Qa'ida launch a successful aerial attack on the Twin Towers in New York and the Pentagon in Washington, D.C., on September 11. More than three thousand people are killed. The United States responds by invading Afghanistan, where the Taliban government had been harboring al-Qa'ida leader Usama bin Ladin.

2003   Citing fears, later shown to be unfounded, that Saddam Husayn was storing weapons of mass destruction, the United States and some of its allies launched the Second Gulf War. 'Iraq is occupied and Saddam goes into hiding. He is found and captured the following year, brought to trial, and hanged.

2011   The Arab Spring uprisings beginning in January lead to the overthrow of dictatorial regimes in Tunisia, Egypt, Libya, and Yemen. Attempts to oust the Alawite/Shi'a Syrian president Bashshar al-Asad by the largely Sunni Free Syrian Army have to date been unsuccessful. Usama bin Ladin is tracked down to a hideout in Abbottabad, Pakistan, and is taken out by a U.S. Navy Seals raid on May 2. Islamic religious parties, led by the Muslim Brotherhood, win control of Egyptian parliament.

2012   Muhammad Mursi becomes the first Muslim Brotherhood president of Egypt and first Islamist head of state in the Arab world in run-off elections on June 16 and 17.

Appendix 3
Table of Shi'a Imams

The Twelver (Ithna'ashari) Canon

1. 'Ali Ibn Abu-Talib, martyred at the hands of a Kharijite assassin in 661 and buried at his shrine in al-Najaf, 'Iraq.
2. Hasan Ibn 'Ali, the elder son of 'Ali and his wife Fatima al-Zahra (The Radiant), only surviving child of the Prophet Muhammad. He was allegedly poisoned by one of his wives in Medina in 670 on the orders of the first Umayyad caliph, Mu'awiya, and buried there.
3. Husayn Ibn 'Ali, the Sayyid al-Shuhada' (Lord of the Martyrs), the younger son of 'Ali and Fatima, killed in 680 at the Battle of Karbala on the orders of the second Umayyad caliph, Yazid I, and later buried at his shrine in Karbala', 'Iraq.
4. 'Ali Ibn Husayn, Zayn al-'Abidin (Beauty of the Faithful), the only son of Husayn to survive the battle of Karbala'. He was allegedly poisoned in 712, according to Shi'a sources, and buried in Medina.
5. Muhammad al-Baqir, allegedly poisoned on the orders of the Umayyad caliph Hisham Ibn 'Abd al-Malik in 732 and buried in Medina next to his father.
6. Ja'far al-Sadiq, allegedly poisoned on the orders of the Abbasid caliph al-Mansur in 765 and buried in Medina next to his father. His tomb and those of his father, Muhammad; grandfather 'Ali ibn Husayn; and great-uncle Hasan Ibn 'Ali were destroyed by the Wahhabis in 1925 during the conquest of the Holy Cities of Mecca and Medina by Sultan 'Abd al-Aziz Ibn Sa'ud of al-Najd (later king of Sa'udi Arabia).
7. Musa al-Kadzim (Kazem), allegedly poisoned on the orders of the Abbasid caliph Harun al-Rashid in 799 and buried in the great mosque/shrine of al-Kadzimayn in Baghdad.

8. 'Ali Ibn Musa al-Rida (Reza), allegedly poisoned on the orders of the 'Abbasid caliph al-Ma'mun and buried in a mosque/shrine dedicated to him in Mashhad in eastern Iran.

9. Muhammad Ibn 'Ali, al-Jawad al-Taqi, allegedly poisoned on the orders of the 'Abbasid caliph al-Mu'tasim in 835 at the age of twenty-five and buried next to his grandfather in the great mosque/shrine of al-Kadzimayn.

10. 'Ali Ibn Muhammad al-Hadi, poisoned (he is said to have died a painful and lingering death) in 868 and buried at the Golden Mosque of al-Hadi and al-'Askari in Samarra, 'Iraq.

11. Hasan al-'Askari, son of 'Ali al-Hadi, lived most of his life under Abbasid house arrest and was poisoned in 874, aged twenty-eight, and buried at the Golden Mosque in Samarra.

12. Muhammad al-Mahdi, disappeared after his father's death in the crypt of the Golden Mosque, 'Iraq, at age five and is believed by Twelver Shi'a to have entered into a state of occultation (*ghayba*) from which he will emerge to bring in the Last Days.

The Fiver (Zaydi) Canon

1–4. The Zaydis accept the first four Twelver imams but believe their fifth, Zayd Ibn 'Ali (al-Shahid, or Martyr, 695–740), was the correct successor to his father because, unlike his brother, Muhammad al-Baqir, he fought against Umayyad injustice. His successors established an imamate in Yemen that survived until 1962, when the 111th Zaydi imam, Muhammad al-Badr (1926–1978), was overthrown by an Egyptian-backed republican military coup.

The Sevener (Isma'ili) Canon

1–6. The Isma'ilis accept the first six Twelver imams but believe their seventh to have been Isma'il Ibn Ja'far, one of the sixth imam's two sons by his first wife. According to Sevener tradition, Ja'far proclaimed Isma'il to be his successor, but at some point after that, Isma'il predeceased his father. The Twelvers reject this, recognizing a younger son of the sixth imam (by a second wife) who survived his father, Musa, as the rightful seventh imam. Isma'il is buried at the Maqam al-Imam (Shrine of the Imam) in Salmiyya, Syria. The Isma'ili imamate continued through Isma'il's son Muhammad and his heirs. Prince Karim IV Aga Khan (b. 1936) is acknowledged by his followers as the forty-ninth successor through the Nizari branch of the Isma'ili imamate, established after the fall of the Isma'ili Fatimid Empire in 1171, and bearer of the sacred aura, "Light of God" (Nur Allah).

For three generations, the princes of the Isma'ili royal family have produced heirs by women from other than their own community. Although Prince Karim's fifty-to-twenty-million Sevener followers, apart from several hundred thousand Arabs in Syria and the Arabian Peninsula, are entirely of Iranian, Afghan, Pakistani, and Indian origin, he, however, has very little Isma'ili ancestry—and his son and heir even less. His grandmother was an Italian ballerina with the Monte Carlo opera, and his mother the daughter of a minor English aristocrat, making him 75 percent of European heritage. Karim's heir, Rahim, is the second child of his first marriage to an English model, making his son seven-eighths European. Rahim announced his engagement to an American model of European ancestry in the spring of 2013, which means that if they have an heir, there may be an Aga Khan Sevener imam who is only one-sixteenth Isma'ili.[1]

Prince Karim's grandmother was the second of four wives of his grandfather, Sir Sultan Muhammad Shah, third Aga Khan (1877–1957) and the forty-eighth Nizari Sevener imam. His father, the well-known international playboy and bon-vivant, Prince Aly Aga Khan (1911–1960), married Prince Karim's mother, in May 1936, shortly after her divorce from a member of the Guinness family became final. Their son was born seven months later. Prince Aly divorced Karim's mother in 1949 and was famously remarried to the American actress Rita Hayworth the same year in a ceremony and reception that defined ultra-wealthy excess—pounds of Beluga caviar and endless bottles of the finest Champagne. Concurrently he had many mistresses, including the Democratic Party fund-raiser and later U.S. ambassador to France, Pamela Digby Churchill Harriman. Because of Aly's profligate ways, his father, on his death in 1957, overlooked the playboy prince in his will and declared his grandson, at the time a Harvard undergraduate, to be his successor as the forty-ninth Isma'ili imam. Prince Aly died in a car crash three years later in Paris and was buried in the Isma'ili Shrine of the Imam in Salmiyya, Syria. In 1969 Karim married his English first wife (they were divorced in 1995 after she accused him of multiple infidelities), by whom he had three children, including his heir, Rahim, in 1971. Prince Karim has spent much of his adult life pursuing international business ventures including the famous Costa Smeralda resort for the rich and famous in Sardinia, Italy. On May 1, 2013, Prince Rahim, a graduate of Brown University, announced his engagement, at age forty-two, to a twenty-four-year-old American "super model" from Seattle.[2]

One cannot help but wonder what pious and abstemious Sevener imams like Muhammad al-Baqir and Ja'far al-Sadiq would make of the extravagant example their more recent successors have set for the hard-working and generally frugal Isma'ili faithful around the world. One of the few things they have in common, like their Druze first cousins, is their undeniable and commendable benevolence.

Notes

Introduction

1. Robert Betts, "The Real Islam: Robert Betts Sees a Divided Culture," *The (London) Tablet,* January 30, 1988.

1. The Rise of Islam and Its Early Divisions

1. Acts 2:11 (King James Version): "Cretans and Arabians, we do hear them speak in our tongues the wonderful works of God." Gal. 1:17 (King James Version): "Neither went I up to Jerusalem to them which were apostles before me, but I went into Arabia and returned again unto Damascus."

2. Andrew Louth, *Saint John Damascene: Tradition and Originality in Byzantine Theology* (Oxford: Oxford University Press, 2002), 78, 80

3. Dante Alighieri, "Canto XXVIII," in *The Portable Dante,* trans. and ed. Mark Musa (London: Penguin, 1995), 151–52.

4. Abd al-Malik Ibn Hishām, *The Life of Muhammad, Apostle of Allah [by] Ibn Ishaq,* ed. Michael Edwardes (London: Folio Society, 1964), 129; and W. Montgomery Watt, *Muhammad at Medina* (Oxford: Clarendon Press, 1956), 214. Polygamy is specifically mention in the Qur'an only in chapter 4, notably verse 3, and stresses that the primary reason for allowing it is the protection of widows and orphans and not (by implication) the satisfaction of sexual desire. Other verses and Hadiths stress the importance of treating all wives and children equally. In many secular Muslim societies, like Turkey, polygamy is illegal. Overall, only a tiny fraction (an estimated 1–3 percent) of Muslims worldwide are participants in multipartner marriages.

5. Edwardes, *Life of Muhammad,* 139.

6. Watt, *Muhammad at Medina,* 219.

7. This Hadith quotes Muhammad as saying that "the Jews have 71 sects, the Christians 72, but my religion will have 73." This famous Hadith occurs in a number of collections. My citation is from Book 40, #4579, of the *Kitab al-Tahurah* (Book of Purification) of Sunan Abu Dawwud (d. 888).

8. Matti Moosa, *Extremist Shiites: The Ghulat Sects* (Syracuse, NY: Syracuse University Press, 1988), 84.

9. So rigid is the Druze attitude to marriage that once divorced a couple may never remarry each other nor are they allowed to be present together in the same house. Aharon Layish, *Marriage, Divorce, and Successsion in the Druze Family* (Leiden, Holland: E. J. Brill, 1982), 181–82.

10. Robert Betts, *The Druze* (New Haven, CT: Yale University Press, 1988), 26–27.

11. Moosa, *Extremist Shiites*, 398–99.

12. According to an Ottoman tradition—which Bayezid himself had begun with the death of his father, Sultan Murad I, at the Battle of Kossovo (1389)—all younger surviving sons of a dead ruler were strangled immediately on his death in order to prevent a power struggle over succession. Since Bayezid was in captivity for nearly a year before he died, his sons had time to build up their own power bases, and thus when the sultan's death became known, three of them were strong enough to keep the succession in dispute for almost eleven years.

13. Edwardes, *Life of Muhammad*, 148.

14. Mohammed Iqbal, "Ajmer Dargah Head to Boycott Pakistan PM," *The Hindu*, March 9, 2013.

15. Vali Nasr, *The Shia Revival: How Conflicts within Islam Will Shape the Future* (New York: W. W. Norton, 2007), 236–37. According to Patrick Cockburn, author of *Muqtada al-Sadr and the Battle for the Future of Iraq* (New York: Scribner, 2008), the city of al-Dammam has only one mosque for the city's 150,000 Shi'a inhabitants. In late September/early October 2011, violent protests by Shi'a in the nearby town of al-'Awamiyya prompted strong Sa'udi efforts to quell the unrest. See Patrick Cockburn, "Saudi Forces Pull Back: Iron Fist Tactic Suspended (for Now)," *Counterpunch*, October 6, 2011.

16. E. S. Drower, *Peacock Angel: Being Some Account of Votaries of a Secret Cult and Their Sanctuaries* (London: John Murray, 1941), 91.

17. There are many references to the Druze refusal to observe this common Muslim practice, one of the earliest being the rediscoverer of the ruins of Petra, John Burckhardt. "The Druses do not circumcise their children; circumcision is practiced only in the mountains by those members of the Shihab family who continue to be Mohammedans." John Lewis Burckhardt, *Travels in Syria and the Holy Land by the Late John Lewis Burckhardt* (London: John Murray, 1822), 203. Over a century later, the French author Narcisse Bouron alluded to it when he noted that "La circoncision, chez les Bedouins, est l'occasion de fêtes bruyantes. Au Djebel [Druze] on ne la fête pas" ("Circumcision for the Bedouins is the occasion for noisy celebrations. In the [Druze] Mountain, one does not celebrate it"[since it is not practiced]). [Capitaine] Narcisse Bouron, *Les Druzes: Histoire du Liban et de la Montagne Haouranaise* [The Druze: History of Lebanon and the Hauran Mountain] (Paris: Editions Berger Levrault, 1930), 300.

The author has knowledge of a Lebanese Druze family in which only the eldest of the six sons was circumcised, and that by accident when the father, an army officer, was away at work in a predominantly Muslim town in the Biqaʻ Valley where he happened to be posted, and the teenaged, illiterate mother of his first-born son did not know enough to refuse the suggestion of the local Muslim cleric who was passing by that she allow this operation to be performed. When the father returned from work, according to family accounts, "he was furious."

18. Otto Meinardus, "The Ethical Issue of the Hymenorophy," *Acta Ethnographica Academiae Scientiarum Hungaricae* 17 (1968): 369–73. Also Nicholas D. Kristof, "A Rite of Torture for Girls," *New York Times*, May 12, 2011, www.nytimes.com/2011/05/12/opinion/12kristof.html.

19. Qur'an, 4:171. I am citing from T. B. Irving's "Modern English" translation (1985). Irving produced the first American-English translation of the Qur'an, although Canadian.

20. In the fourth sura of the Qur'an, verse 157, we are told that "they killed him not, nor crucified him, but so it was made to appear to them." ʻAbdullah Yusuf ʻAli, *The Meaning of the Holy Qur'an: Complete Translation with Selected Notes* (Kuala Lumpur: Islamic Book Trust, 2006), 106.

21. Judith Dupré, *Full of Grace: Encountering Mary in Faith, Art, and Life* (New York: Random House, 2010), 88–89. Much of the scant biographical detail we have of Mary's life comes from the *Protoevangelium of James*, not the Bible, including the names of her parents, Joachim and Anna, and her presentation in the Temple as a young girl. The Arabic name of Christ's mother, Maryam, unlike that of Jesus himself, is the same for both Arabophone Muslims and Christians and popular as a given name, though with the latter it is often encountered in a Western version, Marie, Mary, or Maria.

22. Dupré, *Full of Grace*, 88, 101–102.

23. Kamal Salibi, *Who was Jesus? A Conspiracy in Jerusalem* (London: I. B. Taurus, 1998).

2. The Sunni-Shiʻa Divide in Modern Times

1. Declan Walsh, "Pakistan Reels with Violence Against Shiites," *New York Times*, December 3, 2012.

2. Anita Joshua, "Hounded for Being Hazara," *The Hindu*, February 28, 2013.

3. Nasr, *The Shia Revival*, 88.

4. It comes as no surprise that the author would choose a Hazara boy to be the subject of the dramatic male rape episode early in the book, and later that the boy's son suffered a similar fate as a *ghulam* (in Arabic a young male slave who performs his master's bidding, but in Afghanistan Pashtun culture specifically an effeminate dancing catamite) at the hands of the same protagonist, by now a senior Taliban official, who had assaulted his father. In Afghanistan, the practice of *bacha bazi* (beardless "boy-play") is widespread and attributed

by Western sociologists to the complete isolation of Afghan women. It is not considered "homosexual" in the Western sense since there is no relationship involved other than sexual gratification for the man and no attraction on the part of the boy for his "master," but in Pashtun society the boy's turn will come in time. Both Sunni and Shiʻa religious authorities have condemned the practice, as have Taliban leaders. Nevertheless, their proscriptions are openly flouted, and the Taliban stronghold of Kandahar is popularly referred to as "the pedophile capital" of the region in an area where the degrading practice has been rampant for untold centuries.

5. See D. M. Dunlop, *The History of the Jewish Khazars* (Princeton, NJ: Princeton University Press, 1954).

6. Shiʻa leaders in Lebanon regularly boast that their co-religionists outnumber Lebanese Sunni, but no one has gone so far as the author Vali Nasr, who, in a recent article in the *New York Times*, made the very dubious claim that Lebanese Shiʻa number "up to 55%" of the total population, or nearly double what most observers, including myself, estimate. That would mean that more than half of the country's population would be crammed into less than one-quarter of the tiny country's inhabited area. The Shiʻa are, like most of Lebanon's sects, very geographically confined, in their case over 90 percent of them, to the southern suburbs of Lebanon, the area between the Mediterranean and the coastal mountain range of Lebanon from the city of Sidon south to the Israeli border, and an isolated concentration in the northeast in and around the cities of Baʻalbak and Hermel. In the remaining three-quarters of the country, they are confined to a few small pockets—in the hills east of Byblos/Jubayl, for example—or otherwise nonexistent. See Vali Nasr, "If the Arab Spring Turns Ugly," *New York Times,* August 27, 2011, http://www.nytimes.com/2011/08/28/opinion/sunday/the-dangers-lurking-in-the-arab-spring.html?pagewanted=all.

7. Michael Young, "March 14 May Regret Boycotting Mikati," Beirut *Daily Star,* June 16, 2011, http://www.dailystar.com.lb/Opinion/Columnist/2011/Jun-16/March-14-may-regret-boycotting-Mikati.ashx#axzz2M2qDJxw7.

8. The French spelling is "Amchit," but to Anglicize it to "Amshit" is a bit ambiguous, hence the double e's to indicate both the correct pronunciation (!) and stress.

9. Joshua Hammer, "Samarra Rises," *Smithsonian Magazine,* January 2009, www.smithsonianmag.com/history-archaeology/Samarra-Rises.html.

10. Cited in *Maps of ʻIraq with Notes for Visitors, Revised and Enlarged Edition* (Baghdad: [British] Government of ʻIraq, 1929), 5.

11. On July 6, 2011, Muqtada al-Sadr announced "that his movement would not accept countrymen who had worked with 'the Americans' unless they had genuinely repented." He also said that "translators were also to remain outcasts." "Sadr Says Iraqis Employed with US Are Outcasts," AFP, July 6, 2011.

12. For the author's assessment of Christians in 'Iraq under Saddam Husayn's rule, see Robert Betts, "Christianity on the Tigris," *The (London) Tablet*, May 6, 1989.

13. That the poor, southern border town of Dar'a (Deraa) should have sparked the Arab Spring in Syria, rather than the major urban centers of Damascus and Aleppo strikes one as highly improbable in retrospect, but it is not the first time Dar'a has achieved international attention. In his memoir published in 1922, T. E. Lawrence ("Lawrence of Arabia") wrote that he was beaten and sodomized by the local Turkish commander of Dar'a, described by Lawrence as "an ardent pederast" (a charge vehemently denied by the commander's family), on November 20, 1917, forcing him to sacrifice his "bodily integrity." This incident was dramatized famously for millions of cinema-goers by David Lean in his classic 1962 film "Lawrence of Arabia." The veracity of this incident has, however, been seriously questioned by critics and attributed by some to a probable figment of Lawrence's repressed homosexual, sadomasochistic fantasies. There is, in fact, reasonable doubt as to whether he was even in or near Dar'a at the time of the alleged attack. True or not, Dar'a is forever linked to the story.

14. Anthony Shadid and David D. Kirkpatrick, "Promise of Arab Uprisings Is Threatened by Divisions," *New York Times*, May 21, 2011.

15. "Closing of Qatari Embassy Adds Pressure on Assad," *International Herald Tribune*, July 19, 2011. The article also noted that while the population of Homs is only 20 percent Alawite, because of "preferential treatment by the state, they hold 60% of the public sector jobs in the city."

16. Daniel Brode, Roger Farhat, and Daniel Nisman, "Syria's Threatened Christians," *New York Times*, June 28, 2012.

17. Lara El Gibaly and David Jolly, "8 Bahrain Activists Get Life Sentences," *New York Times*, June 23, 2011.

3. The Future of Militant Islam

1. It came as something of a surprise to the author, therefore, when, on visiting a friend in lower Manhattan several years ago, a stroll to the liquor store across the street introduced me to the two owners—Shi'a brothers from al-Nabatiyya in southern Lebanon. I am not sure who was the more surprised—myself to be buying vodka from Shi'a purveyors, or they to learn that I had been to al-Nabatiyya during 'Ashura'.

2. The Rev. Ted Pike, "Gaza, Flotilla II threaten Israel's Dream," http://www.truthtellers.org/alerts/11_5july_GazaFlot2ThreatenIsrealsDream.html.

3. Yeghani Torbati, "Iranian Share Prices Surge in Face of Crippling Sanctions," *New York Times*, December 13, 2012.

4. Cited in the prologue of Jack Ross, *Rabbi Outcast: Elmer Berger and American Jewish Anti-Zionism* (Washington: Potomac Books, 2011), 1.

5. Following the breakdown in diplomatic talks between the two governments, Prime Minister Erdogan stated, "Normalization of relations between the countries is unthinkable unless Israel apologizes for this illegal act which is against all international law and values." "Turkey: Israel Must Apologize to Repair Ties," Beirut *Daily Star*, July 9, 2011. Speaking at a meeting with Palestinian leaders two weeks later on July 24, 2011, Erdogan reiterated that "[n]ormal ties with Israel are impossible unless it 'officially apologizes' for its deadly raid on a Gaza-bound flotilla last year." He also said that Israel must pay compensation to the families of the victims, one Turkish-American and eight Turks, and lift its embargo on Gaza. "We did not and will not forget the massacre of our brothers." *International Herald Tribune*.

6. Uri Avnery, "Bibi and the Yo-Yos," Antiwar.com, May 26, 2011, http://original.antiwar.com/avnery/2011/05/25/bibi-and-the-yo-yos/. He went on to say that "it was worse than the Syrian parliament during a speech by Bashar Assad where anyone not applauding could find himself in prison."

7. The full text and list of signatories of the April 6, 2011, Israeli Peace Initiative can be found online at "Signatories," Israeli Peace Initiative, http://israeli-peaceinitiative.com/israeli-peace-initiative-english/signatories/.

8. Ethan Bronner, "Israel's West Bank General Warns Against Radicals," *New York Times*, October 11, 2011.

9. Anne Barnard, "Mr. Netanyahu's Strategic Mistake," *New York Times*, December 4, 2012.

10. "UN's Ban Ki-Moon Warns Israel of 'Fatal Blow' to Peace," BBC, December 3, 2012, http://www.bbc.co.uk/news/world-middle-east-20576201.

11. Dan William, "Israel Pushes on with Plans for 6,000 New Settler Homes," Reuters, December 18, 2012, http://www.reuters.com/article/2012/12/18/us-palestinians-israel-settlements-idUSBRE8BH14020121218.

12. Margaret Besheer, "UN, EU, Russia Condemn Israeli Settlements," *Voice of America*, December 19, 2012, http://www.voanews.com/content/un_eu_russia_condemn_israeli_settlements/1568322.html.

13. Philip Pullella and Mark Heinrich, "Pope Tells Abbas of Hope for Mideast Solution after U.N. Vote," Reuters, December 17, 2012, http://www.reuters.com/article/2012/12/17/us-pope-palestinians-abbas-idUSBRE8BG0M720121217.

14. Reuters, quoted in "Pope Tells Abbas of Hope for Middle East Solution," Beirut *Daily Star*, December 18, 2012.

15. Jeffrey Goldberg, "Robert Gates Says Israel Is an Ungrateful Ally," Bloomberg, September 5, 2011, www.bloomberg.com/news/2011-09-06/robert-gates-says-israel-is-an-ungrateful-ally-jeffrey-goldberg.html.

16. "Bill Clinton: Netanyahu Isn't Interested in Mideast Peace Deal," *Haaretz*, September 23, 2011, www.haaretz.com/bill-clinton-netanyahu-isn-t-interested-in-mideast-peace-deal-1.386222.

17. Aron Heller, "Rand Paul Visits Jerusalem, Calls for Gradual Reduction of U.S. Aid to Israel," *Huffington Post*, January 7, 2013, http://www.huffington post.com/2013/01/07/rand-paul-israel_n_2424275.html.

18. Richard Baehr, "The Jewish Demographic Divide," *Israel Hayom Newsletter*, April 30, 2012.

19. Fareed Zakaria, "Bibi Is Mired in a World That Has Gone Away," *The Beirut Daily Star*, May 28, 2011, http://www.dailystar.com.lb/Opinion/Columnist/2011/May-28/Bibi-is-mired-in-a-world-that-has-gone-away.ashx#axzz2M2qDJxw7.

20. Harriet Sherwood, "Palestinian Prisoners End Hunger Strike," *Guardian*, May 4, 2012, http://www.guardian.co.uk/world/2012/may/14/palestinian-prisoners-end-hunger-strike.

Conclusion

1. Richard Silverstein, "An Attack on Iran Will End Israel as We Know It," Mideast Peace, June 10, 2011, http://www.richardsilverstein.com/2011/06/10/an-attack-on-iran-will-end-israel-as-we-know-it/.

2. Ibid.

3. See www.GlobalFirePower.com.

4. Simon Adams, "The World's Next Genocide," *New York Times*, November 15, 2012.

5. "Syria Endgame," *Daily Star*, December 14, 2012, http://www.dailystar.com.lb/Opinion/Editorial/2012/Dec-14/198429 syria-endgame.ashx#axzz2 PqMRDLEz.

6. The relationship between Maronite Catholics and Shi'a Muslims in Lebanon has a long and convoluted past that predates the founding of Hizbollah and even the Lebanese Republic. See Hilal Khashan, "Lebanon's Shiite-Maronite Alliance of Hypocrisy," *Middle East Quarterly* (Summer 2012). Khashan, a Palestinian-American scholar, is chairman of the Department of Political Studies at the American University of Beirut.

7. Suzanne Maloney and Ray Takeyh, "Ahmadinejad's Fall, America's Loss," *New York Times*, June 15, 2011, www.nytimes.com/2011/06/16/opinion/16Takeyh-Maloney.html. See also Charlie Savage and Scott Shane, "Iranians Accused of Plot to Kill an Ambassador," *New York Times*, October 11, 2011, www.nytimes.com/2011/10/12/us/us-accuses-iranians-of-plotting-to-kill-saudi-envoy.html; and Robert F. Worth, "Iran's Power Struggle Goes Beyond Personalities to Future of Presidency Itself," *New York Times*, October 26, 2011, http://www.nytimes.com/2011/10/27/world/middleeast/in-iran-rivalry-khamenei-takes-on-presidency-itself.html.

8. The Justice and Development popular vote was nearly double that of the secular Republican Party (26 percent) who won majorities only in European Turkey, the Aegean coast (Izmir), and the heavily Alevi district of Tunceli

deep in the Anatolian interior. Despite this impressive victory, Erdogan's party's numbers in parliament were reduced from 341 out of 550 to 327 (44 of them women), far short of the two-thirds majority (367) required to propose changes to the military constitution of 1982 without a referendum. Interestingly, an independent candidate, Erol Dora, became the first Syriac Christian ever elected to parliament, and the first Christian since an Armenian was elected in 1955, perhaps reflective of Erdogan's warming relations with Turkish religious minorities. Statistics from Wikipedia, "Turkish General Election, 2012."

9. Editorial, "The New Turkish Order," *New York Times*, August 3, 2011.

10. Heba Afify and Isabel Kershner, "A Long Peace is Threatened in Israel Attack," *New York Times*, August 19, 2011, www.nytimes.com/2011/08/20/world/middleeast/20egypt.html; and David D. Kirkpatrick and Isabel Kershner, "Nations Race to Defuse Diplomatic Crisis Between Egypt and Israel," *New York Times*, August 21, 2011, www.nytimes.com/2011/08/21/world/middleeast/21egypt.html; also Hannah Allam, "Egyptian Protesters Reject Israel's 'Regrets Over Deadly Border Clash,'" *Miami Herald*, August 20, 2011, http://www.miamiherald.com/2011/08/20/2367861/egyptian-protesters-reject-israels.html.

11. Roger Cohen, "Come Home to Israel," *New York Times*, December 5, 2011, http://www.nytimes.com/2011/12/06/opinion/cohen-come-home-to-israel.html.

12. Anthony Shadid, "Turkey Warns Syria to Stop Crackdown," *New York Times*, August 15, 2011, http://www.nytimes.com/2011/08/16/world/europe/16turkey.html?gwh=B5042528582867681FF3E0FBBA48328D.

13. Michael S. Schmidt and Yasir Ghazi, "Iraqi Leader Backs Syria, With a Nudge from Iran," *New York Times*, August 12, 2011, www.nytimes.com/2011/08/13/world/middleeast/13iraq.html.

14. Michael S. Schmidt, "Iraq Leader Says the Arab Spring Benefits Israel," *New York Times*, August 19, 2011, www.nytimes.com/2011/08/19/world/middleeast/19iraq.html.

15. Schmidt and Ghazi, "Iraqi Leader Backs Syria"; Schmidt, "Iraq Leader Says the Arab Spring Benefits Israel."

16. Reuters, "Somalia: Turkey Makes Embassy Plans," *New York Times*, August 19, 2011, www.nytimes.com/2011/08/20/world/africa/20briefs-Somalia.html.

Appendix 3. Table of Shi'a Imams

1. Reginato, James, "The Aga Khan's Earthly Kingdom," *Vanity Fair*, February 2013.

2. Ibid.

Selected Bibliography

Abu-Izzeddin, Nejla M. *The Druzes: A New Study of Their History, Faith, and Society.* Leiden: E.J. Brill, 1984.

Betts, Robert Brenton. *The Druze.* New Haven, CT: Yale University Press, 1988.

Bill, James A. *Roman Catholics and Shi'i Muslims: Prayer, Passion & Politics.* Chapel Hill: University of North Carolina Press, 2006.

Bouron, Narcisse. *Les Druzes: Histoire du Liban et de la Montagne Harouranaise* [The Druze: History of Lebanon and the Hauran Mountain]. Paris: Editions Berger-Levrault, 1930.

Cockburn, Patrick. *Muqtada al-Sadr and the Battle for the Future of Iraq.* New York: Scribner, 2008.

Dadoyan, Seta B. *The Fatimid Armenians: Cultural and Political Interaction in the Near East.* New York: Brill, 1997.

Drower, E. S. *Peacock Angel: Being Some Account of Votaries of a Secret Cult and their Sanctuaries.* London: John Murray, 1941.

Dunlop, D. M. *The History of the Jewish Khazars.* Princeton, NJ: Princeton University Press, 1954.

Dussaud, René. Histoire et Religion des Nosairîs. Paris: Bouillon, 1900.

Edmonds, C. J. *Kurds, Turks, and Arabs: Politics, Travel, and Research in North-eastern Iraq, 1919–1925.* London: Oxford University Press, 1957.

El-Bendary, Mohamed. *The "Ugly American" in the Arab Mind: Why do Arabs Resent America?* Washington: Potomac Books, 2011.

Gonzalez, Nathan. *The Sunni-Shia Conflict: Understanding Sectarian Violence in the Middle East.* Mission Viejo, CA: Nortia Press, 2009.

Guest, John S. *Survival among the Kurds: A History of the Yezidis.* London: Kegan Paul International, 1993.

Harik, Iliya F. *Politics and Change in a Traditional Society: Lebanon, 1711–1845.* Princeton, NJ: Princeton University Press, 1968.

Hazleton, Lesley. *After the Prophet: The Epic Story of the Shia-Sunni Split in Islam*. New York: Doubleday, 2009.

Heffelfinger, Chris. *Radical Islam in America: Salafism's Journey from Arabia to the West*. Washington: Potomac Books, 2011.

Hodgson, Marshall G. S. *The Order of Assassins: The Struggle of the Early Nizari Isma'ilis against the Islamic World*. 's-Gravenhage, Netherlands: Mouton & Co., 1955.

Ibn Hishām, 'Abd al-Malik. *Ibn Ishaq: The Life of Muhammad Apostle of Allah*. Edited by Michael Edwardes. London: Folio Society, 1964.

Jacquot, Paul. *L'Etat des Alaouites, Terre d'Art de Souvenires et de Mystère*. Beirut: Imprimerie Catholique, 1929.

Lewis, Bernard. *The Origins of Isma'ilism: A Study of the Historical Background of the Fatimid Caliphate*. Cambridge: W. Heffer & Sons, 1940.

Luke, Harry Charles. *Mosul and Its Minorities*. London: Martin Hopkinson & Company Ltd., 1925.

Makarem, Sami Nassib. *The Political Doctrine of the Isma'ilis: The Imamate*. Delmar, NY: Caravan Books, 1977.

Momen, Moojan. *An Introduction to Shi'i Islam: The History and Doctrines of Twelver Shi'ism*. New Haven, CT: Yale University Press, 1985.

Moosa, Matti. *Extremist Shiites: The Ghulat Sects*. Syracuse, NY: Syracuse University Press, 1988.

Mottahedeh, Roy. *The Mantle of the Prophet. Religion and Politics in Iran*. London: Chatto and Windus, 1985.

Nasr, Vali. *The Shia Revival: How Conflicts Within Islam Will Shape the Future*. New York: W. W. Norton, 2007.

Olson, Robert. *The Ba'th and Syria, 1947 to 1982: The Evolution of Ideology, Party, and State, from the French Mandate to the Era of Hafiz al-Asad*. Princeton, NJ: Kingston Press, 1982.

Pearse, Richard. *Three Years in the Levant*. London: Macmillan, 1949.

Seale, Patrick. *Asad of Syria: The Struggle for the Middle East*. London: 1988. Published in the United States in 1989 by UC Berkeley Press.

Tabataba'i, Allamah Sayyid Muhammad Husayn. *Shi'ite Islam*. London: George Allen and Unwin, Ltd., 1975.

Trimingham, J. Spencer. *Christianity among the Arabs in Pre-Islamic Times*. London: Longman, 1979.

Van Dam, Nikolaos. *The Struggle for Power in Syria: Sectarianism, Regionalism, and Tribalism in Politics, 1961–1978*. London: Croom Helm, 1979.

————. *The Struggle for Power in Syria: Politics and Society under Asad and the Ba'th Party.* London: Croom Helm, 1996.

Watt, W. Montgomery. *Muhammad at Mecca.* Oxford: Clarendon Press, 1953.

————. *Muhammad at Medina.* Oxford: Clarendon Press, 1956.

————. *Bell's Introduction to the Qur'an.* Edinburgh: Edinburgh University Press, 1970.

————. *Islamic Philosophy and Theology.* Edinburgh: Edinburgh University Press, 1962. Second ed., 1985.

Weulersse, Jacques. *Le Pays des Alaouites.* Tours: Arrault & Co., 1940, 2 vols.

Index

About the Author

Robert Brenton Betts is a retired professor at the University of Balamand, Lebanon, and at the American University of Beirut. He holds a PhD in international relations and Middle East studies from the Johns Hopkins School of Advanced International Studies and is the author of three previously published books: *Christians in the Arab East: A Political Study* (1978), *The Druze* (1988), and *The Southern Portals of Byzantium* (2009). He lives in India.